In **The Wind in her Hands**, popular author Margaret Gillies Brown turns her attention to the life of her own mother whose extraordinary achievements stemmed from humble beginnings as the daughter of a North East farm. Defying conventions and the social expectations of a tight community, Jessie Isobel Jaffray has the strength of mind and spirit to go her own way in 1900s Scotland. An inspiration to modern women finding their own head in a contradictory modern world.

Margaret Gillies Brown is the author of several books and lives in Perthshire.

about the author's previous books . . .

". . . two books that must surely become classics of Scottish autobiography"
Duncan Glen

"brilliant insight"
The Big Issue

"you can't help but warm to this"
Farmers Weekly

"pioneers like these are the kind of Scots we should hear more about"
The Local News (Govanhill & Gorbals)

"an easily readable style, the book is an uplifting experience"
Fife & Kinross Extra

"I loved this book because of the atmosphere it creates"
Elizabeth Sutherland

"a heart-warming story"
The Leopard

"compellingly personal, (a) vivid portrait"
Scotland on Sunday

previous books by the author

Far from the Rowan Tree (Argyll, 1997)
Around the Rowan Tree (Argyll, 1999)
Of Rowan and Pearl (with Kenneth Steven, Argyll, 2000)

The Wind
in her Hands

MARGARET GILLIES BROWN

Argyll
publishing

First published in 2002 by
Argyll Publishing
Glendaruel
Argyll PA22 3AE
Scotland
www.skoobe.biz

The author has asserted her moral rights.

**British Library Cataloguing-in-Publication Data.
A catalogue record for this book is available from
the British Library.**

ISBN 1 902831 41 1

Acknowledgement is made to the estate of
Alexander Gray for quoting lines from his
poem 'Scotland' on p243

Cover design: from an original idea by Cloe Gillies

Origination: Cordfall Ltd, Glasgow

Printing: Mackays of Chatham

To the memory
of my mother

'Behold thy daughter
She hath the wind in her hands
But for a short time only.'
{From the Arabic}

Ancestors

. . . And here we are again in this strange land
To feel the pull in sinews, blood and bones,
This walled in graveyard swept by ocean winds
Where farmers lie with fishers from St Combs,
Here, where all strife ends, I read the names engraved
And marvel at the height and strength of tombs,
Our ancestors, the far flung empires of their days,
Reach out and touch us in surprising ways.

Margaret Gillies Brown

Acknowledgements

Help came from many sources in the writing of this book. First and foremost I am grateful to my mother who told me much, when I was young, about how it was to be brought up on a small Buchan farm at the beginning of the last century. Also for the many long holidays she took us on to that place, before and during the World War II, when things hadn't changed much in centuries with the girdle, cheesepress, churn and the open peat fire all still in daily use.

I am grateful also to my Aunt Peggy who told me many stories of the old days and who guarded, with her life, a small black case, to which I fell heir, containing birth, marriage and death certificates and other important documents plus a few milestone letters and photographs from which I was able to piece together the whole story.

I would also like to acknowledge the help derived from Aberdeen Central Library for its microfiche of old Aberdeenshire newspapers, plus books showing how Aberdeen looked in days gone by.

To friends and relations I owe a great deal: to Jean Ramsay, born and bred in Buchan, to whom I gave my manuscript to read and correct anything I had got wrong in language or custom. She also lent me books from which I learned. One was especially useful for the information gleaned, *Farm Life In North East*

Scotland, 1840 to 1914, The Poor Man's Country by Ian Carter. I would like to record my thanks to the author for this informative and clearly written book. I have only one quibble with it. The word peasant is used quite often within its pages to describe small farmers and crofters. They never saw themselves as peasants and would never have used the word.

Silvie Taylor, too, was of great assistance to me by the lending of books and who very quickly at my request found correct quotations. She it was, also, who found Dartfield Farm for me when I had failed to locate it in the welter of winding roads that is East Aberdeenshire. George Hill gave me valuable information on the Malaya that was before the World War II.

My thanks go also to Richard my oldest son who put a lot of the script up on the computer and who gleaned useful information from the internet and who was always around when my computer went wrong. Thanks go also to my cousin Allison Jaffray for sending me most useful, well-illustrated books from South Africa about Kenya as a young colony.

I would like to thank Christopher Moncton, whom I met once by happy circumstance, while trespassing with my husband through his wooded policies of Crimonmogate. When I apologised for the intrusion and explained the reason, which was that my mother was once factor there, and that I was writing a book about her, not only did he not chastise us, but said we could explore the grounds as much as we wished and then invited us round to Crimonmogate House where he would show us over the sixty five room mansion. Up till then I had desperately wanted to see inside the house but hadn't thought it possible. Not only did he show us over the house, but he and his charming wife entertained us to afternoon tea.

Last but not least I want to thank my husband Henry for his patience and unstinting help in giving me the space in which to write and in driving me to all these windy hidden places.

Margaret Gillies Brown, August 2002

CHAPTER ONE

The One with the Sparkle

'BEHOLD thy daughter,' the doctor said. His eyes were smiling as he handed the bare, newly born child into the arms of her mother. This was what being a doctor was all about – the birth of a healthy child to a healthy mother – joy palpable in the room. Young Mrs Jaffray was full of it after the strenuous but straight-forward birth – a girl, what she had secretly wanted. She already had two small sons so this would even things up a bit on the farm – make it not quite so much of a man's world in the future.

'Waa, Waa,' roared the new-born infant and then all of a sudden was silent and for a moment small watery eyes opened and the tired, fond mother fancied she saw a sparkle there.

'She was aye the ane wi the sparkle,' was said of this new human being almost a century later' – said by Miss Kilgower, an old lady, who remembered vividly running over the fields to Dartfield from Lonmay Station, where her father was station-master, to fetch butter for her mother. She came to know the family well – all eventual seven of them.

The rays of the early morning sun danced through the dormer window of the stoutly built stone house welded to the ground as strongly as a winkle is secured to rock. It needed to be. The strong winds coming straight from the North Sea, six miles away, would have made short work of it had it not been. Today a light wind gently lifted the white muslin curtains as it entered the small bedroom window to welcome the new-born child.

'Close that window, please,' said Doctor Blackhall to the young woman in the long grey skirt and grey apron who had just knocked at the door and entered.

'Leave it open a wee bittie at the bottom.' Mrs Jaffray's orders superseded the doctor's. 'That's ane o the reasons I wanted you at the birth and no Betsy the midwife,' she said. 'She doesna like fresh air getting into the hoose ava – she'd like it hermetically sealed and she wouldn't approve of all the lilac in the room.'

The tall slim doctor with hair greying at the temples looked around him. Right enough – vases and vases of lilac blossom were placed about. The air vibrated with the sweet smell of the white and mauve blooms clustered together in mad profusion.

'Aye fegs, the howdie would likely have thrown them aa oot,' Mrs Jaffray half spoke to the doctor and half to herself. 'Betsy's afa superstitious. Would tell you it's bad luck. Such rot. I dinna believe in those kind o superstitions and you'll no either,' she said looking down at the newly born babe. 'I winna lat ye. I've always loved lilac – my favourite flooer. Look,' she said to the doctor, nodding towards the small squares of embroidered lilac motifs scattered over the sparkling white quilt. It had been washed recently and dried in the sun in the small orchard at the front of the house. 'I embroidered these when I was a quine and making things for my bottom drawer.'

'Aye you're a wee bit different from the rest of them,' said the doctor, 'and certainly with a mind of your own.'

'And tak a keek oot o the window,' Mrs Jaffray said. 'Just look at the lilac ootside. I've never seen better flourish – the blossoms are as big as mountain peaks this year.'

His main job done the doctor went over to the window and looked out. The lilac bushes tossed in the breeze beside the old apple and plum trees and the one or two rowans not long come into leaf. Mrs Jaffray was proud of her garden. Farmers as a rule didn't bother with gardens as they always needed seeing to at busy times on the farm. It was left to the farmer's wife whether there was a good garden or not. Apart from the trees there was a narrow border of flowers, a corner with raspberry canes and a bush or two of blackcurrants, redcurrants and gooseberries. There was also a large patch for vegetables – nothing fancy, just carrots and leeks, cabbage and kale. Kale could survive in all sorts of weather and was the countryman's standby for soup. So much so that soup in the country districts was often called kale. Its strong, dark green leaves were almost indestructible unless the pigeons got at them when they were almost starving after snow had been covering the land. Then they would soon strip off every leaf.

The doctor returned to the bedside of his patient. Mrs Jaffray didn't mention the other reasons for not wanting the services of the howdie. For a start she was gossipy. Not that she minded a wee bit gossip herself at her few afternoon tea parties in the back parlour with some of the neighbours' wives. But there was gossip and gossip. Worst of all, it was said, the midwife wasn't all that given to cleanliness. To Mrs Jaffray cleanliness was paramount. It had been dinned into her when young by her mother before her. At childbirth especially it was necessary. How many mothers died of childbed fever. There was a suspicion that puerperal sepsis was caused by cross infection and young Mrs Jaffray believed it. So far she had escaped the fever.

She had been lucky to have had the services of the doctor. In this part of the world they didn't always attend straightforward births – they left it to the howdie. But Doctor Blackhall lived nearby in the same kind of house welded to the cold Aberdeenshire ground. His housekeeper was her sister Maggie – Miss Urquhart to the doctor and most other people. She had been with him for twelve years now – ever since he had come to this practice from Edinburgh University where he had done his training. Originally from the softer south there was something about this hard northern land that he liked and its sturdy, brave inhabitants who had to deal with it. They had plenty smeddum in their veins.

They had to be tough to survive the rigours of the winter's cold if nothing else. He had to venture out in his pony and trap in all weathers, day and night. At times, when snow was drifting, patients could be difficult to reach and he was never going to make a fortune. There was too little money about. Often he took nothing at all for his services. There was just nothing to give. Sometimes he got paid in kind – a bag of tatties here, a few neeps there – and then there was his housekeeper, Miss Urquhart.

Inwardly he knew that he had grown to love her. Perhaps one day he would defy convention and ask her to marry him – there never seemed time. That was the problem. If she agreed to marry him he knew he would have a battle on his hands contending with the subtle hierarchies of this land where everyone had their place in society. A doctor would not marry his housekeeper even supposing she was a farmer's daughter – she would be seen as a degree beneath him. He was getting to know these people but it took time. It seemed they had been walled up in this forgotten, harsh corner of the world from time immemorial. The spartan graveyards with their grey stone walls and grey tombstones were full of the same names from generations past.

There had been little movement until the trains came. Movement was still slow but it was beginning to pick up with the more adventurous ones getting away from this hard land to something better. Not everyone wanted out, of course, and only now was it beginning to happen – trains were a lifeline to the vast outside world and other people. These two Urquhart sisters, for instance, seemed quite content with the way things were, brought up as they had been to be hardworking and Godfearing.

Maggie, although he never called her that in public, seemed perfectly happy in her quiet busy way. Self effacing, he instinctively knew she would never leave him. He knew she could have married several times over with her gentle ways, grey eyes, strawberries and cream complexion and soft brown hair. He was being selfish, perhaps, by always hoping she would remain with him but he knew that they were happy working together at a common cause – the well-being of the country people in the district, a close-knit community many of whom were related.

He also knew instinctively that Maggie would probably like to be married and have children. He loved children. He would have liked to have children of his own. He was denying himself although to lose one would be heartbreaking. So many children died – diphtheria, tuberculosis, scarlet fever – it was impossible to save them sometimes. Nor could he give the answer why some families almost died out with these diseases while others survived. So far, the Jaffrays hadn't been hit by serious illness and he fervently hoped they never would be.

The girl in grey, who had just entered the room, went over to admire the baby lying in her mother's arms. She loved babies, loved children. Although life was hard at times with always so much to do and Mrs Jaffray a fairly strict task mistress, she liked working for the Jaffrays as nursemaid.

'I'll rin doon noo and get the kettle off the sway.' She knew the score – she'd done this before – the baby must have its first bath. Soon she was back up again carrying the heavy black kettle with steam still billowing from its spout. She went over to the marble-topped washstand and took the tall jug of water out of its matching basin. The set, white porcelain with large pink flowers embedded in elegant curves, had been a wedding present to the Jaffrays from her brother-in-law John and his English wife living in the neighbouring farm of Lums.

Annie Willox, for that was the girl in grey's name, poured equal quantities of hot and cold water into the basin, rolled up her grey sleeve and tested it with her elbow as she had been taught to do. Still a bit hot. More cold was added until it was just right and then she went over to get the baby from her mother's arms.

The doctor had gone.

'He's awa tee tell the maister,' Mrs Jaffray said. 'He'll be walking impatiently up and doon the parlour fleer wondering what's happening.'

Annie had just got the baby into the long flannelette nightgown that Mrs Jaffray had made for the new arrival, when the door burst open and a sense of excitement filled the room with the coming of William Jaffray and the doctor. She could tell they had already had a dram in celebration. William Jaffray went over to the bed and kissed his wife on the forehead.

'Clever quine,' he said. She could see the tears brimming in his eyes – tears that he would hope no one could see.

Annie handed him his new daughter. He carried the baby awkwardly which Annie thought was strange when he was so good and confident with new lambs or calves.

'Gyang doon and bring the loons up tae see their new sister,' instructed Mrs Jaffray, 'and tell Jenny to bring up that tray I laid oot for the occasion. She'll ken which ane I mean.'

Soon there was the sound of feet on the stairs and a small boy burst into the room. Willie, aged two and a half, had brown hair and the distinct stamp of his father about him. He led the way, with one year old John, an attractive dark-haired child, following behind in the arms of his nursemaid, Annie. Jenny, with a large tray holding glasses, a bottle of Elderflower cordial, a jug of water and a flask of the all-important whisky, brought up the rear. Of whisky Mrs Jaffray didn't approve at all. It caused one or two of the very few fall-outs she had with her husband. Not that he usually over-indulged but, because they had to scrimp and save every penny and whisky cost money, they could ill afford it.

However today was different – this was a morning for celebration. William Jaffray bent down on one knee to give the boys a closer look at their wee sister. John wanted to poke her to see if she was real. His older brother, already aware of his responsibilities, wouldn't let him. By now the baby was quiet and drowsy after her first bath. William Jaffray laid her carefully in the wicker moses basket made by the tinkers that had been used for all their babies. Soon there were drinks all round to celebrate the birth – a new life coming into the world.

'Here's tee the new bairn,' said William Jaffray raising his glass.

'What's her name,' piped up small William. All the adults in the room knew what her name would be. The same as her mother's, of course, just as wee William was the same as his father.

'Here's tee Jessie Isobel Jaffray,' said William Jaffray raising his glass once more.

Mrs Jaffray didn't particularly like her own name but knew she would have no say in the matter.

Chapter Two

Visiting

AT FOUR YEARS OLD Jessie Isobel Jaffray was a bright precocious child. She was not exactly what you would call pretty – her mouth was a little too wide for that, her jawline broad and her eyes set, perhaps, rather too far apart. The brose bowl haircut, given to her by her father, didn't help her looks, accentuating these features as it did. She could almost have passed for a boy had she not been dressed in long wide skirts or pinafores.

What saved her from any plainness was the colour of her skin. It was the colour of the cream that rose to the top of the silvery milk pans in her mother's cool dairy and her cheeks were tinged with the same delicate pink of apples in the orchard before they were fully ripe. Her thick hair was as glossy and black as a rook's wing. Her eyes were cloud grey but saved from any dourness by flecks the colour of bracken when it turns coppery gold in autumn. They were eyes that danced with excitement, that glowed with interest in everything they saw.

There was an energy about her that was palpable. She was always wanting to do something new and different which often got her into trouble. But above all she was a happy child and it showed. She had no time for being cooped up in the farmhouse. Annie Willox couldn't keep her out of the farmyard even although the cock turkey 'old bubbly Jock' would chase her and she would come up the yard screaming for Annie to save her. In the end Annie helped her to deal with 'old bubbly'. She gave Jessie a stick, caught the 'bubbly', showed Jessie how to hold it by its long red wattle that hung over its beak and give it a few sharp whacks across the back. Rather to Jessie's surprise it never attacked her again.

She loved also to accompany her mother, or Jenny, the kitchie deem, on the daily chores about the farmyard, looking for and collecting the eggs, feeding the hens and ducks, tending the cows and calves in the byre and at milking time, listening to the frothy sound of milk filling the pail. After it was finished a little warm milk would be poured from the pail into a small enamel dish left there to feed the cats. Sometimes, when Jenny was milking and the cats impatiently mewing about her long skirts, from her perch on the low, three-legged milking stool, she would squirt some milk from the cow's teat directly into a cat's mouth. This always made Jessie laugh.

'Do it again Jenny,' Jessie would say.

After the milking her mother or Jenny fed the calves with fresh milk out of a pail especially kept for them. When they had sucked out the last drop Jessie would stick her hand through the wooden slats that kept the calves in, feel their wet noses and give them a small finger to suck. The sucking sensation on her young skin felt good.

She loved everything about the byre – its low roof, its straw-bedded stalls, its mangers filled with the sweet-smelling hay, and the noises – the lowing of cows needing to be milked, the rustle of straw, the clank of chains that tethered the cows to their stalls. At night time, in the winter, it was even more exciting. Then they would carry a hurricane lamp down to the byre which would often, in the wind, cast great moving shadows.

Next door to the byre were the stables. These were strictly out of bounds to Jessie unless accompanied by an adult. The great Clydesdales towered above her. She was actually a little frightened of them, even although she had heard her father call them gentle beasts. Beside her they looked huge as their iron-clad feet rang and sparked on the cobbles in their stalls and leading out of the stables.

Further up the close was the cart shed and next to it, the boiler house. A large iron boiler stood in one corner and every other day food was boiled up for the hens and pigs. Mostly it was small tatties called chats that were cooked. Sometimes Jenny or her mother would hand her a tattie. Had ever anything tasted so good? To begin with it was so hot that she would juggle it from hand to hand until it was cool enough to eat.

In Spring time there were the clocking hens to attend to. They were kept in boxes in a wee dark house next to the boilerhouse. The clocking house was low and had a musty smell. Each hen sat in a straw-lined box with a lid and a stone on top to prevent the hen from leaving the nest. Not that they probably would have but it was a precaution. As soon as they were released however, the hen would jump out and peck at the scattered grain. Jessie loved to watch them pecking away with relish and drinking from the enamelled dishes of water. Down their heads would go, time after time, and then right up in the air – down and up, down and up. She liked also to hear the clucking noises they made, heard at no other time, and see how they strutted around, feathers all ruffled into a ball.

'We'll gi them half an oor,' her mother would say, 'syne we'll come back and lift them into their boxes if they hivna come back themselves.'

Then there was the exciting day when the chickens hatched and the eggs were all cracked and broken as a faint cheep, cheep, cheep was heard beneath mother hen. As if by magic, it seemed to Jessie, there were yellow fluffy chickens peeping out from underneath her feathers, all over the place.

'Let me cairry ane, mither,' and her mother would hand her a chicken so light it was like a ball of fluff.

'Noo you must hud it afa gentle and nae squash it. They're delicate craturs.'

After the chickens were hatched they were put into coops and placed in a grassy part of the garden. Open air runs were attached. There the mother hens would proudly lead the chickens up and down encouraging them to eat. The only problem was, however often she was told, Jessie would not leave the chicks alone and Annie or her mother would find her there playing with them on the grass, never mentioning the sore pecks a protective mother hen had given her. Sometimes the chicks would escape and weren't always easy to recapture and sometimes the grey-backed hoodie crows would carry them off when no one was looking.

It was for this and other reasons of mischief that Mrs Jaffray was relieved when her sister Maggie sometimes came for a visit of an afternoon and would take Jessie back to the doctor's house. Maggie wanted to help her sister who had now two more children, a little girl, two years younger than Jessie, called Fanny Ewerdine after her English sister-in-law and a boy Andrew who had also been given a family name although one that had been in abeyance for a generation. Andrew had been one of twins, his brother dying in infancy. Even although the bigger boys were at school now, Mrs Jaffray and Annie Willox had their hands full.

At the doctor's house there was a small bedroom set aside for Jessie should she want to stay overnight. The doctor loved this precocious child. She was the light relief he sought after a distressing day at work. Jessie was always bright and loved being there. She always got special attention which was elusive at home these days with so many other children. She had long conversations with her aunt and the doctor when time allowed. They spent time teaching her to read before she went to school. She was an apt pupil and couldn't learn quickly enough although she often made stumbling mistakes. She wasn't perhaps the cleverest pupil in the world but if determination counted for anything she would soon be fairly proficient. From an early age books fascinated her and she very much wanted to know what they said. In the doctor's parlour there was a whole wall set aside for books. She would ask him about them.

'What div they aa say?'

He would remove different ones and explain to her that some were poetry and some prose and would read her an excerpt from a chosen few – Byron, Burns, Wordsworth, Thackery, Scott, Dickens. She loved the stories and the rhythmic sound of the poetry and as she grew older learned many of the poems off by heart for which she would get much praise.

If she liked the doctor's parlour she equally loved his kitchen. There it was all hustle and bustle, baking or preparing food. The kitchen faced west and sometimes in the evening it would be filled with sunlight. The kitchen window had many small panes of glass and from the top sill hung a cage with a canary. Often the kitchen would be filled with birdsong.

'Why div you hae a canary, Doctor Blackhall?' Jessie asked one day.

'Because a lady who knew I liked canaries gave me one.'

'Did it cost ye muckle siller?'

'No it didn't cost me anything.'

'How was that?'

'Well this particular lady had very little money and as she was quite ill over a long period of time I had to attend her quite a lot. She tried to pay me with what very little she had but I refused to take payment. I knew if I did she would have nothing to buy food with. One day she begged me to take the canary. She died shortly afterwards.'

Sometimes, with all this special attention given to Jessie by the doctor and everyone else around his house, she did get a bit above herself. In Scotland this would never do.

One day when she was sitting on the doctor's knee by the parlour fire she took to boasting a bit of how she was going to be a princess when she was grown up. The prettiest in the world!

'Are you sure?' the doctor teased.

'Yes I'm sure, the prettiest in the world!'

'Ah but I know a prettier little girl than you.'

'What other little girl?' She was instantly deflated – that this man who had become a second father to her should have someone else he perhaps liked better and thought prettier devastated the world she had made up for herself. She never forgot it.

'Och but jist wait till you see me in my braw Sunday dress that my mither has made for me. Then you'll think ither.'

Next time Aunt Maggie came for her she insisted on wearing her new Sunday dress. It was made of cloud-grey velvet and had a red collar and cuffs. The deep greyness brought out the colour of her eyes.

Her mother wasn't too keen to let her wear it knowing the mess her little daughter could get into. But that day her mind was much distracted with other things and in a weak moment she allowed it.

'Noo dinna ye get in a sotter. We'll niver get tae church on Sunday if I've got tae tak stains oot o your dress.'

The Jaffrays didn't always go to church on Sundays. The church was a mile or more away and it was a struggle getting everyone ready in time. Besides, often the weather was inclement and she didn't want the children to get colds.

'I dinna care whit the meenister thinks,' Mrs Jaffray would say to her husband. 'I'll gyang when I can and when the weather is aa richt.'

Just the same Mrs Jaffray enjoyed going to church because of all the friends and neighbours she would meet there. The sermons she didn't enjoy much. They were long, drawn out, and sometimes it was a struggle to keep awake. Having all these children with them didn't help matters either. Until Sunday school time they were all so fidgety. She didn't much care for the Minister. He drank, it was gossiped, more than was good for him. How could you look up to someone like that?

Aunt Maggie, with Jessie in her new frock, set off across the fields on the shortcut to the doctor's house. It was a fresh spring day with the air loud with lark song and bubbly with curlews. All the birds were nesting. Jessie walked as sedately as she could over the rough ground. The doctor wasn't in when she arrived which was a disappointment but he would be in later and she would be very good till he came and not run wild in the garden or anything.

The kitchie deem and the cook were busy Spring cleaning. They had all the doctor's silverware out on the kitchen table giving it a good clean. How each piece glinted and sparkled once it was polished up. They stopped long enough to admire Jessie's new dress and afterwards she sat watching them overawed by it all. The tea set, jug, water jug, teapot and sugar bowl, all of heavily embossed silver – the silver cups and bowls, candlesticks, the bone-handled knives and forks and the large silver-bellied pot with a small round pot underneath.

'Fit's that for?' Jessie was curious.

At that very moment the doctor came into the kitchen.

'It's a silver tea-kettle,' he said and he showed her how it worked. The little round bit at the bottom held in the methalated spirits that fed the round wick whose flame kept the silver tea-kettle always at boiling point.

'Ladies use it for their polite afternoon teas. It's fashioned on much the same principle as the Russian samovar which is also used for making tea but is much bigger, made of metal and heated by charcoal.'

Samovar, here was a lovely new word for Jessie and prefixed by Russian gave it a wonderful far-away mystery. She would call it a samovar. It sounded so much more romantic than tea-kettle.

'I got it left to me not long ago by my mother,' said the doctor, 'but I have little use for it really.'

'Its pretty,' said Jessie.

'I suppose it is but mostly I keep it locked away in its wooden kist.'

'I widna dae that,' thought Jessie to herself. 'When I'm big I'll hae a big hoose stappit fu wi siller and ornaments.'

'By the way,' said the doctor, 'you're looking very pretty today.' He thought he had teased her enough lately. He hadn't meant to hurt her feelings the other day and he knew he had.

'That's a lovely dress. Is that your new Sunday one?'

'Aye it is,' replied Jessie. 'Mither lat me wear it but I have to be careful to nae get it in a sotter.'

Just then there was the sound of a galloping horse passing the window. Jessie recognized the neighbouring farmer's son. There was a frantic knock at the door.

'It's ma faither. He's faain face doon in a dwam. Come quickly, doctor.'

CHAPTER THREE

Bread was for Sundays

FOR HER EIGHTH birthday the doctor and Aunt Maggie gave Jessie a bike. There could have been no better present. Her delight was obvious to everyone. She knew her mother and father would never have been able to afford a new bike for her. They made a precarious living off the hundred and twenty acre farm and, depending on the weather and current prices, sometimes had a disastrous year. So every penny was important and used only for necessities. A new bike for one member of the family would have been out of the question.

The bike gave Jessie the freedom she craved. Freedom to see what lay beyond the narrow confines of her life. It gave her freedom also to bike over to Doctor Blackhall's whenever she felt inclined. Her busy mother and father gave her a certain amount of leeway, warning her not to go too far and not to get lost. They knew the narrow roads were fairly safe. Motor cars had come into existence but there were not many of them about. There would be ponies and gigs, horses and carts, a few riders on horseback and on bicycles and people walking, but all were comparatively slow moving. All the country people knew each other for miles around. There were few strangers and there was little harm she could come to. She was told to beware of tinkers but on the whole they were harmless. If she did get lost all she had to do was say she was William Jaffray of Dartfield's daughter and she would be put in the right direction for home.

There was a wonderful maze of narrow roads servicing all the crofts and farms, roads bounded by shelter belts of stunted trees that had been there for a long time. The trees were sculptured by the wind from the North Sea and in winter time, when shorn of leaves, looked as if they had all had similar haircuts sloping up to the horizon which made it easy to guess the direction of the prevailing wind. Jessie liked to cycle along these roads even if there was a cold north-easterly blowing. She had rarely known life without it.

This was part of all the life she knew, this wind, these twisting roads, many of which could so easily fill up with snow and stay like that for weeks in winter. Some were little more than sheuchs waiting for the wind to blow snow into them from the higher fields. The farm road up to Dartfield was such a one – a narrow twisting track bounded by high banks which could quickly become impassable in winter. In springtime, with the snow gone, these same high banks could be full of light and warmth with the broom in flower, a blaze of yellow light rivalling the sunshine. Instinctively Jessie appreciated these things. Inside herself she always saw the beautiful. Optimism started at an early age for Jessie. Always a romantic, this countryside enthralled her without her realizing.

'Folks like us hae bidden here for a lang lang time,' her father often told his children. Sometimes, after a long day at the plough, her father would come home, take off his boots and his nicky tams (leather straps that were buckled on just under the knee hitching the breeks up enough to keep ends clear of water and mud) and after leaving them in the back porch he would put his hand in his pocket and tell one or other of his children to close their eyes and stretch out a hand. Into that hand would drop something cold and hard.

'Anither dart,' he would tell them. 'That's hoo this fairm's caa'ed Dartfield. Aince lang ago there was a battle focht ower

25

here and I still pick up these auld stone flint heeds till this day, ilka time the couter throws them oot. Naebody seems tae ken fit the battle was aboot or when it took place but aince there must hae been ane ower this land.'

The new bike did have several disadvantages. Her mother had fixed a carrying basket on to the back seat.

'Get on your bike and tak this poond o butter to Mrs Ironside. She's having a bairn shortly. She'll nae be able to come hersel.'

The village of Lonmay was a mile and a half away and not Jessie's favourite road but she didn't like anyone else riding her bike so there was no option.

'Och, mam,' she would say, but never refused. She knew there would be trouble if she did and in the end she usually enjoyed it – nearly always being given a bap or a girdle scone spread with homemade jam for her trouble and coming back with news. She always took a great interest in what went on in the world beyond her doorstep.

'Mrs Ironside has had her bairn. It's a loon. I got a wee hud o' him.' Or 'Cairnbog hae feenished their hairst. Aa the stooks are inby.'

The bike had another disadvantage. It had aroused jealousy in some of her siblings. Older brother John was intensely so and whenever he could lay his hands on the bike just took it and went off. Jessie was furious. Tears rolled down her cheeks.

'John's awa wi my bike again, mam.'

'You'll jist hae to larn where to pit it so that he canna find it,' was often all her mother would say. John was her acknowledged favourite. Everyone knew that he would be more leniently treated by her than the rest. He was a handsome, dark-haired boy who from a early age could talk to grown-ups with apparent ease. Mrs Jaffray had plans for him. She would discourage him from going into farming. Encourage him instead to go to university, become a lawyer, doctor, banker – get away from these endless rounds of disaster that was farming in Aberdeenshire.

William Jaffray was not so lenient with John but, because he was out working in the field for such long hours, he had to leave much of the disciplining of the children to his wife. He knew John often did things just to annoy Jessie. Hang her rag dolls up by the legs in trees was another of the ways he found to aggravate his sister. Jessie loved her dolls and this was sacrilege. Occasionally John came back with the bike damaged and then trouble arose and he was severely reprimanded and punished by his father.

The other contender for the bike was her sister Fanny, two years her junior. At six she still couldn't ride one and there was no other bike small enough for her to learn on. She kept pestering Jessie.

'You canna even reach the seat yet,' Jessie would make excuses. Then one evening she relented.

'I'll teach you,' she said and she did in the long summer evenings holding on to the back of the seat of the bicycle until she felt Fanny had got her balance and then let go. There was many a fall and much laughter. Afterwards she allowed her to ride her precious bike from time to time but there was always unhappiness over it until the English Aunt, whom Fanny had been called after, gave her a second-hand bike. It surprised everyone. Aunt Fanny was not known for her generosity.

Once Fanny became proficient, she and Jessie went off together. There was always rivalry between the two sisters. For years they were much the same height and although they didn't look all that alike some people thought they were twins. Sometimes they pretended they were and many years afterwards, when Fanny would write from Africa or the southernmost tip of Ireland, she would still sign herself, 'Your beloved Twin.'

Jessie wasn't altogether selfish with her bike and was willing to give anyone a shot of her prize possession but she hated it being taken without her sanction. She never took it to the village school. It was a couple of miles away and all the Jaffray children had to walk there and back. Most country children walked to school. It was the norm so no one thought much about it. On the whole Jessie liked school. She loved to read and write. She loved all the new worlds it opened up to her. The schoolmaster, in the little two-roomed school, was on the whole a kind man if somewhat strict.

'Learning is the thing,' he would tell them. 'You must learn.' He knew he had parents backing him especially those who didn't want their children to have to stay in farming. For those who wanted to get out of the poverty trap learning was the answer. But he knew most children would rather be out playing than sitting at desks. He had an increasingly large family of his own but the heart had been taken out of him when two of them died at a young age of the dreaded tuberculosis.

'Why? Why his family?' he would ask himself when many of the farming families escaped the scourge – there must be an answer. One day they would know all about tuberculosis. They were making great strides in medicine. Learning was the thing – all important.

Learning was very important in the Jaffray family also and they were all encouraged to do their homework. A peat fire was put on for them in the parlour as soon as they came back from school and Annie Willox set to preside.

'Especially the loons. The loons must larn,' their mother would say.

'Why especially the loons?' Jessie would argue.

'Because they have to gyang oot and earn a living. We're nae rich. I dinna see hoo we can ever be and we winna be able to start all the boys aff in fairms even if they wanted ane. For you quines, it doesna maitter so muckle. You'll all hopefully mairry weel-tae-dee fairmers. You must learn to be guid hoosewives. Jessie, I notice you are guid at sewing but not very diligent at any kind o hoosework – far tae scatter-brained and Fanny, you're no muckle better.'

Jessie, always ready to take the argument further would say, 'But what if we dinna want tae mairry?'

'You will,' was all that her mother would say in reply sighing to her self and wondering where these two rebellious daughters got their ideas from at such an early age.

There were eventually seven children in the Jaffray family. After Fanny came Andrew and his twin Robert who died in infancy, then Peggy the following year and Charles three years later in 1900. Eight babies in ten years if you count the one that died. Life was a struggle because money was always short.

While the children were small, Mrs Jaffray was able to keep Annie Willox and Jenny employed. The maids got little pay but got free board and good wholesome food. This was the way things were in the country. The maids' parents couldn't afford to keep them anymore and so they were put out to service until such time as they would marry. Annie and Jenny got a day off on Sunday when they would usually visit their own homes. They got off early on Saturday evening and had to be back on Sunday evening. Mrs Jaffray was kind but strict with the maids. She didn't pry too much into their private lives but if she suspected they had been out with a lad at the weekend a concoction containing Epsom Salts was made up and the girls ordered to drink it.

'Guid for the constitution,' she would tell them with no further explanation.

The maids shared a bedroom in the farmhouse next to the kitchen. There they both slept on deep downy mattresses of feathers and were covered by coarse blankets and patchwork quilts. They had to be up before six in the morning. It was Jenny's job to hang the great black kettle on the sway and make up the peat fire underneath it. The fire was in a great open hearth. On it all the cooking was done for the men on the farm and the family, either in a great black pot hanging from the sway or in smaller pots on small fires made at the side.

At six am the men came stomping into the kitchen ready for the day. The long scrubbed table at which they sat was sparsely set with two bowls, a plate, a spoon and a knife for each man.

The bowls were either white or ringed with blue. One was a quarter filled with oatmeal, the other filled with milk – whole milk it had to be before any cream was skimmed off to make butter. At the centre of the table was a huge platter brimming over with what was generally known as 'breid' or 'cake' – oatcakes, always baked on Tuesday. Beside them was a glass dish containing syrup. Jessie was never to forget the big cans the syrup came in. On the front of the green and gold can was a picture of a lion and the words 'Tate and Lyle's Golden Syrup'. When she was very small words sometimes got mixed up. Syrup was spirit in her mind. God she was told was a spirit. So God became for her a great golden lion like the one on the syrup tin. This misunderstanding slipped out one day at breakfast. Everyone laughed but Jessie.

As soon as the men entered the kitchen they took their bowls of oatmeal over to the singing, spluttering kettle. They knew the exact amount of water to pour into each bowl and then with the handle of their spoons mixed the water into the already salted oatmeal. Now it was ready to eat which they did with relish, dipping a spoon full of brose into the bowl of milk. The milk was last evening's, fresh from the cows. The oatmeal was last season's, oats grown by themselves then taken to the mill nearby and ground. It was then kept in a girnal (a huge wooden box) in the dark passageway next to the kitchen. From the girnal also came the oatmeal that went into the baking of the oatcakes. It would take half a day to bake enough 'cake' to last the week. Baker's bread or loaf as it was called was seldom used except on Sundays as a special treat

William Jaffray ate along with the farm workers, sitting at the head of the table. He was always there before them and enjoyed the chance of discussing the day's work in the comfort of the firelit kitchen. Not all farmers did this. The more acres they had, the more inclined they were to eat in the back parlour.

Before work in the fields could begin and before breakfast, the animals had to be seen to. The horseman went to his horses to water and feed them and saddle them up for the day's work. In winter time the cattlemen went to sort the 'nout' (as the cattle were called) in the large open-slatted reeds. The women were responsible for milking the cows and seeing to the pigs and poultry.

Looking after the children was not the only job Annie Willox had to do. It was just one of many. Before she got them up in the morning she had to wash the men's breakfast dishes to let Jenny get to the milking. After this chore was done she got the sleepy children up for school. There was much complaining, some squabbling but eventually they all had their brose and were out on the open road. Then Annie would attend to the smaller ones, the busy day well into its stride.

Life didn't change much from day to day except with the change of the seasons and so it had been for ages past. Illness, of course, took its toll but mostly grown-ups worked through it and the young also, though more care was taken with them and bed rest was the cure for many things, the only cure there was with very few medicines about. There were only the old remedies that had been handed down for generations. The Jaffrays were fortunate that no TB got into the family and no diptheria.

William Jaffray could get gloomy sometimes when these diseases were mentioned. 'Five o my brithers and sisters died o diptheria when they were jist bairns,' he would often lament to his wife. 'Five o them. Thank God there was anither six o us or I dinna ken fit my mither and faither would hae daen. It was afa. I can aye mind the dour times o gloom and sadness. Pray to God it never happens tae us.'

Mrs Jaffray refused to think along these lines. What was the use? Do your best and don't worry about things that may never happen, was her outlook on life. However it was a constant source of fear and each evening William Jaffray took out the bible before the children went to bed, and in the parlour, glowing in the light of the peat fire and the paraffin lamp, he would conduct a small service.

All the children were gathered together and Annie Willox

and Jenny. The farm workers were also welcome to attend but often, exhausted after a day's work, they chose to remain in their chaumers, the Aberdeenshire equivalent of bothy, one of the many Aberdeenshire words derived from the French language.

A passage from the bible was read out. Jessie didn't always understand what these passages meant but she loved the sound they made, the music of the language, and she would learn pieces off by heart. Afterwards, prayers were said asking God to keep them all safe, and that the harsh weather would allow them to get sufficient crops in to sustain their way of life.

These small services were to have a stabilising affect on Jessie for the rest her life. She never became anything approaching a religious enthusiast, but Jesus was there for her to turn to if the times got tough. In this small community there were few doubts that he was there for them – sometimes to punish if they did wrong – sometimes to help – but there. And they needed something to sustain them, something other than everyday contact with other people who were fallible. Sometimes they got a 'fire and brimstone' minister who would warn them they would burn in the eternal fires if they didn't reform their ways. Some rather enjoyed this kind of preaching but more often it was a lower key sermon that was in favour. The Gospel according to St Paul was a great favourite.

For the fisher folk living on the seaboard it was different Loss of life could be an every day occurrence for them. Who knew when a fishing boat would turn turtle when the seas were running high. Their lives and livelihoods were always in danger. Their church had to reflect their preoccupations. Some fisher folk attended the Church of Scotland but many of them liked there religion hotter and their churches tended to be Baptist, Methodist or Brethren both closed and open. It seemed sometimes to Jessie that even though they lived so close to them, they were a race apart. She seldom visited St Combs on her bike, the nearest village on the sea's edge six miles away, even although there was a golden beach there. It was a different country – this eastern seaboard.

Chapter 4

Trespassing

ON THE WHOLE Jessie's life when she was very young was a happy one. There was always a lack of money but the Jaffray parents didn't let this affect the family any more than they had to. Mother Jaffray was thrift itself – knitting, sewing, mending in the long winter evenings while the children played or did their homework. Sometimes their father would read to them from some of the classics. There weren't many books around – books were expensive – so almost everything was read that they could lay their hands on. Jessie loved books and was fortunate to have access to more than most as Doctor Blackhall had a good collection and he was only too pleased to have them read.

'Anytime you like,' he would say. 'You can take one or two home with you but look after them. Give them to your father and remember to bring them back.'

From an early age Jessie was a great romantic and once she got into the stories of Sir Walter Scott, Thackery, Dickens or George Elliot she became completely absorbed in other worlds.

Poetry also interested her. To begin with, it was more the sounds of the words and the rhythms that pleased. She learned many poems by rote, indeed quite often had to, for school. The headmaster, or dominie as they called him, liked having her as a pupil. She was bright, intelligent, hard-working and above all interested and enthusiastic. He had an assistant teacher but also used older pupils to teach the younger children. Jessie was good at this because she was able to convey to the younger ones a sense of excitement.

'She'll make a good teacher one day,' confided the dominie to his wife.

'If they ever have enough money to send her to university or teachers' training college,' she replied.

'They'll probably try to, because Jessie herself has set her heart on going already, even although they have a big family, if they're all spared,' he sighed, heavily overcome for a moment by the recent loss of a cherished daughter. 'There is so much poverty around and so many bright pupils in farms and cottar houses keen on learning. You feel so helpless sometimes.'

'You do a great job,' said his wife. 'And every year the government is trying to improve the school situation and give the really bright kids, who could never afford to go to university, bursaries to help them pay for it.'

'It's all too slow,' said her husband impatiently.

Jessie looked up to the dominie as if in some ways he was a God. How could anyone know as much as he did? One day she would know a lot, go to university, be able to teach others. Her mother wasn't altogether encouraging.

'Nae many quines gyang tae university,' she'd say. 'You really have to be afa clever, so hoo on earth do you think you'll get there?' She felt at times this daughter of hers was getting a bit above herself.

'And I'm gaun too,' piped up Fanny. 'If Jessie gyangs, so do I.'

'University is for loons,' said their mother. 'I dinnae ken what's got into you twa quines. Noo look at your wee sister Peggy. Already she's a dab hand at sweeping the fleer and setting the table withoot even being asked. But you twa, ach! Peety your peer husbands.'

Just the same Mrs Jaffray saved every penny to help them if

she could. It wasn't easy with money getting tighter and tighter.

'Thank guidness for the sales o butter,' she would sometimes be heard to say.

'I dinnae ken hoo we would manage withoot it.'

The worst nightmare was the shoe bill.

'They're aye sae hard on their sheen and they grow oot o them sae quickly and I want them to grow up with feet that arna aa calluses and bunions. We micht hae mair siller if it werna for these damned shalties,' she would sometimes be heard to mutter. 'Hoo aften hae I telt him but he winna listen. Goes his ain dour wey.'

And William Jaffray did in this particular instance. Once a year just before sowing time when the grass was becoming green on the land, he had got into the habit of going to Skye to buy ponies and truck them back by train to Buchan where he would let them feed on the good Buchan grass. Later in the year he would sell them at Aiky Fare on a Wednesday in July when it seemed that all Aberdeenshire trooped there and a thousand or more ponies and horses of all sizes were sold. The whole family went. It was a great day out. Aiky Brae, where it was held, wasn't far away and they always took a picnic with them.

'You'll never mak muckle siller oot o they shalties if ony. Some years you definitely lose money though you'll never admit it but it disna stop you gaun tae Skye ilka Spring. It's jist a holiday. That's fit it is and an expensive ane at that.' William's feisty wife didn't mince her words.

Holiday was a word that was hardly known in Aberdeenshire among the farming community at that time. Holidays were for the gentry who were always shooting off down to London or taking long trips abroad, something that was never even considered among the ordinary farmers of the north east.

'There's nae ony question o me getting a holiday,' Mrs Jaffray would sometimes grumble, 'or the bairns for that maitter.'

'It's nae a holiday. It's wark! You want to get oot o the bit, don't you?'

'Oot o the bit – into the hole mair like.' For years this bone of contention was unresolved and William Jaffray would return from Skye telling of the wonders he had seen.

'You should jist see it,' he would say.

'It's afa bonny in quite an ither wey frae here. Aa thae braw lochs and mountains and the colours are richt fine even afore the trees come intae leaf. Ilka shade o green, broon, goud, mauve, mingled a thegither. The air is safter than it is here and the folk mair relaxed, generous with their whisky, douce and kind.'

'Generous wi their whisky – douce and kind!' his wife would splutter, dangerously about to explode.

'You could gyang wi me next year if you wanted to. We could manage the fare somehoo and Annie Willox could look aifter the bairns and hoosehold. What a boon she's become.'

'I dinnae seek tae gyang,' said Mrs Jaffray. 'Besides Annie's got a lad noo and is like to be marriet by next year.'

Without ever meeting anyone from the west, Mrs Jaffray had grown prejudiced about the people there and managed to instil this into her children. She saw the folk as deceitful and lazy – Celts all. A different people from those in the north east. Here the ethos was for hard work and frugal living and thrift to the point of meanness. It was the only way to live. The Buchan folk were the folk and she was Buchan through and through as everyone was, born within sight of Mormond Braes, that bonny frugal hill they saw every day of their lives. Her folk were still at Corsgellie where they had been for generations and where she had spent all of her childhood. It was at no great distance from Dartfield. Mrs Jaffray was also somewhat prejudiced about the fisher folks who lived at the wild sea's edge.

'They're a different race tae us, an ither breed,' she would tell her children. 'Their weys are no oor weys.'

She was friendly enough, however, with Betsy the fish wife who came once a week with her creel of fresh fish and her voluminous black skirts. Here was a hard-working woman like

36

herself who needed every penny and walked the six miles from St Combs to get it. Mrs Jaffray always bought fresh fish from her for a few pennies as well as buying a barrel of salt herring every year and a goodly quantity of hard fish, cod that had been dried in the sun and would keep for a long time.

This food was needed in the winter when no one could move for snow. The hard fish was a special favourite – soaked first of all before use to soften and remove salt and then boiled until the flakes fell apart. It tasted of sun, salt and sea. Mixed with chapped tatties and mustard sauce it was a favourite filler not only in winter. Its popular name was Hairy Tatties because of the hair-like appearance of the fish mixed through the mashed potatoes.

Salt herring, too, if it was properly treated and cooked, could make a healthy nourishing and palatable meal. First the salt herring was left overnight under a running tap of cold water to rinse salt away. Next day tatties, in their skins, would be scrubbed laid in the foot of the pot and herring packed on top and then cooked. The tatties helped to soak up the salt that was left.

Apart from commerce the farmers had little to do with the fisherfolk. They lived very different lives. Many of the fisher people had their own churches although several came to nearby Lonmay Church where, in the graveyard, they buried their dead, spending a fortune on bigger and better gravestones than anyone else – not the way of most of the farming folk at all.

Mrs Jaffray rarely went to St Combs nor did William but, when they were older, the children went there occasionally on bikes during the long summer holidays, not to play on the beach so much as to smell the sea, marvel at its power or watch the fishing boats going out or coming back in with their catches.

That was the extent of holidays for the Jaffray children, that and a picnic or two up Mormond Braes with Annie Willox. Always memorable occasions. The rough feel of heather on bare legs, the smell of it, the tough climb, and the view from the top far out to sea. Their picnic basket was always full of home baking and they carried flasks of diluted elderflower cordial made by their mother that they would pretend was wine. It was wine to them. Everything about these excursions was wine – the wind and the sea, the smell of the heather, the freedom to run and jump and laugh and push each other over in the heather, and laughing, scramble up again in this land where their ancestors had worked and played from time immemorial, seeing the same view, smelling the same smells, hearing the same calls, curlew, lapwing and gull in from the sea.

In the long summer months Jessie would escape on her bike all on her own. Sometimes she went to nearby Lonmay station. Here there was a whole other world for her to watch. The trains were frequent, carrying fish, coal, grain, animals or passengers. It was the people-carrying coaches that intrigued her most. Amazing to think you could travel to London from Lonmay and that people from Buchan did just that. Richer farmers went to London from time to time – those with bigger farms than Dartfield – but mostly the long distance travellers were those they called 'The Coonty'. They were always at the station either going off somewhere exciting themselves or with friends, arrriving or departing. They also owned the few cars that were about as Jessie was growing up, beautiful models all polished and gleaming. They spoke loudly in English voices and were fashionably dressed. The women walked with nipped-in waists, flowing, long Edwardian gowns and wonderful wide-brimmed hats. Jessie took in every detail. especially the hats. One day she would wear hats and clothes like these even if she had to make and sew them herself.

She had learned to sew from her mother. She liked to sew. And one day, her romantic mind would flow into the future, one day she would get to know these people, perhaps even live their lifestyle. Didn't her mother always tell the children when they said 'I can't do it' that there is no such word as can't in the dictionary?

Jessie would sometimes spend hours at the station just

waiting for trains to come and go. Trains that took people out of this tight corner of the world called Buchan where the same names appeared on the gravestones generation after generation and where the Doric had become so local that even people in the town of Aberdeen couldn't understand what they were saying. At school the dominie tried to teach them to speak English.

'That is the language of advancement,' he would tell them. 'You will get nowhere if you don't speak English.' And Jessie never doubted that this was so. Didn't these rich Coonty all speak English in loud confident voices as if it was the perfect thing to do. Her mother wasn't against it either.

'Aye, English is the thing. You do as the dominie says and you winnae gyang far wrang.'

And so Jessie tried to cut out some of the rich, warm, expressive words of her motherland and use English words instead. Fanny did likewise but if they got too posh the boys would make fun of them and a fight would ensue.

'You loons will never get anywhere in the world if you don't speak English,' Jessie would tell them. 'And think of what you would be missing – all these wonderful things to do, places to see, worlds you've never dreamed of.'

The boys continued to scoff but within Jessie's words the seed was sown, the realisation there was another world outside Buchan.

There were discussions, sometimes, about what was happening in the outside world. The *Aberdeen Journal* was a great source of news. The Dartfield Jaffrays couldn't afford it but Uncle John at Lums got it daily and passed it onto his brother. Increasingly it had news within its pages of what was happening in Britain's far-flung Empire. There were amazing opportunities here for young explorers. There were fabulous places to see, new worlds to be discovered, riches to be made. Jessie read the paper with interest and wished she was a boy. It was always men they were needing. Why not women? She also read of the work of the suffragettes and, although she never felt like becoming one of them, she could foresee a future when women would be able to do what they wanted. Things were definitely looking up for women.

Her mother was fearful.

'A woman's place is in the hame,' she would tell her daughter, 'and I dinna want you to get ony fancy ideas. If you want an education, fine, but you'll get mairriet ae day and there is nae mair important job than bringing up bairns.'

'Hoo ald-fangled can you get!' said her tempestuous daughter and Fanny as always chimed in to agree with her sister.

'You'll see,' was all their mother would answer.

Exploring on her bicycle Jessie was always careful not to trespass on other people's property. Farmers had a strict code of conduct which they instilled in their children.

'You dinna gyang rinning ower ither folk's grun wi'oot invitation unless on an erran or because there is snaw and the roads are drifted.' And so Jessie was careful not to trespass with one exception.

One day she became unbearably curious to see Crimmonmogate House. This was the big house where the 'County' lived. They owned the big estate on which Dartfield and Lums stood. The house itself was surrounded by two hundred acres of policies, mostly trees so that at no angle was the house actually visible from the road. Jessie desperately wanted to see the house where some of these people lived. Feeling a little bolder than usual she decided to risk it. There was no one about. She went in at the North Lodge – an impressive old two storey house where she knew the factor lived. She got past that successfully. All was quiet. She pedalled on in some trepidation through the deep woods with their maze of paths, soft with years of fallen leaves. There was nothing to see but trees and more trees until she came to some stone buildings. This was no doubt the stables. She had heard her father talk of them. Here the original house had stood before it was burned down. She knew from hearsay that the house, built in the middle of the nineteenth century to replace it, was further on.

Amazingly all was quiet. Nothing stirred. It was midday – dinner time. Everyone would be in for their dinner she reckoned and she had heard that the owners, Earl and Countess of Southesk, were staying at their other estate in Forfar at the time. Before she was quite expecting it the huge house loomed in front of her. How enormous it was. It took her breath away. The leaf soft track led comfortably past the back of the house but Jessie wanted to see the front. Would she dare bicycle up that drive that would take her there?

'I've come this far,' she thought.

'If I get caught father's gyang tae kill me if he hears aboot it.' Slowly, fearfully she walked her bicycle up the drive and round to the front of the house. How wonderful. How like a picture out of a book – the green grassy lawn, the summer drive and the magnificent house itself with its many huge windows and enormous porch whose roof was held up by tall pillars of granite. She was just about to turn her bike and speed off with her mission completed when all of a sudden she became rooted to the spot with fear. Coming towards her was a man and a horse.

CHAPTER 5

The Factor

JESSIE STOOD with one foot solidly on the ground and the other on the peddle of her bike. Normally her instinct would have been to get on her bike and get out of there as quickly as she could but something in her made her unable to move. Fear had welded her to the spot. Not fear of some unknown stranger – she knew who he was. She'd seen him from time to time riding round the estate on his fine chestnut gelding. She knew his name. It was Captain Chaplin and he was the factor for the estate. The man her father paid the rent to. He would be sure to tell her father where she had been and she would be in real trouble this time.

There was also a certain fear of him but not that he would harm her in any way. This fear was more related to awe. This man was one of the upper crust who spoke English in a loud voice and with the tone of authority. If he spoke to her what would she say to him? Would he understand her Buchan speak. He trotted towards her on his horse. A handsome man in his mid forties with a military bearing and not an ounce too much flesh anywhere. Jessie knew something of his background also. She'd overheard her father telling his sister, her Aunt Margaret from Maud, about him. Her father hadn't realised that Jessie was listening and taking it all in.

'Aye, they say he got into some bother when he was young

and was sent doon frae Cambridge. At ae time he was engaged to be mairriet to the Errol o Southesk's sister. I'm no richt sure what happened there but the mairriage never cam off. Aye fegs, he must o gotten intae mair bother, I jalouse. He was reputed to be a bit o a gambler and a little ower fond o the bottle. I suppose it was aifter the break-up o the engagement that he went intae the army and eventually became a Captain. Anyroads, aff he gaes tae Africa biding there for a guid while. It's a wild place, they say. He was a peer looking soul when he left the army and cam here. Wouldn't hae gie'n tuppence for him. He'd taen blackwater fever or something and was invalided oot, a changed man I believe. The Earl, who'd aye been his freend, took peety or him and offered him the job o factor for his twa estates. Captain Chaplin accepted and he's been here ever since. It was grand hoo he recovered aifter he came here. When he first came back he was gaunt and grey. Noo look at him – quite the dashing Captain again and he's aa richt as a factor, disna bother ye much, is reasonable when listening to complaints and I've been gey late in payin the rent this last wee while. Aye fegs, times are hard.'

Captain Chaplin had reached Jessie by this time and was looking down at her from what seemed a great height.

'Well well, little girl and what might you be doing here?'

Some of Jessie's fear left with the annoyance of being called little girl. She was now all of ten and anyone could see she was no longer small. Her legs were long under her cotton skirt which reached near to her ankles. How often she wished she was a boy and could wear trousers. The older she grew the more attractive she had become. A lovely rosy complexion shone through the light tan of her skin and her thick and shining black hair was scraped back into one thick plait which hung down her back almost to her waist. She was quite unaware of what a picture she made standing there at the edge of the green lawn, her face flushed with annoyance.

'I'm nae that wee,' she said. 'I'm ten noo.'

She was surprised at herself for speaking out like this and she found, by doing so, she had lost some of her awe of him but there still remained the big fear that he would tell her father.

'I'm sorry for trespassing,' she said. 'But I jist wanted to see for mysel where the grand folk lived. My faither aften described it to me but it's no the same as seein it for yoursel.'

'Well now you've seen it, scamper,' the man on the horse said in a not too unfriendly voice.

'You'll no tell my faither will you?' she pleaded. Captain Chaplin looked down into her earnest grey eyes.

'Well, well, that remains to be seen,' he said.

Jessie had a horrible feeling he was laughing at her and she couldn't bear to be laughed at. What kind of answer was that to give a body. It wasn't yes and it wasn't no. She made up her mind. She didn't like this man.

'And what do you think of the big house now that you've seen it, young lady,' asked Captain Chaplin changing his tone somewhat.

'Oh, it's fair grand,' she said. 'I'd like to live in a muckle hoose like that one day but it must mak you feel sma whatever hicht you are. How tall these pillars are and what a big porch. It's enormous.'

Jessie was surprised she was able to say so much to some one she had been in awe of only a short time ago. Suddenly she wanted to be on her bike and away.

'Straight home now, naughty,' the Captain shouted after her.

She waited for days in fear and trepidation that Captain Chaplin had told her father but there was no mention of it. When the day came to pay the rent her father donned his best suit and went off in his pony and gig. She waited in fear for him to come back. When he did, there was nothing said.

William Jaffray was always in a good mood after he had paid the rent. It was Saturday and one of these spontaneous parties in the kitchen sprang up that evening. William had unearthed a bottle of whisky, much to his wife's annoyance, and the men came from the chaumers with their fiddles and a few neighbouring farmers came over, one with an accordion. The children were allowed to stay up late on these impromptu nights that were brimming over with the joy of life.

There was much country humour bantered about and much laughter. Even plump, apple-cheeked mother, the lines in her face caused by worry, hard work and constant childbirth, softened by lamplight and relaxation, would jig round the stone-paved kitchen floor with her husband to music played with muscle and zest. More peat was heaped on the fire and the flames gave off just about as much light as the paraffin lamps hanging from the ceiling. Soon the children were dancing too. Jessie loved to dance. As usual, before going to bed that night, there were bowlfuls of hot oatcakes in milk for the children.

Jessie slept soundly after all the brisk dancing and was up next morning before the others. Her father was just about to go out when she appeared downstairs.

'Jessie, seein you've risen will you come and help me shift some sheep. I should hae done it yestreen. It's nae a difficult job. The dogs and I could probably do it oorsels but an extra pair o legs wouldna come amiss.'

It was a pleasant summer's morning and, for once, not cold, no wind coming up from the sea. The clouds were high and herringbone in the eggshell sky and, as always, on days like this, Jessie marvelled at the amount of sky there seemed to be compared to earth. They walked to the far park in a companionable silence. This was an uncharacteristic thing for Jessie to do. She was by nature a chatterbox. She was still afraid her father might say something after being with Captain Chaplin the day before but nothing was forthcoming. She began now to feel a sense of guilt. Jessie as a rule was a straightforward girl and didn't like to be deceitful.

As predicted the sheep were easy enough to shift. The two

dogs did it for them with a few whistles from their master and a few crisp orders.

'G'way by. Steady noo Nell, steady.'

Jessie loved to watch the dogs at work, sleek, fast as the wind, eager to run and always attuned to commands. All she had to do was open a gate or two or stand in certain positions so that the sheep wouldn't go the wrong way.

'Thank you, Jessie,' her father said once the sheep were safely enclosed in a field of fresh grass, emerald green and shining after yesterday's rain.

William Jaffray gave a big sigh.

'What's the sigh for, faither?'

William, who hadn't realised he had sighed, thought a moment and said,

'I suppose it's a sigh of relief aifter yesterday. It always feels guid to pay the rent and, man, whiles it's a real struggle, an gettin waur ilka year.'

'Do you go to Captain Chaplin's hoose to pay it, the ane that's ca'd the North Lodge.'

'Aye, that's the Estate Office as weel.'

'Div you like him?'

'Wha?'

'Captain Chaplin.'

'He's nae bad. There's a lot waur folk than him.'

'He didn't say onything did he?'

Jessie had taken her father's rough and callused hand and lengthened her stride to keep pace with his. They passed the peat moss where low hillocks of peat were drying in the sun. Jessie loved the peat moss with its rich black seams. At this time of year it was starred with bog cotton shimmering in the air or blowing sideways in the wind. It always seemed to Jessie that its creamy white tufts gave the sensation of silk rather than cotton. From an early age she had a great awareness of beauty.

Three oystercatchers above them were making an awful noise

– two chasing the third one off. Jessie knew there could be nestlings cowering in the ground not far away but it would be a waste of time looking for them. They were so like the colour of the peaty earth that she would just about have to stand on one before she saw it. If any danger was near they were preconditioned to roll into tiny inconspicuous balls and keep absolutely still whenever they heard the warning cries of their parents.

'Say onything? Fit are yi on aboot?'

'He didn't say he was talking to me, did he?'

'Talking to you. When could he hae been talking to you?'

Jessie hesitated and took a deep breath. She wanted to get this off her chest. This was probably her best chance.

'Well,' she said tentatively, 'I hope you winna be ower roosed wi me but he foond me trespassing the ither day.'

'Trespassing. Far? Hoo aften hae I telt ye. . .'

She felt his anger rising but she would have to go on now.

'You ken hoo you whiles mention that you cannae see Crimmonmogate Hoose frae ony angle frae the road?'

'Fairly at, it's surroonded by trees. You're nae supposed tae see it. That's fit the Coonty like to dae, keep themselves tae themselves so that you cannae see what they're up tae.'

'Well for ages I've longed tae see that hoose far they bide. I've seen them in their fancy car and at the station and I jist wanted to see far they bide.'

'You didna go in there did ye?'

'Aye I did. I didn't particularly mean to but last week when I bicycled past, aifter delivering Mrs Murdoch's butter, it seemed quiet and I kent the Earl and Coontess were awa frae hame. So I jist bicycled in by the North Lodge and foond it.'

'And you bumped richt intil the factor?'

'Nae at first. There wisna a soul to be seen to begin wi. It was denner time, I suppose, nae ane aboot, that is until I took a keek roond the front o the hoose and there he was, Captain Chaplin, on that great horse of his.'

Jessie took a quick look at her father. He had his stern face on but she had the feeling that he was pleased to be told, pleased that she had confessed.

'Your nosiness will get ye into real trouble ane o these days,' he told her.

'But I so wanted to see it.'

'A weel what did you think o it?'

'It's afa grand isn't it, and afa muckle. I think it must mak folk feel like pygmies to live there.' Jessie had been learning about pygmies at school.

'Aye, they like their big hooses richt eneuch, but they're no bad folk jist the same. Oor folks hae been tenants to their folks for generations back. Some are better than others, just like folk aa ower, but the present Earl's nae a bad chiel. We aa hae respect for him and he's earned it. Even the Southesks are nae aa that rich though they put on the style. Fegs aye, and what did the Captain say to you? Gave you a richt telling off I hope.'

'Waur than that. He ca'ed me a little girl and I think he was laughing at me. I don't like him. I'll not trespass again. How old do you think he would be?'

'Aboot my age I would think.'

Jessie knew better than to ask what age that was. Her parents' age was never discussed in the family. That sort of information was sacrosanct. She glanced sideways at her father and had to admit that he looked a lot older than Captain Chaplin.

So being wicked didn't necessarily age one, but hard work did. Her father's face had lines on it that were as deep as some of the furrows he so assiduously ploughed each year and there were great crinkles round his eyes when he laughed, as he did a surprising amount although there was often little to laugh about. His nose, never his most attractive feature, always a little too big, now stuck out boldly on his gaunt face and his chin which sported a short grey beard on the underside, likewise. His hair was iron grey, and his skin was darkened and shrivelled by constant battering from wind, rain and sun. It didn't help that he wore no teeth. He had them taken out years ago. He had a false set in a drawer upstairs mixed up with various nuts and bolts but he wore them only for going to the market and church or the few occasions when he and her mother went visiting.

She didn't mind how her father looked. She loved him and wished she could make life easier for him. Why did he have to work so hard while the Coonty could sit in their big hooses and tell others what to do?

'And what wicked things did he dae, the Captain, I mean?' Jessie had been intrigued by what she had once overheard. She was always making up stories about people in her mind using what material she could find. One day she would write a book that people would want to read – about people – real people. She knew she was good at writing. Hadn't the dominie praised her school essays more than once and read them out to the class?

'Fit are ye on aboot noo?'

'I heard you and Aunt Margaret talkin oboot him aince.'

'You shouldna hae been listening to a conversation that wasna meant for you.'

'I couldna help it.'

'It's not for the likes o us to ken directly what goes on wi thae folk. They live in a different warld tae us and onywey you're far ower young to ken aboot these things.'

This statement from her father whetted Jessie's appetite all the more. One day she would find out for herself.

CHAPTER 6

The Growing Family

FOR THE NEXT TWO years life went on much as usual for Jessie. With seven children now in the household there was always noise and excitement.

Jessie noticed that her mother and father often looked tired and trauchled these days. She knew it wasn't easy getting enough money to educate, clothe and feed all these children. Mother Jaffray scrimped and saved more than ever. She held fewer afternoon teas, and seldom went out visiting any more. She wished that Jessie and Fanny would help more in the house and were a bit tidier. She was impatient with their reluctance and ineptitude and it often seemed easier to do the job herself. Peggy was different but she was barely old enough to do much, even though she was willing to try.

From time to time however Jessie and Fanny were landed with some jobs to do that they did not like. Jessie's pet hate was churning. The butter took so long to 'come'. She would sit on a hard wooden chair placed on the middle of the paved kitchen floor and turn and turn the handle of the wooden barrel churn for what seemed to Jessie to be ever. After a while she kept stopping the churn to have a look at the wee glass window at the top to see if the glass was clear, a sure sign that the butter was ready. When that happened the buttermilk became separated from the butter and the churn would begin to make a different soft thumping noise while the separated buttermilk gave a distinctive woosh.

'I think there maun be something wrang wi this milk the day,' she would sometimes say to whoever would listen. 'The butter's just never gaun tae come.'

'If you would jist get on wi it – keep caain and no be always keekin at that wee windae it would come an afa lot quicker,' her mother would tell her.

And of course cream eventually did become butter. Just as Jessie was about to give up her mother would proclaim it ready and open the lid. There it was – the lump of butter as yellow as buttercups in a swill of buttermilk as pale white as the moon in a morning eggshell sky. The rest of the process belonged to her mother who would squeeze out any excess fluid and weigh the butter out into pounds, half pounds and quarter pounds. Then with butter clappers and much dexterity learned over the years, she quickly fashioned it into shapes. She had little stamps made of her own design, some of thistles and various wild flowers, others depicting small calves or lambs, pictures to make each pat of butter look more interesting. She knew all about presentation. It wasn't for nothing that her butter was famed far and wide for being the best in Buchan. She knew exactly what it needed, the exact amount of salt to bring out the rich flavour of milk from cows fed on good grass, straw and turnips.

Occasionally, at the end of the winter when straw and hay, fed mostly to the horses, was becoming short, the cows had to be fed a larger proportion of turnips and the milk began to taste faintly of turnip. There wasn't much she could do about this other than to complain to her husband and pray that the snow would disappear quickly and the grass come through and let the cows out to graze. The money for the butter was the perquisite of the farmer's wife – her pin money which she sorely needed to buy clothes and shoes for the children.

She also made cheese but the girls weren't allowed any hand

in this process. Everything had to be just so. Jessie would watch her mother setting down great shallow steel pans of milk on small fires of peat she had made from the larger fire in the centre and heating them until they were just the right temperature. After testing the milk with her forefinger and finding the heat acceptable she would measure out spoonfuls of rennet, the exact amount needed to make it curdle. Once the curds were ready for pressing, they were put in a round tub with holes in the bottom to let out the whey. This tub was first of all lined with a piece of muslin or scrim. Afterwards the curds were put into a chessel (cheese press) that stood outside the back door which was then screwed firmly down to get rid of any excess moisture. Once it was pressed enough the individual cheeses were often put up on the window sills of the dormer windows of the bedrooms. Here the wind came in wafts from the sea and would dry off the cheese. The children's bedrooms would smell faintly of goose feathers and cheese.

Baking day was Tuesday. As soon as the men's dinner was over, out would come the baking equipment. Oatmeal was mixed up with measured amounts of baking soda, cream of tartar and salt in a big bowl – white on the inside, yellow on the outside. Water and dripping were added and then the raw lump of wet oatmeal was taken from the bowl onto a baking board and pummelled about a bit. Afterwards it was rolled to the required thinness with a huge wooden rolling pin and fashioned into a round that would fit exactly onto the black girdle.

While the oatcakes were in the making the greased girdle was heating on the sway over the red peat fire. Before putting the oatcakes on to the girdle, oatmeal was spread over the top of the round to prevent it from sticking and then a second baking board of exactly the same size was placed on top and the whole thing deftly turned over. The bottom board was taken off and the round sprinkled with oatmeal on its other side after which it was ready to shuffle onto the hot girdle. Before the oatcake began to harden a knife was taken to cut it into sections. At just the right moment each section would be turned with a palette knife and, when deemed ready, all were removed from the girdle leaving it empty for the next batch. The v-shaped sections were then placed round the big fender and left to grow faintly brown and curly at the edges in front of the fire.

Sometimes, of a cold winter's afternoon, when the children had battled home in a biting and wet east wind with wet shoes, wet clothes, cold and tired, Annie would give them each a bowl of milk with broken bits of newly baked hot oatcake dunked in it. In later life these children remembered how good it tasted.

Apart from the Sunday loaf, mother Jaffray didn't buy much from the horse-drawn baker's van that came round the farms from Maud once a week. She deemed it too expensive. Besides she was a good baker herself. Once a week she also baked scones, thick brown or white girdle scones made with bought-in flour which was kept in a separate girnal. It wouldn't matter how long they were snowed up for in the winter, they would not go hungry. Sometimes she would make treacle scones with dark black treacle taken from a large tin that was mostly used as medicine to give to an ailing cattle beast.

The girls were not encouraged to attempt any baking, only watch.

'Fanny and I jist get aa the borin wark,' Jessie would complain. 'Like washin eggs or churning butter.'

Eggs were washed in the small back kitchen with water that was carried in from the pump in the yard. They had to be washed in cold water using a little scouring powder if the stains were hard to remove. Sometimes, on a winter's day, fingers would become numb with the cold water. The eggs must be perfectly clean and great care taken not to break any. Eggs were also an important source of income for the growing family.

The job the girls hated most of all, however, was the washing and drying of dishes especially if there was a big pile of them. For this job water had to be heated in the great heavy black kettle.

The children were not allowed to unhook the kettle as it was heavy and awkward. Once, when Charlie was two and a bit, Jenny put Jessie in charge in the kitchen for a short time. When the kettle boiled, Jessie took it off the sway just as wee chubby-cheeked, bare-footed Charlie came towards her and a splash of boiling water landed on his foot. He gave a howl of anguish. Mother Jaffray came flying into the kitchen. The suddenness of her entrance made for complete silence.

'Fit's wrang?' Mother Jaffray demanded to know.

Nothing was said for a moment or two and then Charlie's gruff little voice piped up.

'Jessie's burned my foot.'

Jessie was in trouble again.

Another job, perhaps equally as unpopular with the girls as the washing of dishes, was the cleaning of lamp globes. A dirty job this, black paraffin smoke was hard to remove.

Washing clothes was done on a Monday mostly by Jenny and Annie using a scrubbing board and a large wooden washing tub set on a sturdy wooden stool made for the purpose The tub and its stand were set in the middle of the kitchen floor and the tub filled with water, all of which had to be carried from the pump and heated over the peat fire.

Fanny and Jessie both thought they might like ironing but that was probably because it was forbidden. Irons were dangerous things for children to use. The red hot v-shaped blocks had to be taken out of red embers in the peat fire with long tongs and slipped into the hollow irons. They were easily dropped. Annie and mother Jaffray did most of the ironing. Many an afternoon when the children came home from school they entered a kitchen sweet with the smell from the ironing of clean clothes brought in from the sun and wind.

Saturday nights were bath nights for the children. These took place in a hip bath placed in front of the kitchen fire with screens put round for privacy.

There was one job that mother Jaffray did trust Jessie with, more and more as she grew older – a creative job – a job that Jessie liked – the making of clothes. Out would come the old, well-oiled, treadle sewing machine and Jessie was trusted to sew up seams. Hour after hour she would do this quite happily and never get bored. It surprised her mother that this bright-eyed, volatile girl should take so easily to sewing. She seemed to know instinctively how to make things and loved working with the paper patterns her mother occasionally bought. Jessie began to take more interest in what clothes she wore and began to make skirts for herself and Fanny using the same material so that they could look like twins.

Very occasionally she went into Peterhead in a gig with her mother and father, a day of great excitement. It was a bustling place and the nearest she had ever been to a big city. Together she and her mother would visit the drapers' shop and choose materials for the clothes that were needed. They never could afford the more expensive sort, or all that they fancied, but Jessie was a great improviser and the draper, attracted to this bright-eyed enthusiastic and excited girl, would give her odd bits of material for nothing of which she would make great patchwork use. Sometimes the bits would be large enough to make a shirt for Charlie and a pretty apron for herself. Narrow pieces would make bright ribbons for her hair.

How she loved these days in Peterhead going from shop to shop buying things for the household and afterwards going down to watch the fishing boats in the harbour.

'Aberdeen is far bigger than Peterhead,' she was often told. She couldn't imagine it. She couldn't wait to get there but there was never enough money for such luxuries. Before she was twelve years old, however, something happened, something quite unexpected, that was to change Jessie's life.

CHAPTER SEVEN

A Visit to Aberdeen

JESSIE had been aware for sometime that her beloved Aunt Maggie had not been well. Everything that had once been a joy to her was now a trauchle. Once plump and rosy-cheeked she was now thin and occasionally snapped at Jessie which was so completely out of character that Jessie knew she must be ill.

One bright June morning just before she was twelve her mother woke her early, shaking her gently so as not to wake her sleeping sisters with whom she shared a bed.

'Come doon stairs and get some breakfast. Put on your Sunday claes. Dress as fast as you can. I hae a surprise for you.'

Down in the quiet kitchen, the men having just left the long scrubbed breakfast table, her mother was mixing up a bowl of brose for her.

'Eat this up,' she said, and then your faither is gaun to tak us in the trap for the early train to Aberdeen.'

Jessie couldn't believe her ears. 'Aberdeen,' she spluttered, 'But why?'

Your Aunt Maggie's no weel. Doctor Blackhall's taen her tae a nursing home in Aberdeen and she's ettlin to see us baith.'

A look of anxiety came over Jessie's face at the thought of Aunt Maggie being in hospital. Mother Jaffray saw it and was quick to try and dispel fear in her daughter.

'Dinna you worry, she's in the richt place. She hasna been weel for some time but they'll maybe be able tae dae something for her in the nursing hame.'

Jessie brightened at this and was almost sick with excitement at the thought of going to Aberdeen. She had wanted to go there for so long. Knowing of the excitable nature of her daughter, mother Jaffray hadn't told Jessie about the plan the night before, thinking she might not sleep.

Mother put on her Sunday coat and hat and they were ready. Father had the gig at the door to take them to the station even if it was barely half a mile away. There was a bit of bustle. One or two of the bigger farmers were off to the cattle sales in Aberdeen and the Crimonmogate Riley was there, chauffeur-driven, taking some guests of the Earl and Countess to catch the train back to London, a man and his wife.

'Oh mither, jist look at her elegant traivelling dress and her bonny hat. I'd love to hae a dress and hat like that when I'm big but I canna imagine myself ever looking that guid.'

'There's no sic a word as can't in the dictionary,' said her mother using her favourite adage. She might have enlarged on it had it not been for the train steaming into the station.

Jessie loved the familiar sight of the long snaking train trailing clouds of steam, the smell of tar, the clanking of wheels across rails, the sharp banging of doors. How often she had watched a train approaching and now she was really going on one and all the way to Aberdeen. The guests from Crimonmogate elegantly stepped into a first class carriage. Mother Jaffray looked for a suitable second class one and was fortunate enough to find one that was empty. They both climbed in and mother Jaffray lowered the carriage window by the strong leather strap so that they could wave to William who was standing there in his working clothes ready to hoe turnips. Jessie could not help contrasting the man who had just stepped into the first class carriage in his smart London suit and her father in his old working clothes.

'Faither should hae pit on his best suit to see us aff in,' said Jessie.

Mother Jaffray read the drift of her daughter's mind.

'None o that noo, Jessie. Your faither's just as guid as onybody and a sicht better than some. Dinna be too in awe o the Coonty. Like us they cam wi nothing and they'll gyang wi nothing. And if you ever hear onyone ca us peasant fairmers, ignore it. There's no such things as peasants in Scotland – aa Jock Tamson's bairns as Burns tells us, all important in the sight of God, no a sparra fa's. Awbodie's a wee bit different, jist the same, even within faimilies. Look at you with your black hair and grey een. No one else in the faimily is really like you. Nae doobt you are some hark back to some earlier ancestor o oors.'

'French maybe,' said Jessie her eyes flashing with interest and remembering the story her father told them from time to time. A story she could never hear too often. She went over it in her mind once again.

The Jaffrays in Buchan had all come from a common ancestor, a French sea captain who was drowned along with his wife in the seventeenth century when his ship was wrecked off the dangerous Rattray coast not far from Dartfield. It had been a wild wild night. Some fishermen had noticed the ship in distress towards midnight but there wasn't much they could do about it until morning light. By morning the ship had sunk without trace. The fishermen scanned the rough seas for survivors. It was unlikely there would be any in such fearful conditions but in the dim dawn light they saw something afloat, a raft, and there seemed to be someone on it. The raft was making its way inland on the incoming tide. The fishermen launched a boat and went out to help it in over the still towering waves. Much to their surprise, when they reached it they saw what looked like two babies strapped on. With great difficulty and courage they managed to rescue them from the raft into a fishing boat. The babies were badly affected by cold but miraculously still alive. The seamen massaged some warmth into their tiny limbs and wrapped them in fisherman's jerseys. Once ashore they were taken to the nearest house.

Astoundingly both of them lived. That was about all that was ever salvaged from the wreck – the twins and the ship's log which was also strapped to the raft and from which they learned that the captain had been travelling with his wife and twin sons. It was never known if any of the twins' family had been looked for in France and, according to legend, one boy was brought up by the fisher folk and the other one by farmers.

'And that's where wi aa cam frae,' William Jaffray would tell his children with a certain pride.

Jessie had taken this story more to heart than any of the others.

'I really dae feel afa French, mither. Dae yi think it's possible that I'am a hark back. I want tae tak French when I gyang tae university. The dominie's aye tellin us that a lot o the words that we use in Buchan have their origins in France. Oh hoo I would love to gyang tae France sometime. I am sure it would feel like stepping on the soil of my mitherland,' she said dramatically.

'Calm doon,' said her mother. 'Stop getting cairriet awa by your imagination. We're gyang to Aberdeen today – ae thing at a time.'

Jessie and her mother spent most of the rest of the journey looking out the window and taking in all that they saw – the green growing fields of oats and barley, the lush pastures, interspersed with peatbogs, the sheep still in their winter wool, the sleek cattle putting on fat day by day. From the minute those scrawny, lacklustre beasts were herded out of their winter enclosed cattle courts or reeds, as they were called, their appearance changed amazingly quickly once they got on to the strong Spring grass.

As the train drew nearer to Aberdeen they caught glimpses of the long seascape. Jessie had little aptitude for painting but she wished that she could do so and in this way be able to capture and hold the beauty of the sea, blue today with reflection from an azure sky. Gentle billows, tipped with white spray, came rolling in and on the horizon the boundaries between sea and sky were almost invisible, only a hazy blue mistiness dividing them. It wasn't always like this.

They stopped at several stations on the way. Their carriage soon filled up mostly with people going to work in Aberdeen How smart and neat they were, Jessie thought. At the stop just before Aberdeen two ladies entered, all dressed up ready to go shopping. Jessie would have liked to speak to someone but she was too shy to start up a conversation and her mother didn't seem inclined to either. She watched and listened, taking everything in. She wondered what sort of lives they led. Were they very different from her own?

Jessie and her mother, lifting up their long skirts, stepped carefully down the tall steps from the train into the vaulting Victorian station at Aberdeen. Jessie thought she had never seen quite so many people all together except perhaps at Aiky Fair, but that was different. Where were they all going? What did they all do?

Soon they were in Union Street with all the shops open. Jessie had not imagined such big shops displaying so many goods nor such imposing buildings on either side of the broad street. Today with the sun shining on their granite walls they sparkled and winked at her just as if every building were alive. The streets were busy with every sort of traffic, a car or two, horse-drawn carts and carriages, trams on steel rails, bicycles, everyone going about their business in their own way. Well-dressed ladies out for early shopping were descending from horse-drawn carriages to stroll along Union Street at a ladylike pace looking at the displays in the various windows.

'We'll leave gaun to see your Aunt Maggie till the aifternoon. That's when the doctor said would be the best time,' said her mother. 'We'll spend the morning looking at the shops – maybe buy ane or twa things. I've taen some o the butter money that

I've saved for a rainy day. It's no a lot but it'll gi us something each. I micht get a new hat if I see ane I like. It's your birthday soon Jessie. Fit div you seek?'

What a decision to have to make. She loved clothes and would dearly have loved a new red silk blouse. She loved red and knew it suited her but even more she loved books and books were hard to come by.

'Div yi ken what I would really like? I'd love to learn French. Could we find a bookshop wi a book that teaches French grammar. The dominie said he would help me if I could get hud o a book.'

Mother Jaffray was taken by surprise with this request. Would she ever understand this daughter of hers.

'If that's fit you want we'll find a bookshop later on.'

Mother Jaffray did find a hat that suited her and Jessie thought she really did look nice in it and told her so. It was blue and would go with her blue skirt and match her blue eyes.

They also found a bookshop. Jessie had never seen so many books all together. She would have liked to stay there all day just browsing. Mother asked the young shop assistant about the best book for the teaching of French. It was rather more expensive than she had bargained for but she bought it for Jessie who was happy indeed with the purchase. As soon as she got home she would start to learn French. One day she would go to France.

At lunchtime they went into one of Aberdeen's big restaurants. It was full of people – women shoppers mostly, all chattering. Mother Jaffray feared it would be too expensive but the prices were more reasonable than she had expected. Both Jessie and she chose a dish with sausage the main ingredient. It was modestly priced. They had a sweet cake to follow and a cup of tea. Everything to Jessie tasted different and special. Mrs Jaffray thought she could make better cakes at home.

After lunch Mother Jaffray bought some June roses from a flower seller in the street and they found a cab that would take them to the nursing home which was in the rich end of town.

Jessie was amazed at the sight of one big granite house after another. How did people need so much room to live in? The nursing home was just a big house like its neighbours, not quite what Jessie had expected. Not that she really knew what to expect. Inside it was all thick carpets, velvet curtains and silver ornaments and nurses in stiff starched white uniforms. They were escorted upstairs into a big room with a wide bay window. There were four beds in the room discretely curtained off, one from the other. The nurse drew back the curtains in the bed at the far corner.

'Visitors, Miss Urquhart,' she said. 'Visitors to see you.'

After the happiness of the morning Jessie got a shock when she saw her aunt. She was even thinner and her skin had an unhealthy yellow palour about it. When she saw them Aunt Maggie's smile was as bright as ever.

'How winnerfae tae see you – how unexpected.'

Jessie and Mother Jaffray both kissed her on her thin hollow cheek. Her sister handed her the roses.

'Aren't they afa bonny and what a grand smell,' she said burying her nose in the bouquet.

'Hoo dae you feel?' asked her sister. Try as she would she couldn't keep a worried note out of her voice.

'Afa tired,' said Aunt Maggie. 'But I'm real comfortable here. Hoo guid o the doctor tae tak me tae sic a grand place. I just wish I felt well eneuch tae enjoy it. He's comin the morn tae see me.'

They chatted away pleasantly enough but Maggie began to look strained and Mother Jaffray thought it was time to go. Before they went Maggie took hold of her niece's hand.

'Promise me,' she said, 'that if onything should happen tae me you'll still gyang and see the doctor. He's very fond o you, you ken, as I am Jessie. We see a grand future for you. It's almost as if you're oor wee girl. Big girl noo.'

Tears came into Jessie's eyes. 'But auntie, you will get better. I know you will. Nothing can happen to you.'

'Dinna worry, Jessie. I'll probably be oot in a week or twa

but jist in case. Weel you niver ken in this warld.'

Tears were beginning to run down the cheeks of Mrs Jaffray also by this time. Maggie quickly changed the subject.

'Have you teen Jessie to see the university buildings, Marischal College and King's College?'

'Nae yet,' said Mrs Jaffray, wiping her eyes with her handkerchief.

'Oh she maun see them. Have you time to tak her there afore you get the train hame? You ken hoo muckle Jessie ettles to gyang tae the university.'

'We'll gyang there noo,' said mother Jaffray regaining her composure. 'And we'll come back and see you next week, Maggie, if you're no hame by then.' And with these parting words and a few hugs and kisses they left.

True to her word, Jessie's mother hired a cab and went to see both university buildings. Marischal College seemed like a fairy palace to Jessie. It was a sunny afternoon and the light danced and sparkled off the light granite building but King's College impressed her even more. It looked as if it had been there forever welded to this North Eastern soil and the houses around it looked old and sombre and dignified. She could hardly imagine herself being there. And yet that is where she meant to be one day, no matter what.

It was late afternoon by the time they caught the train home. William Jaffray was there to meet them when it came in to Lonmay station.

'Hoo is she?' he asked.

'No ower weel,' was all that Mrs Jaffray would say in front of Jessie. Next week, before they could pay a second visit, Maggie Urquhart was dead.

CHAPTER EIGHT

The Snowstorm

THE DEATH of Aunt Maggie was the first time that Jessie had come up against real grief. She had seen the effects of grief in others. Some of her companions at school had lost someone close to them – a father, a mother, a brother – but she hadn't ever faced the fact that it could happen to her. She had only been three years old when Andrew's twin brother died in infancy and she didn't really remember. The death of someone close was a shock to the always optimistic Jessie. Aunt Maggie had been like a second mother to her. In fact perhaps more of a mother. She had spoken more to Aunt Maggie than to her own mother who was always busy and had so many other children. The day in Aberdeen with her mother had been an exception – a happy one. Never had she had her to herself for so long a time at a stretch.

Jessie didn't feel the same about going to the doctor's house anymore. The memories of Aunt Maggie would be too strong but she knew she had to go. She remembered very clearly that Aunt Maggie had said if anything happened to her to look after the doctor.

A few days after the funeral she paid him a visit arriving just after the time when she knew he had his evening meal so that she would have a chance of catching him in. It was strange going there without Aunt Maggie. Now that there was a new housekeeper would she have to knock at the door? She supposed she had better.

Mrs Anderson, the new housekeeper (temporary Jessie came to hope) answered.

'Fit dae you want?'

'Could I see the doctor please.'

'Fit for?'

Jessie didn't think it was any business of hers but said politely but firmly. 'Because he's my freen.'

'He's jist had his supper and doesna want to be bothered but I'll find oot. Bide here.'

Jessie found it very odd to be left standing at the door at what had been for so long a second home. She wasn't left standing long. The doctor himself came to the door.

'Jessie, I'm so pleased to see you. What on earth are you standing at the door for as if you didn't belong here. Come in.'

How tired and old he looked all of a sudden, Jessie thought, and her heart went out to him. Her arm went round his waist in a voluntary hug of sympathy and they stood together in silence for a moment or two.

'Come through to my study.' He always called his book-lined cosy sitting room his study. A peat fire danced merrily in the hearth. The two armchairs still sat one on either side of the fireplace.

'Sit down, Jessie,' he indicated the chair, upholstered in horsehair with a strong mahogany frame, on which Aunt Maggie had sat of an evening when all the chores, apart from the darning, had been done. Aunt Maggie had always felt it wasn't her place to sit there but the doctor had always insisted she should. Tears sprang into Jessie's eyes.

'I know how you feel.' It was the doctor's turn to give sympathy and put his arm round Jessie's shoulder.

'We've both lost someone very dear to us.'

Jessie didn't know what to say. She had come to cheer him

up and now she was on the verge of bursting into tears.

The doctor spoke first. 'I hope you'll come and see me whenever you can, Jessie. You are the one link I have left with your Aunt Maggie and we were both very fond of you. You really are like a breath of Spring on a bleak day.'

Jessie was far from feeling like one.

'And you don't need to knock. You know this is your second home. Mrs Anderson's a bit grim but she's efficient, although no one will ever replace your aunt. I get such feelings of guilt sometimes. We should have got married. I bitterly regret that we didn't but somehow we were always so busy and the right time just never seemed to come along. Your aunt was always frightened it would harm my career in some way – my status as a doctor. What nonsense – I shouldn't have listened to her. She was a very fine woman, gentle and kind, always willing to do things for others without considering herself. A true Christian come to think of it. It's a cruel old world. Terrible how it can take away the best but nothing could have saved your aunt. She had cancer of the liver and by the time there was much in the way of symptoms it was too late. Your aunt never complained. It all seems so unjust. All the same, don't let anything ever make you give up your Christian faith, Jessie. It's a lifeline. I've always found it to be so.'

The doctor occasionally had been in conversation with Jessie about religious matters and knew that, young as she was, her faith was strong. It was true, Jessie did have strong leanings towards religious matters and wondered how the doctor could think she could doubt Christianity.

'Of course I winna,' said Jessie, 'and I dinna think you should feel guilty aboot onything. My aunt loved warking for you, doctor – looking aifter you and aa the patients who cam to the door. She loved you and her job, and jist aboot the last thing she said to me in the nursing hame was that I was to look aifter you if onything happened to her, so I'll come and see you whenever I can if you want me to.'

'Of course I do. What else did your aunt say to you in hospital?'

'Oh she wisna a bit depressed only very tired. Jist afore we left she asked mither if I'd been up tae see the university buildings. When mither said no, she said she must tak me there.'

'And did she?'

'Aye.'

'And what do you think?'

'Jist oot of this warld. I would really love to gyang there someday. I'm gaun to wark as hard as ever I can at my lessons for you ken, doctor, I'm not the cleverest person in the warld. There are ithers at school cleverer than I am. I don't think it will be easy for me to get a bursary but I'm really gaun to try. I'm determined to gyang there some wey or ither.'

The doctor laughed and teased her gently.

'You're much more modest than you used to be. Remember when you were a little girl and I was teasing you by saying I knew a prettier little girl than you and you said, Oh, but you haven't seen me in my new frock?'

Jessie laughed.

'I was a conceited wee thing then,' she said. 'But I've had plenty knocks since and ken better noo. I'm useless at maths for instance, but English I'm nae so bad at and it's the subject I like best – English and French. The day we went to Aberdeen to see Aunt Maggie, mither said I could buy ae thing and she gave me the choice. I chose a French grammar and the dominie says he'll help me wi't. You see', she went on explaining, 'my faither tells us aften aboot oor French ancestors and I feel sometimes I micht be a hark back to them.'

'Well you never know.' The doctor didn't laugh at her fancy but took it seriously. 'Your aunt told me that story once, about your ancestors. I've got one or two French books you can borrow. As I've said, borrow what books you like from the shelf but look after them and put them back.'

Jessie had taken advantage of this offer before. There was nothing she enjoyed more than to curl up with a book in some hidden place like the hayloft where she wouldn't be disturbed and become totally absorbed in a story, enter another world.

They talked of this and that for quite some time but mostly about Aunt Maggie, both finding comfort in remembering little things she did, keeping her alive. They spoke as if she wasn't dead at all but was still with them until they were interrupted – a knock at the door – the midwife was having trouble. Mrs Michie's baby was coming the wrong way. The doctor was needed at once.

After that evening, whenever she could, Jessie popped over to see the doctor. But life was getting much more hectic for her these days. She had her lessons to think about and also helping out in the farmhouse. More and more, now that Annie Willox had gone, with all these growing children to look after, her mother needed help. Quite often too, when she did get the opportunity to go over the doctor he would be out – away in his gig. He threw himself into his work more than ever and often, when she did catch up with him, she found him exhausted. He didn't seem to care how he felt anymore.

Winter came early that year – well before Christmas they had hard frost and flurries of snow. One night there was a heavy fall of snow with considerable drifting. Dartfield's farm road quickly filled up with snow blowing off the fields. It had been a struggle getting out of doors at all that morning. When the back door leading into the farmyard was opened a mound of snow fell into the house.

The men had to dig their way out of the chaumers to get to the cattle reeds, the stable, the byre. The first essential was to keep the cattle and horses warm and fed. Breakfast came afterwards. Aberdeenshire farmers were provident and forward thinking – they had to be and enough turnips had been brought in for just such an eventuality. A month's supply or more was near at hand and the lofts were stacked full with hay and straw.

Similarly in the farmhouse there was no shortage of food. The girnals were full of oatmeal, hams hung from hooks screwed into the kitchen ceiling. Cheese, butter and eggs were always in good supply. They could withstand a siege. Their father would tell them, however, that the climate was changing. Winter's were milder now than when he was a boy. It was seldom nowadays that they got snowed up for too long.

'Noo I mind, when I was a loon,' and he would go on to tell of winters he had known when they were snowed in for months on end. 'The winters noo-a-days are no half as bad as they used to be. Rather than sna, yi get sheets o rain driven in frae the sea by that cald east wind that disna half gae through you. I think I preferred the sna o the ald days. There was mair sunshine. Noo it's aa weet and grey growling skies.'

However much hardship it entailed (children and all having to clear snow) Jessie loved these snow-filled days when the sun came out and every particle of it glittered in the covered fields around them. Sometimes it was almost too bright for the eyes to bear. The winter trees took on a new look when snow stuck to every branch and twig. The rowans especially became a delicate tracery of fine twigs and slim wands and in the few fir trees white satin cushions furnished the dark green branches. The duck pond had ice thick enough to skate on. Sometimes too, if the snow lasted long enough, the older children would go up Mormond Braes to sledge on mother's iron trays or the one solid sledge their father had made for them.

Jessie liked when the snow lasted for a while and the family was altogether – no school, a warm kitchen, a time for games and storytelling, a time for just existing with nothing outside to interrupt their way of life. The younger members of the family, however, didn't always realise the danger of snow although sooner or later they would encounter it.

One day, during the second winter after the death of Aunt Maggie, it was brought home to the children very forcibly. A couple of weeks after the New Year, when they had all returned to school, the skies blackened alarmingly as they were eating their lunchtime snack and snow began to fall. The schoolmaster sent all the children from outlying districts home and so John, Jessie, Fanny, Andrew, Peggy and Charlie, who had not been at school long, started off on their mile and a half trek home. The first half mile or so was fun. The younger ones skipped and danced along glad to be out of school early.

As they continued the wind rose and the snow worsened. The big flakes, fluttering and dancing down like small chicken feathers, changed to much smaller flakes and were so close together that they became a blinding white curtain that made it difficult to see where they were going. Small drifts were beginning to form. But the worst thing was that familiar landmarks were disappearing. Would they be able to recognise Dartfield road end when they came to it? Wee Charlie began to cry with fear and the cold. John and Jessie took charge. Jessie carried Charlie for a bit but, small though he was, he was heavy and it was too much for Jessie against so strong a wind. She had to put him down, taking hold of his hand and half pulling him along. John went in front of the little band of children. For once Jessie was impressed by her brother. He shouted to them over the noise of the wind, encouraging them on, leading the way.

'This is fit faither ca's a blin smoor. It really is dangerous. We'll hae to be afa canny and no get lost. But you'll be aricht. We canna be far frae hame noo. Jist follow me and aa keep thegither and gyang as fast as ye can.'

On they trudged valiantly forward. Sometimes the wind gusted so strongly that it was an effort to breathe let alone speak or rather shout as they had to do over the wind. Then all of a sudden John stopped and beckoned to the straggling line of children to cluster round him.

'It's nae the ferm road end yet,' he shouted, 'but I recognise that ald hake o faither's. There's nae other jist like it and it's at the corner o the park that leads stracht tae the hoose. There's a fence aa the wey. It wad be much safer tae climb ower the fence and gyang this wey keepin close tae the fence so that we dinna lose oor direction.' John knew how easy it was to get disorientated in these conditions even if you were just yards from home.

The others did not doubt his judgement and started to struggle up the snow-covered bank to reach the fence. It was at that moment that two ghostly apparitions suddenly appeared out of the snow – Willie, who at fifteen had left school and was working for his father, and father Jaffray himself. A whoop of joy went up from the beleaguered children.

'It's faither, it's faither and Willie,' they all shouted above the wind.

'Thank God ye're aa here,' was all that father Jaffray could say when he saw them.

John shouted to his father what he was intending to do.

'You're richt John. I'll gyang afore you and lead the wey. You gyang at the hinner end Willie, and see that none faas ahint.' And so they set off on the last tortuous lap, that brave little band of children led by their father, battling the elements.

All of them struggled home somehow with father at the head carrying the exhausted Charlie. They tumbled into the porch like so many snowmen. What a wonderful feeling to be out of the wind and into safety. They took off their snow-covered coats and boots and went into the warmth of the kitchen. Soon their faces were glowing and their hands and feet beginning to thaw out. Mother Jaffray, like an anxious hen, gave her husband a big dram from her hidden bottle kept strictly for medicinal purposes. William Jaffray didn't often get this privilege nowadays. For the children she made up a warm pan of saps from the white pan loaf she kept for Sundays. Into it she put sugar and a few raisins. Never had it tasted better or been more welcome.

Jessie knew the dangers of snow all right but it came as a great shock to her a few days later when drifts were cleared and news got through to learn that Doctor Blackhall was dead.

He canna be, he canna be,' she cried. 'I saw him last Saturday. There was nothing wrang wi him.'

Her father put his arm round Jessie.

'It was that nicht of sna, quine. He was battlin his way through it tae deliver a bairn and drappet deed on the doorstep wi a massive heart attack.'

Jessie was hard to console – her beloved doctor.

'Weel at least he'll be wi Maggie noo, I've nae doobt. They were baith bra folk,' said her father.

These words were of some consolation to Jessie. All the prayers and the teachings of the bible had seeped in, all the promises made. She didn't understand how God let those good people die but she supposed he had his reasons and yes she was sure they would be together. She knew the doctor was not happy with Aunt Maggie away. He had not recovered from his loss. It was little more than eighteen months since she had died. It was a hard cruel world she was beginning to discover.

'Gentle Jesus, meek and mild / look upon a little child / pity my simplicity / suffer me to come to thee.' That night, as she said her prayers, she prayed that the doctor and Aunt Maggie would be together united in bliss. She also came to a new understanding. 'Gentle Jesus' – that prayer was getting too childish now. She was a child no longer. She had been through the fires – she was adult and must accept what had to come, face up to responsibility and realise that, however optimistic she might feel, things went wrong sometimes. But it wasn't God's fault. It was just life, how the world was and to have God and Jesus to turn to was a wonderful consolation.

The doctor had been right. It did help enormously. She knew some people did not believe in Christianity and had no religious faith. How did they withstand all this grief. 'My rock and my redeemer' – these words came into her mind. The minister repeated them every Sunday before he began his long sermon which, to be truthful, she often never listened to. But how she loved the way he pronounced rock, ending the word quickly, making it sound so solid and permanent, immovable. From now on God would be her rock. She wasn't quite sure yet what redeemer really meant.

William Jaffray attended the funeral. In some ways it was a bleak affair. The day was dark with leaden skies threatening more snow. The church was grey, the tombs were grey, the trees were grey without their leaves. There were very few relatives present, only a brother and uncle up from the south, but the little church was packed full of sober-clad men there to pay their last respects to a good man. The minister's eulogy to Doctor Blackhall brought tears to the eyes of most of these strong men. Not that they needed to be reminded they had all lost a friend – a helper in time of trouble.

'He cared for us more than for himself,' said the minister. 'No one followed the second commandment better than he did. He died in the course of duty. Who can ask for more? When will we see his like again?'

Many a bowed head nodded in agreement and a warmth grew within that cold dark kirk with the icy wind coming in from the sea – a comradeship in struggle was felt among them.

When William Jaffray returned home Jessie asked him eagerly about the service. 'It was grand,' said her father. 'The Meenister did him prood.' He told Jessie something of what had been said. Jessie found it a consolation to think her doctor was so well thought of.

'And anither thing,' said her father.

'Doctor Blackhall's lawyer was at the funeral and muckle tae my surprise I saw this mannie coming towards me. 'You're William Jaffray, I believe, the father of Jessie Jaffray?'

'Aye,' I said. 'Well could you bring your daughter into my office in Aberdeen sometime soon. I have something important to tell her.'

CHAPTER NINE

The Will

THE NIGHT after Doctor Blackhall's funeral the air softened a little and the snow fell again in earnest – great huge soft flakes of it. Somewhere towards midnight the wind rose and by morning the Jaffrays woke to a white world once more. The field immediately in front of the house had been swept by the wind and looked like a threadbare white carpet, but the farm road was full of snow and would have to be dug out. No school today – the children inwardly applauded. A few days later there came a partial thaw and things began to get back to normal. Snowploughs had managed to make enough inroads to let traffic move again and the railway line was open once more and then the frost set in hard and grim and meaning to stay. William Jaffray was glad the appointment with the lawyer wasn't till the following week.

The day dawned frosty and bright. This time William was going to take his daughter to Aberdeen – this was man's business. There was no problem getting Jessie up that morning. She was ready before her father, dressed in her Sunday best. He also put on his Sunday clothes but, over his dark formal suit, he wore his overcoat which had seen better days. On his head a black lum hat covered the thinning grey hairs and he had his teeth in. They were delayed somewhat because he couldn't find them. William looked his daughter over and thought she didn't look warm enough.

'Hae you nae a warm scarf or somethin?'

Mother Jaffray, fussing around the pair of them, came up with a hand-knitted scarf and a fur muff for Jessie's hands. The muff was her own and Jessie had often fancied it. She loved to stroke its silky softness.

Jessie marched off proudly with her father. He looked like a real gentleman today in spite of the age of his overcoat. She could hardly believe what was happening to her – never in Aberdeen in her life before and now twice in eighteen months. It was just a pity they had to be such sad occasions, she thought. Still, with effervescent youth on her side, it was difficult being downhearted on a day like this. The sun shone from a clear sky making a million million diamonds sparkle in the snow.

Father had said, 'I think we'll walk to the station today. It'll be easier than getting the gig oot and haein the loon to tak us.'

They started off down the winding farm road on the small track that had been dug out. On either side the banks of snow rose higher than Jessie. To her it was like being in an enclosed world, just herself and her father. She loved the sound her boots made on the snow, a squeaky interesting noise. This was adventure and what would they find by the end of the day. She suspected that Doctor Blackhall must have left her his books. He knew she loved books and they would be precious to her. How wonderful it would be to have all these to read anytime she wanted. Her father suspected there might be a little more to it than that – a small legacy perhaps but said nothing to Jessie.

Soon they were on the open road which was virtually free of traffic until the sound of an engine and a loud horn made them jump. They stood well into the snow at the side of the road while the Riley from Crimonmogate passed. It was packed with people. Jessie mused that perhaps it was also going to the station.

It took them some considerable time to find the lawyer's office which was in a sidestreet off Union Street. Unpretentious, it was a bolthole with a brass plate stating the lawyer's name studded on to a stout wooden door that stood open. There was no bell, just the brass plate. They supposed they were just meant to enter. At first they went through a narrow stone-flagged passage and then up wide and winding stone steps with a landing halfway up that dipped badly where the earth had presumably sunk under the old building.

Jessie had just finished reading David Copperfield and Macawber and Uriah Heep were still vividly in her mind. Would the lawyer be like one of them, she wondered. This place looked and felt Dickensian. At the top of the stone stairs there was another stout door with a brass plate – 'Murdoch and McDonald, Lawyers' and below, 'Please Enter'. They pushed open the door to be confronted with a high wooden desk behind which stood a tall thin scrawny man with red hair. Uriah Heep, Jessie immediately called him to herself. William told the young man that they had an appointment with Mr Murdoch at eleven thirty. Young Uriah Heap beckoned them to two high-backed chairs.

'Take a seat please while I find out if Mr Murdoch is ready to receive you.'

He was gone for some time. Jessie was shivering with excitement and apprehension. Eventually they were led through to an enormous room with a huge window. An equally enormous stout table stretched the full length of the room and was piled high with brown paper parcels tied round with string. There was hardly a spare inch of table top visible and behind this table, in the middle and facing them, sat Mr Macawber, except he was not at all like how Jessie imagined Mr Macawber. The man behind the table appeared to be small. He had a thin and serious face with a neat goatee beard and he wore on his head a bowler hat. Jessie wondered if he had forgotten to take it off or did he keep it on because it was cold in this vast room, or was he merely hiding the lack of hair. He rose when they came in and came round the table to shake hands.

'And this is your daughter Mr Jaffray,' he said and then

turning to Jessie he held out his hand and gave her a surprisingly warm handshake.

'Pleased to meet you Miss Jaffray,' he said.

Jessie had never been called Miss Jaffray before. It made her feel grown-up and important somehow to be treated with respect like this. The lawyer asked them to be seated at two tall chairs on the opposite side of the table and started to rummage amongst the brown paper parcels.

'Now where. . .'

Eventually he found the bundle he wanted and picked out the knot in the string.

'Ah yes, Doctor Blackhall's estate. Poor man, poor man.'

He searched some time for the paper he wanted – read it over and then began,

'Well it seems, Miss Jaffray, you are a most fortunate young lady. Doctor Blackhall has left you the bulk of his estate in memory of your aunt. His books, his silver and a considerable amount of money. Four hundred pounds in all – most of what he had. The money has to be kept in trust for you until you are seventeen and it was Doctor Blackhall's wish was that it should be used for the university education he knew you desired. If however you should need it before then, for something of real importance to you, it is left to the discretion of the trustees, of which I am one, whether you have access to it or not.'

Jessie could hardly take in what she was hearing. Doctor Blackhall had left her not only his books but his silver, all these things she had so often admired on his sideboard and money. Money enough to go to the university – much more than enough. Four hundred pounds was a fortune.

Her father was taken by surprise too – his daughter with money enough to buy a small farm.

'The doctor wasn't an excessively rich man. It was kind of him to leave you the most of what he had,' continued the lawyer. 'I do hope you will use it well, Miss Jaffray. You want to go to the university I believe. Not many women get that opportunity yet but why not? Why not, indeed.'

'Aye,' said William. 'She's a clever quine, Jessie is, and fit's mair, she sticks at things and is no a quitter. It will be a grand chance for her.'

For the first time Jessie realised that perhaps her father was more on her side about girls going to the university than her mother was. She began to see him in a new light.

Once out on the street again Jessie felt she was walking on air. Was there ever such a place as Aberdeen? Snow lay, still white, here and there trimming the edges of buildings in untouched neuks and crannies. Horses and carriages rattled past, also a tram and one or two cars. It seemed like a magical place. To be able to come to the university, live here for a while amid all this exciting hustle and bustle seemed like an unbelievable dream. Perhaps Aberdeen never looked quite so wonderful to Jessie again as it did at that moment. Everything she wanted and had dreamed of now seemed so much more possible. She wouldn't have to ask her parents for money to help her with her dreams. This had begun to worry her lately. Although they never complained to her about the depressed state of farming she sensed it was worrying them more and more.

Jessie's father took her into a teashop and they had lunch. He didn't quite know what to say to Jessie, he was so taken by surprise after the visit to the lawyer.

'I'm richt happy for you. It'll mak your life easier. I jist didn't expect he would leave you onything like that. Aifter aa there are a puckle relatives – he has a brother, an uncle and maybe mair. I ken he and your Aunt Maggie were real fond of you, lookit on you as their wee quine but, fegs, I didnae expect this.'

'He was afa fond of Aunt Maggie, faither. He told me so, that day I went to see him jist aifter she deed. He said he felt guilty that he'd no marriet her. Maybe leaving aa this tae me made him feel less guilty in a wey.'

'Ach weel, you jist niver can tell. There's nowt sae queer as folk. You niver ken fits gaun tae happen neest. You're no even ca'ed aifter your Aunt Maggie. Noo if it had been ony o the loons that had been left aa that siller they could hae set themselves up in a decent size fairm wi it. I dinna ken hoo I'm gaun tae set aa the loons up.' William was now half musing to himself.

'And you think the siller's wasted on me, dae you faither? Wasted on a quine?'

'Na na, dinna think that for a minute. I'm richt prood o you Jessie. You'll gyang places. You'll beat them aa yet. Dinna tak ower muckle heed o my ravins. Things will wark themselves oot.'

But Jessie knew it wasn't all ravings and it was an ongoing worry how he would be able to help so many sons. She knew he would like them all to become farmers like himself, hard though it was. He loved the land. He'd done much to improve it. He didn't own it but he was thirled to it in much the same way as sheep become thirled to their own hillsides. The Laird owned the land but William, like most of the neighbouring farmers, felt a sense of belonging. Generations of his forebears had farmed this land always improving it.

To begin with much of it in the nineteenth century had to be brought into cultivation from bogland or peatmoss, as it was called in these parts. This was no easy task. It was hard graft to dig all the drains that were needed for which they got little recompense for years and years. The laird who owned the land didn't pay the farmers for this work, but let them have it rent free for a time until it began to produce. Once, in the middle of the last century, rents had been lower than they were now and prices for grain and cattle higher. In times of war, the Napoleonic and the Crimean wars, farms had flourished. But for quite some time now, due to imports from abroad, prices were poor and rents on the small farms hadn't gone down. Larger farms had fared better. They made real money for the Lairds and the hard-hitting big farmers had insisted on lower rents. The reward for the small farmer was not so much an increase in profit but more the satisfaction of seeing his place improve, his crops and his cattle flourish. The same sort of satisfaction that he got from a healthy flourishing family – sons who would become farmers after him and daughters who would marry farmers.

'And they'll maybe no aa want to be fairmers,' Jessie said. 'I've heard you ask yersel sometimes, wha would want tae be a fairmer?'

'If they dinna want tae noo, they'll change their minds later. I've seen it aa afore.'

'John disna want tae be a fairmer.'

'But he disna stick into his lessons aa that weel either so fit else is he gyang tae dae?'

'Maybe he'll gyang abroad tae the colonies. A lot o the loons are talking aboot that nooadays. Anyway I can always help oot noo I've got some money.'

'You'll no dae onything o the kind, quine. You'll need every penny.'

In his heart of hearts William didn't want his sons to go abroad. He knew that would be the end of their life in Aberdeenshire and it wasn't all that bad a place really. If you were lucky enough to be a tenant with a good landlord it could be a hard but a happy life. Crimonmogate was a good estate to be on. Unlike some big estates they had not made a policy of pushing out the tenant to make way for bigger farms. If possible, when the old farmer died, his farm was then let to his son or nearest relative seeking it. He had heard tell that in the west many of the big landlords had made a clean sweep, putting out all their tenants to make way for sheep. It hadn't happened here to the same extent. From time to time, however, a few of the more ruthless landlords did take aboard this policy but mostly it was the crofts that went, not the small farms and it was cattle rather than sheep that were responsible for this. The small farmers were needed. They produced the young cattle beasts, or stirks as they were called, for the large farmers with better land to fatten them for the London market. Ever since the steam ships had come into general use beef could be transported down to London. The arrival of the railways made it easier still. Gone were the days when cattle had to be driven on the hoof down to the market at Falkirk and from there further south. William Jaffray remembered, just the same, that once Mormond brae was covered in crofts. There were none now.

When they emerged from the tea room the sun had gone behind a cloud.

'It doena seem quite so cal. It's letting up a bit. Maybe we'll get mair sna. Fit would you like to dae noo? We've a wee while to go afore its train time.'

Jessie would have loved to go round the shops again as she had done with her mother but she knew her father would not like that.

'Lets gyang doon tae the harbour,' she said. It didn't take too long to walk there.

A wind was now coming in from the sea – a cold wind but Jessie barely noticed it. Nor did she notice that the sun had gone and that, to the East, over the sea, the sky was the colour of lead. There was much activity at the harbour. Fearful of bad weather the fishing fleet was coming in. The smell of fish was strong in the air and the cry of seagulls following the boats in eager anticipation of food was deafening.

'Better get back to the station. There's gaun tae be a storm,' shouted her father above the wind.

Jessie laughed, 'There's a storm noo,' she shouted back.

'It can be a gey cal place, Aiberdeen,' said her father when they got back to the comparative shelter of the station. Jessie barely heard him. Right now her thoughts were back home telling the rest of her family the amazing news.

CHAPTER TEN

Effects of a Windfall

THE NEWS of Jessie's good fortune engendered much excitement in a family where money was always short. But Jessie was surprised at the reaction of some. Her mother, for instance, although she did say she was delighted by her daughter's good fortune, also let slip that she thought it a pity her older brother John had not fallen heir to the money instead. He had so much more need of it to help him on in the world. He didn't want to be a farmer but how did one escape and get to the big city without money? John was of the same opinion – money was wasted on girls.

'Hopefully,' mother Jaffray had always said, 'they'll mairry weel, become guid wives, mithers, hoosewives and of some use tae their man. It was a man's duty tae keep his wife.'

John had always been jealous of Jessie and now even more so. Why did she get everything? He wasn't wanting to be like his elder brother, Willie, who at fourteen had left school to work for his father. John knew he would be working for a mere pittance. Up down, up down with the plough day after day in all weathers was what put John off more than anything else. What a boring job that was. To Willie it was better than school. Willie had never been much of a scholar. He would rather be out in the fields working, as he often was, when his father was behind with the farm work and Willie had been kept off school to help.

It wasn't that Willie didn't have dreams for when he was older. He did. He just didn't think to mention them. Sometimes, when looking through his Uncle John's *Aberdeen Journal*, he would read of the Great British Empire of which he was a part and all that was happening there. He occasionally heard of a young man going abroad and, after a while, making a fortune. He knew also of a few farmers' sons who had got the opportunity to do likewise when some entrepreneur, mostly of landed gentry origin, was looking for hardy young men to help them with their schemes for colonising land and bringing good virgin soil into production. These young men, it was said, could end up with a good farm of their own some day at very little cost, something that would not be possible at home.

Entrepreneurs were looking for young men to emigrate to places like Africa, Malaya, Canada. These young Aberdeenshire men, brought up on farms in a fierce climate and working on the land from a very early age were just what was needed – those who survived were tough. Willie knew he was still too young to go at fifteen, but when he was eighteen he would be off if possible. He loved farming. It was in his blood and from what he could gather, there were far better opportunities of acquiring a good farm of your own abroad than at home. Most of the land here was owned by some landlord or other and even supposing it did come on the market it would be almost impossible to afford. In the meantime he would content himself at home, even although he would get very little in the way of hard cash. He knew, however, that his father needed him. One of the bothy chiels had left last feeing time and his father had said that he really couldn't afford to fee another man and would have to work harder himself.

He was secretly pleased when he heard Willie say, 'I'm gaun tae leave school, faither. That's it, that's eneuch for me. I'll gie you a hand on the farm if you like for a whilie.'

Fanny, Jessie's so-called twin, wasn't exactly overjoyed either at Jessie's windfall. She had always been jealous of her sister and now even more so. But she wasn't one to do nothing about the situation. At times their mother got a bit exasperated with these two girls and their ambitious dreams.

There were times when she would say, 'You twa quines just get a wee bit abeen yoursels whiles. I'll hae nane of your Didos here.' Or 'Wha di you think you are – the Queen o Sheba?'

It wasn't that she didn't want her children to have high hopes and ambitions. She knew only too well what the alternatives were. Having a big family and a small farm sometimes meant one or two of the family had to go out to service and that was a definite come-down in the eyes of the farming world, to be avoided at all costs. It was more that she didn't want her children to get hurt when they went out into the real world, didn't want them to get too disillusioned.

Spurred on by Jessie's windfall, ten year old Fanny decided it was time she paid court to her Uncle John and Aunt Fanny. After all, was she not called after her aunt and they had no children. John was called after his uncle but no way would he go near him. They had had a fall-out once when John was younger and his uncle had called him lazy and that was enough for John. Wild horses wouldn't drag him back. Besides, whenever he had gone there in the past, Uncle John had made him work far too hard.

But Fanny thought that perhaps she could take up the challenge. Might she not become their heir in the same way as Jessie had become Doctor Blackhall's and Auntie Maggie's. And they had money too, it was reputed. Aunt Fanny had brought money with her to the marriage and Uncle John had been hard working and provident in his farm of Lums which was a better one than Dartfield. Being the eldest son John had inherited the best.

He had recently given up farming. Some years before he had acquired a piece of land from the Crimonmogate estate by the side of the road running between Fraserburgh and Peterhead. The estate didn't like chopping off bits of their land to give to people to build houses of their own but John Jaffray had got on well with the laird and he had relented. On this piece of land Uncle John had constructed a house which they now lived in. In honour of the Carnegies for allowing him the piece of land, he had called the house Bancar. The Laird was a Carnegie and his wife a Bannerman. The estate had come, unusually, through the female line.

Bancar was only about a quarter of a mile from Dartfield's road end and easy for Fanny to get to on a bike. The house Uncle John had built was a substantial one of granite with big windows downstairs and smaller dormer windows on the upper storey. It was kept in the traditional design of an Aberdeenshire farmhouse but somewhat more spacious. It had a pleasant and very typical Buchan outlook. Immediately across the road was a shelter belt of trees common to this part of the world. In other areas of Aberdeenshire, where the land was stony, provident farmers had enclosed their fields with drystone dykes which served several purposes. Mainly it was a way of using up unwanted stones in the fields while, at the same time, enclosing them and the dykes served as shelter for the stock when a cold north easterly blew or rain lashed sideways. Here in Buchan, a lot of land had been reclaimed from bogland where stones were scarce, so wire fences were erected instead. In order to give protection to the animals, shelter belts of trees were planted. Even with years of growth these belts of beach and oak never grew really tall because of unfavourable soil and the prevailing wind. From the front of Bancar, through gaps in the trees, green fields could be seen rolling to a clear horizon especially in winter. In certain days of northern sun there was a special light that defined everything with a clarity the beauty of which could be overwhelming.

Uncle John had ambitions for Bancar. He started what he hoped would be an exclusive small hotel, where people of substance would come – teachers, doctors, lawyers. This notion was somewhat scoffed at round about but, to a certain degree, he did manage to attract the kind of people he wanted. It was fortunate that the house was situated close to a fairly busy road and as time went on there were more and more cars about. Also it was near Lonmay station which gave it easy access from Aberdeen.

The hotel was Uncle John's domain – he organised it, he ran it, he chose the servant girls whom he thought would be suitable and if they didn't come up to standard they were soon sacked. He hired a good cook with advice from the Carnegies with whom he was friendly and filled a cellar with good French wine plus barrels of rum and beer and kegs of whisky from the distillers further north. The spacious, comfortable sitting room was lined with books and he had playing cards, cribbage and a chess set for the entertainment of his guests. Against the wall opposite the window stood a solid upright piano for any impromptu soiree that might occur. In the dining room stood a sturdy table to which leaves could be added should he have a full house. He made it policy that all the guests should dine together. Many a good conversation got up over dinner.

Uncle John did not encourage families to come to this gentleman's residence. Truth to tell he didn't really like children, perhaps because he didn't have any of his own and felt uncomfortable in their company. He was a man of little patience. He sported a luxurious beard, was as stout as his brother William was thin and had once been the better looking of the two with good features and a tall stature and fond of the good life which he now attempted to have. His impatient nature was well-known in the neighbourhood. When he was farming he rarely kept his men more than a term because he got in such a temper if things went wrong, blaming everyone but himself. A pillar of the kirk, he did not blaspheme, apart from the word damn which he used with such frequency that he was known as 'Damit' rather than Lums, the name of his farm which was normally the name by which a farmer was known.

Sometimes, in his farming days, he had been his own worst enemy. The story was told by his neighbours how one day his reaper broke down in the middle of a difficult harvest. He took it to bits, found the offending piece, removed it and because it was awkward to replace after being repaired, threw the offending and vital part as far away as he could and he and all hands had to spend the rest of the day looking for it amongst the ripe grain. Next day it rained.

He wasn't a farmer at heart and tried to get out of farm work by employing plenty of bothy loons. But suitable loons were getting harder to fee and he found it was becoming less and less profitable to hire them. Farming was not giving him much of a return and he had no children coming up to help him. He had had the idea of having a small hotel in his mind for a long time.

Aunt Fanny also had a rather fiery temper which made it impossible for them to work together. She decided she would like to have a small shop. An extra building was built on to the gable end of Bancar. In this wee shop she stocked everything she could think of from foodstuffs to knitting wool, from garden plants to ribbons. She wasn't nearly so good at running things as her husband and sometimes her shop got into a real muddle and wasn't as clean as it might have been either. Oddly it did have a good turnover. The Fraserburgh road could be quite busy at times.

It was not long after Aunt Fanny opened the shop that Fanny decided to go and visit her aunt and uncle. She was older now and she would see if she could charm them. To begin with she made some inroads with her uncle John. When he didn't have guests to attend to he would enter into conversation with her. He respected intelligence and recognised that she was intelligent and like her sister Jessie, well-read for her years.

Aunt Fanny she found more difficult. However her aunt was in need of help at the time. She was too mean to employ anyone, so she made full use of Fanny whenever she appeared. She was given the job of cleaning and sorting out the muddle. She kept her for ages longer than she meant to stay. Fanny hated any form of housework. The visits became less frequent.

When Jessie realised the effect her windfall was having on the family, she tried to do something about it. She told the younger ones that, when she got access to her money, she would buy them all a bike. To John she suggested that she would possibly be able to help him in any ambition he had. Jessie was very generous-hearted especially with anyone that was family and they knew this.

'I'll be rich by that time,' boasted John.

'I'll get a bursary and go to university under my own steam,' said Fanny. 'So there.'

Jessie couldn't win with these two.

'And fit would you like, Willie?' Jessie asked. Her older brother was a bit of a mystery to her.

'I widna mind the price o a ticket tae Canada,' he said diffidently. 'I hear they're settin up some grand fairms there.' Jessie was full of enthusiasm for this adventurous idea.

'And why not? There'll be plenty for ideas like that,' said Jessie. 'Although I would much raither have Aunt Maggie and Dr Blackhall alive than ony money. Haein it will be a good thing, you'll see. It could help the hale faimily in one wey or anither.'

It was true what she said. The loss of her aunt and beloved doctor left a gap that never could be replaced. But little did Jessie guess how prophetic her words on the value of money to the family were to become.

CHAPTER ELEVEN

Disaster

EVEN WITH the full-time help of young William, things were not going well on the farm. Prices for farm products were poor and there had been several bad harvests in succession with stooks staying so wet in the fields that the grain was spoiled by the time they got them into the stack. The harvest after the death of Dr Blackhall looked as if it was shaping up to be no better.

It didn't seem to matter how hard they worked they were never getting 'out of the bit'. Worse than that they were sliding backward and they were in arrears with the rent. Mother and father Jaffray didn't say much about their troubles to the children but the older ones could sense something was badly wrong. They knew money was becoming tighter and tighter. It was a struggle even to buy them new shoes. Then one after the other, the milk cows started to die. TB was diagnosed. William had bought a beast which, unbeknown to him, had the disease and infected the others. This was disaster. Part of their income came from butter and cheese.

The landlord was understanding about arrears in rent but William Jaffray knew this state of affairs couldn't go on forever. He knew the landlords's patience would wear thin. Always in the past, when they had gone through bad times, hope and optimism had been their greatest assets but this time William could see no way out, no way at all. He had nothing of worth to sell to tide them over bad times. He had no money to replace the all-important cows. He knew he was finished. It was the greatest sorrow to him. He loved his farm as if it were a child. He loved farming. He had no other skills. What would he do?

Not having paid last year's rent and now six months overdue with the present one he went to see the factor. Captain Chaplin was the sort of man you could talk things over with. William Jaffray decided to tell him the absolute truth in this dire situation.

'And you've no assets at all?' asked the Captain.

'No, naethin – naething ava.'

'Well something will have to change,' said the Captain.

'Have you considered giving up the farm?'

'It's the last thing I want to dae but I canna think o ony ither wey oot.'

The Captain felt heart sorry for this man. He knew what a struggle it was for these small tenant farmers, how hard they worked and how independent and proud they were. He knew of suicides when they had to give up. Strong men who couldn't face life any more took the gun they kept for shooting fox and rabbit to shoot themselves. The Captain didn't think this would happen to William. He knew what sort of man he was. He had a big family to provide for. He would not leave them in the lurch but he knew he must help him, let him see a way out.

'It looks as if you'll have to give up the farm Mr Jaffray. Have a roup at the term which will bring you in some money and I'll have a word with the Earl. There's a cottar house on the estate vacant just now, not very big but a wee bit bigger than the usual and perhaps the estate could find a job for you. Failing that, perhaps you could get a job on one of the bigger farms. Perhaps a manager's job although they are hard to come by.'

This was the solution William most feared – going to work for another farmer providing another farmer would have him. But he knew he was going to have to face reality.

That evening he gathered the children and his wife together in the parlour before the usual time for prayers.

It came as a shock to the family. They knew things were bad Things had been bad before and a recovery had been made time after time. This time, leave the farm – this couldn't be happening. There was stunned disbelief. Perhaps Jessie took the news worst of all. It was bad enough at school, just now, as daughter of a small farmer. Some of her friends had fathers who had bigger farms and were in a better position than herself. It was hard enough keeping her end up with them living at Dartfield, never mind the unthinkable flitting to a cottar house. Her poor mother and father, so proud in their own way, it would be the end of them.

'But surely it canna be as bad as aa that, faither,' Jessie piped up. 'Fit if we aa worked an afa lot harder. We could grow mair vegetables, sell them at the end of the roadie at a stall? Onything.' Jessie was feeling guilty that she hadn't done enough to help her family. 'Aa o us can pu thegether and dae somethin.'

'It's ower late for that,' said their father.

'I could get a job on anither fairm. Bring in a wee bit siller. At least I widna cost you ony mair,' said William.

I could leave the squeel noo that I'm fourteen and fin a job as weel,' said John.

'It's ower late. We're ower far ahint in the rent and we've nae milking coos left and the grain will nae be worth onything this year. I didna say to the Captain what I intended to dae but I canna see ony wey oot. We've nae siller and nae wey o getting ony. I was wantin to put you aa in the pictur before I said onythin but something will hae to be daen soon. We canna gyang on like this.'

Jessie went to bed that night in the depth of despair. This just could not be happening to her, to her family which was so important to her. All the dreams gone. It mustn't happen. It would kill her mother and father whom she loved so dearly and suddenly it came to her what she must do. Somehow or other she must get hold of the money that the doctor had left her last year. She knew it might not be easy to get it before she was seventeen but the lawyer had said the trustees would consider giving it out earlier if there was something she desperately wanted it for and if they thought it a worthy reason. Surely it would never be more needed than now. Surely she could persuade them to see that her family was the most important thing on earth to her. Perhaps there would be a little left to see her through university. But that was of less importance, far less importance. Besides she could always work extra hard and get a bursary. That was what she intended to do in the first place. It was now that was important, more important than any other thing.

She knew she would have a problem getting her father to agree to the plan. His attitude would be that it was her money, meant for her use. She must make him see how important it was to her as well as everyone else. The family must stick together and help each other. She snuggled down under the patchwork quilt, more content now that she had come up with a plan. Tomorrow she would speak to her father.

The next day was Saturday. Jessie woke to grey skies and the rain teeming down with that determined feel of being settled in for the day at least. For once Jessie was happy about this because it would give her the opportunity to get hold of her father and talk to him. Her resolve was even stronger this morning. It was the only solution. She waylaid her father when he came in for his morning break.

'Faither, I've something afa important to say to you. Could we gaun intae the parlour.'

'William looked puzzled. Jessie had never spoken to him like this before. He followed her in. There was no fire in the hearth at this time in the morning and it was rather cold but Jessie didn't feel it. She was burning inside with what had to be said.

'Well fit is it, quine?' He took his usual mahogany, horsehair seat at one side of the cheerless fireplace.

Jessie sat down on her mother's chair at the other side and felt very grown-up.

'Faither, there's something you are gaun to have to dae.'

'And fit could that be?' asked her father.

'You're gaun to have tae let me pit my money intae the fairm if I can get the trustees to let me hae it oot early. You're gaun to hae to let me help you ower this hurdle. This canna happen to us. I ken we've gone through bad times afore and survived. You've aye said fairmin's aye like that and we must survive. I want this mair than ony ither thing on earth. Surely I could get my siller oot for such a dire necessity. I ken fine Doctor Blackhall would have wanted this. There is naething mair important to me than the family, every one of you. You hae aften told us yoursel that we should aa stick thegether an help ane anither. Please, please let me help you now.'

'I canna tak your money, quine.'

'Faither I beg o you.'

'Na na, I canna dae that.'

At that moment the door opened and in came her mother.

'Fit are you twa claiking aboot that's sae afa important?' she said. 'It's no that warm in here. Would you no be better in the kitchen?'

Jessie began again and told her mother of her proposal.

'And faither'll no listen,' she said. 'Can you no mak him see reason. Things could be better again. It's nae a bad hairst ilka year. We could buy ither coos, better anes and you could be famous once more for your butter and cheese. I'll try and help mair and nae be so selfish, disappearing aff tae the hay loft to read books. I can see a bricht future.'

Little by little she wore her parents down to see the possibilities and show them that this is what was more important to her than anything else on earth. But still her father flatly refused to sanction the use of her money. Her mother was not quite so adamant.

'Weel, William, it's somethin worth considering. It would be for the guid o aa the faimily and for Jessie jist as muckle as for the rest o us. Dinna lat your pride get in the wey. It's no the time for that.'

'Weel, weel, 'said her father eventually. 'You can gyang and see the Trustees if you like but I dinna think they'll be on for the idea ava.'

Jessie hugged them both. She was happy that her father had at least agreed to get in touch with the trustees to find out the possibility of such a proposition. Hugging was not a thing that happened often in North East families. Undemonstrativeness was not a sign they didn't care – they cared most deeply. It just wasn't done to show too much emotion. Perhaps because life was so precarious and hard, it didn't do to let their feelings run away.

That very morning Jessie bicycled down to Bancar to ask if she could use that new-fangled thing called a phone. Uncle John was curious what she wanted to use the phone for.

'Oh jist to get in touch wi the lawyer. I'm supposed to go and see him some time aboot the legacy I got.' Everyone in the district knew about the legacy by this time.

'Aye you've been a lucky quine. Go ahead and use the phone if you like. I'll show you how.'

Jessie didn't tell Uncle John anything about the trouble the farm was in. She knew her father would never forgive her if she did. She made an appointment to see the lawyer the following Wednesday. She would have to take a day off school but that would be nothing new. She had taken quite a few days off lately to help out on the farm.

William Jaffray offered to go to Aberdeen with Jessie but she insisted on going alone.

'I ken ma wey aboot, faither. I'll easily manage. Besides that would be the waste o a fare.'

Wednesday was again a day of unrelenting rain. It was warm enough in the train but the countryside she saw through the window was dreich and miserable with an overall grey appearance. Where were the blue-as-cornflower seascapes, blue watercolour skies with their whiffs of white, the brilliant gold of ripe corn in the field and in the stook? Only darkened grain and sodden stooks, tarnished and colourless stood in the waterlogged fields. Other farmers must be suffering too. Would this rain ever give up?

She was both excited and nervous by the time she reached Aberdeen. Would she be able to find the lawyer's office again? At least she had the address and could always ask if she got lost. Aberdeen was dull today. Rain came down here too. There was no sparkle from the granite buildings. Today they were not winking at her as she had imagined they were the last time. The voices of the seagulls, floating above her, sounded more strident than usual and the smell of horses and horse manure from those animals pulling carts and carriages seemed more pungent than she remembered.

Jessie found it rather frightening being in this big city all on her own. She felt small and insignificant. She found the lawyer's office, however, without too much bother and soon she was ushered into the same cluttered room with the same lawyer behind the same large table still with his bowler hat on.

'Well, what can I do for you, young lady?'

'Something terrible has happened.'

'What on earth can that be?' the lawyer looked concerned.

For the first time since her father had told her of their dire position Jessie felt like bursting into tears. Large tears filled her eyes but she managed to pull herself together. It would never do to let herself go now. The lawyer would just see her as an over-emotional schoolgirl. She must convince him of the necessity of her mission, how vitally important it was.

'We've, we've got into trouble wi the fairm. We've been unable to pay the rent for a year or twa. We've had several bad harvests and now all oor milking coos have died of tuberculosis and father says this time there is no way out, so we'll have to give up the fairm. I love my family and I love the fairm more than anything else on earth. The family and the fairm are far more important to me than going to the university. I would like to put my money into the fairm for a time to let us get out of this hole. I know it's possible to recover with a bit of help. We've had bad times afore and father's a good farmer and a hard worker. We're all going to work. William, my oldest brother, has left school to help and John is going to do as much as he can. I know we could succeed but we can't without money. Father and mother were not for me coming to you but I managed to get them to let me. It won't be easy persuading my father to agree to taking the money but if I do get him to, I've come to ask you if I could possibly get my legacy from Dr Blackhall soon for this purpose.'

Jessie stopped speaking and took a breath. She was surprised that the lawyer hadn't interrupted her. She had been careful to speak in as good English as she could muster. She had often been told at school that English carried more weight than the Doric.

The lawyer could see Jessie was in earnest. He didn't quite know how to answer her.

'In these circumstances would it not maybe be better if your father gave up farming. He might get a better job somewhere else, perhaps something outside farming that brought in more money.'

Tears came into Jessie's eyes in earnest this time and slid down her cheeks. English was forgotten about.

'Na, na it widna. Faither can dae nocht else but fairmin. The factor's offered us a cottar hoose and micht find a job for him but it wid be the end o aathing. We'll none o us be able tae face it. It will be gaun doon in the warld, no up.

'Dry your eyes, lassie,' said the lawyer. It upset him to see Jessie crying. Across the table he handed her a clean white handkerchief out of his top pocket.

'I'll have to speak to the other trustees and get their opinion and I'll have to see your father and mother. Get them to come in some time if you can. I'll do my best for you lassie.'

With that Jessie had to be satisfied. All the way home in the train she was deep in thought. She felt a glimmer of hope. Yes she had got through to him. She felt sure of that. Not exactly in the way she meant to but she felt his sympathy and knew he would do his best to try to convince the other trustees of the dire necessity of her cause. He had told her she might have to come to Aberdeen again in order to try and convince the other trustees herself if he failed. She would do that. She would move heaven and earth to get the money. Her next task was to try and persuade her mother and father to make an appointment with the lawyer. She knew that wouldn't be easy. Her mother mightn't be so bad but her father. . .

Jessie, however, succeeded in her mission and a date for a meeting between the lawyer and her parents was made for a fortnight hence. It was the longest fortnight of her life and the day her parents went to see the lawyer, the longest day. She couldn't wait for them to come home. She went to meet them at the station. She knew what train they were likely to catch. As they stepped down onto the platform they hadn't noticed Jessie and she saw that her mother was smiling. A feeling of hope surged through Jessie's body. They were surprised to see their daughter there.

'Fit's the verdict?' Jessie couldn't wait to ask.

'Weel,' said her mother. 'The lawyer had seen the ither Trustees and they agree to giving you the money but wi ae proviso.'

'Fit's that?' asked Jessie a note of worry entering her voice.

'Your faither and I were asked to sign a statement they had made oot that stated that the fairm would be liable for you gaun tae the university when the time came.'

'And did you sign?'

'Aye we did.'

Jessie could hardly contain herself for joy. All the way home it seemed her feet didn't touch the ground. The world hadn't come to an end. It was the beginning of a new day, the beginning of a struggle, a challenge, one to which she was looking forward.

It began for Jessie the very next morning. When she came down for breakfast, her father was waiting for her.

'You'll better tak the day aff squeel and gyang and pay the rent.' Yesterday we set up an account for you in the bank and the money will go in there in a day or two. Here's your cheque book. You can date the cheque a week or so in advance.'

'Would it no be better to wait until the money's through?'

'I'd like the rent paid noo. It's lang ower due.'

Jessie saw how important it was to her father to get this debt paid.

'Could you no tak the cheque yoursel, faither? I dinna like that factor mannie muckle.'

'Na, you've tae dae it. It's your siller.'

With these words from her father Jessie knew he considered her a child no longer.

Chapter Twelve

Dealing with Insolvency

IT WAS with some trepidation that Jessie set off on her bike with the rent money, the cheque placed safely in a pouch bag that she had made for herself. She had on her winter coat because, although it was a sunny day early in October, a cold east wind was sweeping in from the sea. She knew exactly where to go – the North Lodge, the substantial house she had passed on her bike the day she had dared to trespass. The North Lodge doubled as the residence for the factor and the office for the estate. Jessie had always thought it a rather gloomy house. It wasn't facing the road as many lodges do but its gable end was at the road edge with the front of the house looking across the drive to a thick wood of trees of unremarkable appearance. Trees also grew thickly behind it and the mysterious drive, passing the front of the house, led into more trees. It was a long two storey house with a small front garden neatly kept by one of the estate gardeners. The red leaves of Virginia Creeper wandered up the wall which somewhat brightened its appearance. It was, however, what the locals called a 'gran hoose'.

Her father had given her directions as to what to do when she got there.

'Gyang tae the front door and ring the bell. Dinna wait for onyone to answer but jist walk in. You'll see a notice that says Estate

Office. You canna miss it. It's richt in front of you as you enter. The door of the office will probably be closed. Chap at the door. It'll probably be ane o the clerkesses who opens it. Dinna gie the rent to her. Ask tae see the Captain himsel. He's usually in in the mornings and I ken he's no awa at the Forfar estate this week.'

It took courage for Jessie to ring the bell and walk in. It took courage for her to knock at the Estate Office door but having come this far, she would have to go through with it. A clerkess did come to the door as her father said she would. She invited Jessie in.

'Can I help you?' she asked politely.

'Could I please speak with Captain Chaplin?'

'And what might you be wanting to see him for?' asked the clerkess.

'A matter of business,' said Jessie, not wanting to divulge what the business was in case the clerkess would take the money. She would like to be able to tell her father she had done as he told her to and had handed the cheque over to Captain Chaplin in person.

'I'll see if he's available,' said the clerkess and went out of the room. Jessie heard her go upstairs. She heard her come quickly down again with sounds also of a heavier foot behind her. The clerkess re-entered the office with Captain Chaplin immediately in her wake.

'Well, what can I do for you?' he said and then with recognition dawning he went on, 'You're the girl I met at Crimonmogate House. One of William Jaffray's daughters.'

'Yes,' Jessie affirmed

Jessie hadn't seen him since that day at Crimonmogate apart from a fleeting glimpse of him on his horse occasionally in the distance. She was surprised how much older he looked now. His hair and moustache had turned completely grey and his face was rather more lined than she remembered. She had to admit, however, that he was still a tall and handsome man with a ramrod straight back and military bearing. His eyes, she noticed, were his most remarkable feature, deep blue, the colour that the sea sometimes took upon itself when the skies were without cloud. Today they had a serious expression and she noticed a certain curiosity in them.

She hoped he wouldn't laugh at her again.

'I've come to pay the rent for Dartfield,' she said simply.

'You've come to pay the rent. Is your father not well?'

'Aye, he's fine,' said Jessie, 'but it's my money so father said I should come and pay it.'

'Your money?'

'Aye.' Jessie didn't feel like enlarging on this. The two clerkesses were listening and she didn't think it was any of their business. Jessie opened her pouch and took out the cheque.

'It's postdated because the money's nae through to my bank yet but faither wanted you to get it the day.'

Captain Chaplin gravely took the cheque, looked it over carefully, and then wrote the amount into a big ledger.

'Thank you very much, Miss Jaffray. I'll send you a receipt.'

Here she was, being called Miss Jaffray again. It gave her a renewed confidence in herself. It certainly made her feel grown-up and although the Captain was a tall man, six feet or more, he wasn't on his horse this time and didn't tower over her as much. Also two years had made a difference to Jessie's height. She was tall for a girl. At five foot seven she was already taller than her mother.

Business over, the Captain politely saw her to the office door and opened it for her. The front door likewise. They stood in the morning sunshine.

'I hardly recognised you. You've grown so,' he said.

Did she detect laughter in his eyes? She hoped not. Was he implying she was too tall for a girl. Jessie was becoming very aware of her height, self-conscious about it in fact. Already people were making remarks about it. She hoped she wouldn't grow any more. Five foot seven – that was enough.

'Are things all right on the farm?' he asked tentatively. 'I've been meaning to come and see your father. I know of the struggle you've been having.'

He sounded sympathetic which made Jessie feel like volunteering information.

'They'll be fine noo,' she said relapsing in to the Doric. 'We've had a teuch time lately but things will be better from noo on. We've got a fresh start. In a year or twa things'll be great. You'll see.'

Jessie had no doubts and this conveyed itself to the Captain.

'We're aa pullin thegether, all going to wark as hard as we can. We've got a lot o new ideas. Thank goodness for the legacy just the same.'

'Legacy?' the Captain didn't want to pry but he couldn't help being curious and then he remembered hearing that Doctor Blackhall had left one of the Jaffray girls most of his worldly goods. It must have been this one.

'Aye, Doctor Blackhall left me a legacy. It was supposed to be for me going tae the university and I wasn't to get it till I was seventeen. My faither was dead against takin onything frae me and the trustees weren't too keen either but I said that what I wanted more than onything else in the world was to help my family out in such difficult times. We would never be more in need of the money. To me it was far mair important than the university. I'll get there somehoo but keeping the fairm is important to all of us, mair important to me than onything else.'

'You're a generous young lady,' said the Captain, 'and a thoughtful one.' Jessie detected admiration in his voice and didn't know quite what to say.

'Nae really,' she said. 'You see it's nae me, it's us and all the others are going to do their bit also. We are all gaun to work as hard as ever we can to turn things roon. It'll be hard but it'll be fun.'

The rent paid, a council of war on poverty was held with the whole family that very evening. In fact there was a council of war most nights held in the parlour after prayers. The Jaffray parents had never consulted the children before over affairs of the farm, not even young Willie working full time for his father. But things were different now. Everyone had to be involved. Each must play their part in order to change things. Jessie must be listened to, especially as it was her money that was making it all possible. And Jessie was not short on ideas or enthusiasm. She didn't *think* they would succeed, she *knew* they would succeed and this had a marvellous regenerating effect on the whole family.

It was now her turn to say to her mother, 'There's nae sic a word as can't in the dictionary,' and she believed it.

Privately she thought what a wonderful thing to be able to do. It was wonderful to see her parents looking happy again, less tired, less worried after the worrying months, years for that matter. It was like a renewal of life. She was too young to realise that the great gift she had given her parents was the gift of hope, the attribute that the hard-working north-east farmers, always working against the odds, were not short of as a rule. Hope and humour, these two essentials had worn very thin lately. Her father and mother had come to the point where they could see no hope at all.

Everyone in the family promised to help in whatever way they could. Even wee Charlie was eager to help. He promised to feed the hens and gather the eggs before he went to school.

A plan of action was set up. First of all they must all work together and save what was left of the sodden stooks still out in the fields. In the last week or so a wind had risen to dry them out a bit. They must bring them in to be stacked before the next rain came. Everyone could play a part. They worked till late at night and fell into bed exhausted.

That done, they all agreed that the next most important thing to do was to thoroughly scrub out and disinfect the byre and any other building that had housed calves and cattle. The last of their dairy cows had died and this year they had bought no calves. It had been the custom for William Jaffray to buy in extra calves every year and rear them until they were big enough to sell to the farmers with better grazing land to fatten for the London market. Through lack of money this had not been done recently and so there were no cattle about the place at all. This proved fortunate as it meant they could make a fresh start with new cattle hopefully not harbouring the disease.

They all scrubbed and better than scrubbed the outhouses. Every inch was disinfected and washed over with white lime. Never had they looked so clean.

When the steading was pronounced ready, William went to the market at Maud able to hold his head up high once more. He took young Willie with him. He must be taught the trade. Jessie would have loved to have gone too. Why couldn't girls do all these things? However, she saw it was an unpopular suggestion with her father and realised that he would lose face if he took his young daughter into the market. It just wasn't done. So Jessie didn't pursue the matter. William Jaffray bought some sturdy in-calf heifers. They were a bit more expensive than some of the others but father Jaffray knew they were from a good farm and were bred from a good milking strain and that was important.

That evening the heifers arrived by train from Maud and all the family, apart from mother, went to Lonmay station, half a mile away, to herd them home. Charlie went with them and insisted on having a stick also. The Jaffray children found him a sturdy one. The children might quarrel amongst themselves, from time to time, but not with Charlie. He was exempt. They all loved him. And indeed he was a brave wee boy who looked you in the eye with such innocent honesty that you couldn't help but love him.

Some of the heifers were near to dropping their calves. From past experience it was known heifers giving birth for the first time could have difficulties. So no chances were taken. If a heifer in the evening looked if she were likely to calf by morning, someone was allocated to sit up with her all night in case she needed attention. Eventually all the heifers were safely delivered.

For a time, before the first heifer calved, they bought in a flagon of milk each day from a neighbouring farm. Peggy was allocated the job of walking to collect the milk every morning before going to school. They all agreed to spread no butter on their oatcakes, only syrup or treacle, commodities that were relatively cheap. All sorts of savings were made although the priority was, that the children at least, should have sufficient nourishing food to keep them healthy and fit. Mother Jaffray would no longer have her genteel teas in the afternoon and there would be less Saturday evening kitchen entertainments with the whisky bottle circulating. Impromptu parties in the kitchen would have to make do with mother Jaffray's homemade raspberry or elderberry wine, or so said mother Jaffray.

However, rather to her annoyance, unmarked bottles of what she called fire water occasionally appeared from nowhere. She knew of the existence of a few illicit stills on some small crofts in the Garioch further west belonging to these lawless people, as she privately called them, who lived there. Once many crofters owned a still. It was often what sustained their way of life, but stills had been outlawed. She didn't know how men nowadays dared to make whisky.

To generate maximum cash they decided not to kill a pig that year for home consumption but sell all of the pigs in the litters, apart from keeping a young gilt or two for breeding purposes. They put more effort into trapping and shooting rabbits for the pot. As far as meat was concerned, rabbit and the occasional old hen became their staple diet. Baker's bread, or 'loaf' as they called it, was given up altogether and, apart from barrels of salt herring, fresh herring which was cheap, and hard sundried cod, very little food was bought in at all. Only cracked eggs were used by the family, every whole one kept to sell.

Jenny left to get married. Fanny volunteered to wash the eggs for sale and do other jobs in the house. She rather liked swanning around being important and bossing her younger sister Peggy into getting her to do as much of the work as she could. She did not like working outside, preferring not to get her hands dirty.

Jessie was different. She hated to be, as she saw it, imprisoned in a house. She hated housework but loved to work outside. How often she wished she was a boy. Hard it might be but how much better was the lot of men, she often thought. The work women were supposed to do was so restrictive. She began to understand that farming was in her blood just as much as it was in her father's. She was learning to love this difficult land and was looking forward to the challenge of making it better as her ancestors had done in the past. They had drained it and enclosed it with such hard graft, rescued it from bog land, made it fertile. Now the effort was to try to 'make two blades of grass grow where one had grown before'. Where had she read that? Young as she was she was now truly bound up in the farm. Her money was in it. She knew though she would never fall heir to it. The landlords in the north east usually tried to give the lease of farms to the nearest relative after a tenant retired or died but rarely to a women. Farms were a man's business.

CHAPTER THIRTEEN

The Farming Year

THAT FIRST winter of the new regime, whenever the weather allowed, the family helped to build more pig sties in order to keep more of the female pigs from the litter. At Maud market William bought a new boar, one guaranteed to produce good pigs. He knew Johnny Watt, the farmer he bought it from.

'He's a guid chiel. He widna lat me doon.'

Come Spring Jessie suggested to her mother that they should set every clocking hen available on eggs. A clocking hen was the name given to a hen that stopped laying eggs and went broody in springtime. You always knew them. They went about the farmyard with ruffled feathers making a cluck clucking noise.

'Maybe we could also buy some ald hens that are 'on the clock' from oor neeghbours Hae as mony hatching oot eggs as possible. They could hatch oot turkey eggs as weel. You've aye said hens mak better mithers than turkeys. Turkeys aye seem to manage to lose maist o their chicks.' Jessie was always coming up with new schemes.

'It's the weet and cald that does it,' said her mother. 'Turkey chicks are delicate wee craters that canna stand muckle.'

'Fit about keeping them in the barn wi their mother hens till they grow aller so that they winna get weet.'

'Sounds like a richt guid idea,' said her mother.

Charlie, Peggy and Andrew were put in charge of the chick hatching – the clocking house. Boxes and boxes of hens were put into the low building next to the boilerhouse where the hens' and pigs' food was boiled up. Come Spring, every day, the three children went into the low dark building to remove the stones from the wooden slatted lids covering the boxes and let the hens hop out all clucking, cross and fluffed-out feathered. The hens were glad to get out firstly for a drink and then to peck at the food put down for them. The children left them out for half an hour or so, being careful to close the somewhat rickety door behind them.When they returned, all the hens would be back in their boxes sitting contentedly. No need to turn the eggs underneath them – they had done that themselves. The younger children rather enjoyed being made responsible, even young Charlie. Andrew especially was happy working on the farm. He hated the 'squeel' as school was called in Aberdeenshire and was slow to learn to read and write and couldn't do the sums.

Some whispered he had a 'want' but the parents didn't agree. He just wasn't a scholar but took a great interest in the farm. He knew how things worked and was curious about everything. He loved the huge Clydesdale horses that did the ploughing, Bess and Blossom, Queen and Canny, and couldn't wait till he was older and able to harness and work them himself. He was a tall lad for his age, taller than average and strong. His father reckoned he would make a good farmer one day.

That winter much snow fell and for a considerable time the frost was severe, but all of a sudden the weather changed leaving the soil broken down and friable, in fine fettle for ploughing. The two Williams set to, working every hour they could to make the land ready for the sowing of barley and oats. In these days little wheat was grown north of the River Tay.

The last farm worker had left at the November term. Now that it was Spring and the weather somewhat warmer, John and Willie had moved into the chaumer in order to make more room in the house for the younger children. At Dartfield, as on most smaller farms in Aberdeenshire, the chaumer was in the hayloft above the stable with a ladder leading up to it. Dartfield's one was sparsely furnished, like most others, with two or three beds with chaff (caff as it was known locally) mattresses. Course woollen blankets covered the beds. Usually, round the low walls, stood the men's kists containing all their worldly goods. The only other furniture these chaumers contained was a kitchen chair or two, a small table and that was it. Mother Jaffray tried to make the Dartfield chaumer a bit more comfortable for her sons and there was a war on rats which could sometimes become a nuisance.

Father Jaffray let it be known he could do with another hand for sowing. What about John? John had no heart for farm work and was reluctant.

'Ach faither, I'm feenishing squeel this year. These last exams are important. If I get guid results I've a chance to get a job in the bank in Peterheed.'

Mother Jaffray was adamant about John. He must be allowed to finish his schooling. So John was let off.

'I'll dae it if nae ane else will,' said Jessie. 'I'd love to hae a shot at sowing in the Easter holidays or I could tak days aff squeell.'

Jessie had always loved to watch her father sowing. Her poetic soul thought it looked a graceful occupation. From the canvas seed scoops, called happers, tied to the sower's waist, arms and hands would rhythmically spread out and scatter the seed – first this one then that. There was something biblical about. She was sure there was an art in it but an art that she could master. She did, however, in an attempt to modernise and save time suggest something different to her father.

'Faither, do you no think it's aboot time we boucht a seeder. We would get on so much faster. Most of our neebours hae got ane by noo.'

'Awa you go, quine, they dinnae mak half sic a guid job.' Her father could be stubborn about certain things and this was one of them. He preferred the old-fashioned ways. The ways he was used to.

'Well, will you teach me to sow then?'

'Aye, I'll fairly dae that.'

Jessie was a quick learner and by Spring it was a pretty sight to see this graceful long legged girl with the thick black plaits that almost reached to her waist, pacing up and down the fields scattering the seed, skeins of wild geese overhead, lapwings tumbling about her and within the constant sound of lark song.

Quite a number of days were taken off school to help with the farm work but with the help of the dominie, Jessie also managed to keep up with her school work. He gave her books to take home and set her exercises to do to return to him.

Jessie had moved into the maid's bedroom now that Jenny had gone. This suited her admirably as she would often study at night when everyone else was asleep. Sometimes she set her alarm to wake her up in the early hours of the morning when she would light the paraffin lamp and creep through to the kitchen. With luck the peat fire would still have glowing embers and be easily made up. Here she could study in both peace and comfort.

After Easter the air began to warm and the fields quickly took on an emerald sheen, the curling blades of barley trembling in the wind. There was a great deal of teasing about bare patches, bits that Jessie had been responsible for, although she hotly denied it.

'Jessie dreaming again,' her father chided but said with a twinkle in his eye. He was proud of his daughter. What did it matter what the neighbours said about having his daughter working like a man.

'Why shouldna quines dae what they want tae?' said Jessie. 'It's fit this suffragette movement, you read of in the papers, is aa aboot.'

'I'm no gaun along wi that aathegidder,' said her father. 'A woman's place is in the home looking aifter the bairns and her man.'

'Rubbish,' said his daughter. 'A woman should be able to dae what she wants to dae and what she does best. Why shouldn't women be writers, artists, painters or whatever if that's what they're good at? Why shouldn't they be as good as men? They've got the same parents. They take after the same ancestors.'

These arguments went on endlessly around the peat fire now that the children were growing older. Mother Jaffray darning or knitting and not saying very much and Jessie tacking up some seams ready to sew on the machine.

By Spring several calves had been born and mother Jaffray was back to the milking. Sitting on the old three-legged stool, head pressed into the cow's soft flank, milk streamed out at the sure stroke of practised fingers and landed in the tin bucket first with a loud tinging sound and then with a satisfying frothy ryhthm as the pail filled. Mother Jaffray often sang softly to the cows some of the old songs of her youth, and the cows, contentedly chewing the cud, would relax and let down their milk more easily. From time to time both Jessie and Fanny helped with this job.

The heifers turned out to be good milkers although not yet at their full capacity. There was milk now for resuming the making of butter and cheese. The calves were housed in separate stalls and taught to drink milk out of pails. This was a job for the girls and they loved the feel of the calves' milky noses on the palms of their hands.

The pigs too, in their new styes, were producing well. They were carefully watched when it came time for them to farrow. Father and mother or some of the older children stayed up all night with them if they looked like giving birth to make sure everything went well and to see that the enormous fat pigs didn't lay over any of their tiny piglets.

It was always a satisfying thing to watch these little pigs being born. Out they would pop one after another. One two three. . . eleven, twelve, thirteen. No more than twelve was wanted, though, because the pig had not usually enough teats to feed more. Each little pig had its own teat, the first one got to after it was born, which meant that if there were thirteen the last piglet wouldn't have a teat and just got an occasional suck from one belonging to one of her sisters or brothers when they were asleep or not looking. This little pig was called a runt and never grew as well as the others did. There wasn't much anyone could do about it.

There were a few disasters with the pigs. One had only three piglets, and another managed to lie on two or three and smother them but on the whole things were looking up with the pig breeding enterprise. They had to be always watching though. Pigs took diseases so easily and had to be treated for worms and tiny lice that settled in their skins. They weren't an easy animal to look after. You always knew when they were sick – their curly tails grew straight. Pigs ate a lot too and never seemed to be satisfied. Everyday the boiler in the wee dark boiler house was bubbling away and the air full of the delicious smell of boiling tatties.

In June their was a good crop of hay and fine weather to let it dry in windrows and then to lead it in. When it was dry enough it was gathered into small hillocks called coles. One of the youngster's jobs was to take the huge Clydesdales to these hay coles and drag them to the stack, one by one, by placing a chain, attached to the horse's harness, around each cole. Jessie wasn't fond of this job because it meant having a certain rapport with the horse. They were canny beasts but Jessie was never to overcome her irrational fear of them.

Harvest came early that year. It wasn't as heavy a one as they would have liked but there was a chance they would get it in good order. William Jaffray had a binder which saved a great deal of work. His brother John had sold it to him cheaply when he had come out of Lums some years previously. Before the binder came along farmers had to make do with the reaper which cut the crop but did not gather and bind it into sheaves and a small army of people was needed to gather into bunches and make straw bands to tie each sheaf individually, a time-consuming job.

Before going into the field with the binder, roads right round the perimeter had to be cut by scythe. Jessie volunteered for this job. At the beginning of the nineteenth century and earlier much of the harvest had been cut with the sickle, sometimes by teams of women each of whom could cut about a quarter of an acre a day. This was a job that women were good at, keeping up a good rhythmic pace. For the same reason they sometimes got the job of singling turnips in the Spring time. If there was in the team an outworker woman, as she was called, she would be put in front of the men so that they would keep up with her.

When the scythe superseded the sickle it did the job more quickly but it was a much heavier implement that women found difficult to wield so the reaping of grain became largely a man's job. These women who worked so valiantly in the fields and were paid so small a fee for their labour were considered to be the lowest of the low. Even the kitchin deem came before them in status.

Being tall and strong Jessie found she was able to wield the scythe and rather enjoyed the steady rhythm of it. Always a romantic she saw herself as Wordsworth's solitary reaper.

> Behold her, single in the field,
> Yon solitary Highland Lass!
> Reaping and singing by herself;
> Stop here, or gently pass!
> alone she cuts and binds the grain,
> And sings a melancholy strain;
> O listen! for the Vale profound
> Is overwhelming with the sound.

The grain cut, they got the harvest stooked and led in good order. All of the family had helped. Things were looking up. The farm was not out of trouble yet. It would take several years of both luck and hard labour to achieve that but it was a beginning – a good beginning.

CHAPTER FOURTEEN

The Tennis Match

THE MICHAELMAS term came – time to pay the rent. Once again Jessie bicycled to the factor's office with the cheque, not quite so frightened this time but still rather wary of speaking to the important man himself. Once again he managed to disarm her.

'Congratulations,' he said. 'Dartfield's really looking well this year and I hear that you have a whole lot of new stock. Things are looking up.'

Somehow he made it easy for her to talk to him. He treated her much like Dr Blackhall would have done, with the same interest but with the difference that she was no longer a child.

'Aye,' she said, 'but it's a struggle. Folks dinna want to pay muckle for food and it's nae easy for fairmers to mak a living however hard they work. But my brother John has got a job noo,' she went on with pride, 'in the bank as he said he would. He doesna get much pay but its aye something to bring hame. My mother's real pleased aboot it.'

'Good for John,' said the Captain. 'And how about yourself. How are your plans for going to the university?'

'I dinna richt ken yet. I've at least another twa or three years to go. I'm awa from school a lot working on the farm when faither needs me but the dominie's real helpful. He knows the predicament we're in and lets me tak hame books and sets me exercises to do at hame.'

'What subjects do you like best?' asked the Captain.

Jessie had no hesitation in her answer. 'English and French,' she said. Jessie was surprised that he should be interested. 'French is hard to pronounce but I love it. We have French ancestors from long ago. I think it must be in the blood.'

The Captain smiled, amused at her earnestness. Jessie noticed his expression. Perhaps she was talking too much, telling him too much. But he quickly became serious again.

'I liked English best myself,' he informed her, 'read the Greats at Cambridge.'

Jessie had no idea what 'the Greats' were but it sounded impressive. She knew about Oxford and Cambridge and it was quite something to be talking to someone who had been at one of those universities. Already life was taking on new colour. She forgot all the scurrilous rumours she had heard about him – perhaps they were only rumours. Country folk were great gossips – they often got things wrong. It made their day to have a bit of sensation. Or perhaps there was a good reason for his bad behaviour. By nature Jessie was not judgmental. All she knew was that at this moment she would rather like to be like him, in a female way of course. What made the difference? How could she be more like these people she so very much admired? What could she do about it? Well first of all, she thought, there was the accent. She must lose her Aberdeenshire accent, her coarse Buchan speak. She had been trying to but sometimes her family would laugh at her in her attempts and say she was becoming afa posh. She would persevere just the same. It was important, very important. When she went to university she didn't want to be looked on as the country bumpkin. John, she noticed, was speaking better English.

'You have to in the bank,' he said.

He was beginning to get a bit conceited, she thought, but

then mother made such a fuss of him and she was so proud of him. She was always ironing his shirts, starching his collars and pressing his suit so that he would look smart in the bank. She never bothered about any of the rest of them. They had to iron their own clothes, if they were ironed at all. Jessie was often too tired these days and too preoccupied with all she had to do to bother about her appearance. She had little time to sew nowadays but fortunately seemed to have stopped growing so her old clothes still fitted her.

She bothered less with the girls in her class. She was still friendly with them but their worlds were drifting apart somewhat. The girls that were left at school after fourteen were mostly the daughters of the bigger farmers or those who had risen in trade. Some lived in big substantial houses and were not so much at school to learn as to mark time until they were old enough to be looking for a husband. At home they were taught to embroider or carve laboriously in wood and taught to live like ladies.

Tennis was very much in the fashion and one parent had built a tennis court complete with clubhouse and paid for a coach to teach some of the older children at the school. That year all the talk in her circle of so-called friends was of the forthcoming tennis match that had been arranged at Jeanie's tennis court. It was to be an end of school celebration. There was to be tea served in the small clubhouse and there were to be a few older brothers there to partner the girls. Jessie began to feel very left out until Jeanie said, 'You can come if you like, Jessie. You widna be able to play tennis, of course, but you can bide in the club house and gie oot the teas. We'll bring the baking but there will be sandwiches to mak so that'll keep you busy while we're playing. Maybe you could get yoursel a new dress.'

'Do come,' chorused the others in a condescending fashion.

Jessie would have liked to have told them what to do with their tea in the clubhouse but in a snap decision decided to accept the offer.

But the more she thought about it the more it rankled. How dare Jeanie Birnie, Bessie Laurence, Annie Jack and the others, with whom she had grown up, talk to her in this way. They were treating her as a servant and Jessie was a servant to no one. Who else could go and speak to Captain Chaplin almost on equal terms? What other girl in her school was preparing to go to university? What other girl had money enough to save her father's farm? All the same she must smarten herself up a bit. Appearances did matter.

So busy had she been helping out on the farm and studying that she had neglected her appearance. She hadn't bothered what she wore and her raven-black hair had lost its shining. She took to brushing it every night and morning till it began to shine with the same lustre given off by her mother's black diamond necklace.

One day she bicycled to Peterhead and went to the draper's shop to buy some cloth to make a dress for herself. She had a style in mind, quite a simple one, one she had seen worn by one of the grand ladies who had come up from London to Crimonmogate. It was white with a nipped-in waist and a somewhat flared skirt but what made it outstanding was the contrast of a crimson collar, cuffs and sash. At the time Jessie had said to herself, 'I'll have a dress like that, one day.' Now was the time. She chose enough white cotton to make an underskirt and, for the dress itself, a length of white voile. She chose silk for the collar, cuffs and sash. Not quite the red she wanted, more of a scarlet, but it would do.

They were busy at the hay on the day of the tennis match but her father had let her off work because he knew this was important to Jessie. For one or two nights previously she had stayed up late to make the dress. She cut it out carefully from a simple pattern and she took great care with the sewing of it. It mustn't look in the least home-made. She had also bought a pair of shoes for the occasion – pointed toes, straps across her high instep, the height of fashion – and for the first time in her life she put her shining long black hair up in a style she had seen in a magazine. It took ages and lots and lots of hairpins but at last she got it the way she wanted. As a finishing touch she had taken one of the few roses the wind hadn't torn to shreds in Dartfield's garden and pinned it into the back of her hair. It was scarlet and matched the collar and cuffs of her dress exactly. She went into her parent's bedroom to look at herself in their long wardrobe mirror and even she was surprised at what she saw.

'Oh, but I'm quite pretty,' she breathed into herself and indeed she was. With her dark hair up to the nape of her neck and soft and wavy round her face, bright grey-flecked eyes and fresh glowing skin deliciously sunburnt with working outside. The rather gangly inauspicious girl had indeed become a swan.

'I'm even rather aristocratic looking in this dress,' she thought. And indeed she was with her long legs and her proud bearing when she held her head up high.

She walked downstairs. It was midday and dinner time, Everyone was in the kitchen.

At first when she came into the kitchen they were all too stunned to speak and then Fanny broke the silence.

'You're beautiful Jessie,' she said.

No one disagreed. Her father and mother looked at her with admiration.

'Aye, you're a bonny quine,' her father said. 'You'll fin a guid man ane o these days.'

Jessie declined dinner. There were too many butterflies in her stomach for her to eat. She would just be sick.

'No, no, I'll jist get going,' she said.

'The pony and trap are at the door for you,' said her father.

Usually Jessie went everywhere on her bike or walked but today she had asked her father for the pony and trap.

'It's a white dress I'll be wearing and I'm nae wanting it to get dirty.' So Jessie went off down the rough farm road in the pony and trap. Miss Jaffray she now truly was and someone to be reckoned with.

At first the girls didn't recognise her but when they did, in spite of themselves, there were a few gasps of admiration. Jessie said little and tied the dainty scarlet apron, made out of what remained of the scarlet silk, round her slim waist. From the clubhouse she heard the backward and forward spring of the balls as the tournament got under way. It was a sultry summer's day, threatening thunder. At three o'clock the tennis players all trooped in for tea. She had it ready. Tea for those who wanted it, a fruit punch for others. She had laid everything out attractively and was there at the table pouring the tea, vivacious, alive and vibrant. The boys all left their plainer partners, wanting to speak to Jessie, the girl they had barely noticed until now, the novelty. Jessie wasn't overly shy and had a sparkling line of chatter. She could make the boys laugh. After tea the girls had some problem getting the boys to come out and play again.

'Aye, we're comin but jist wait till we've helped Jessie wi the washing up. It's a shame to leave her to dae it aa. You lassies should be helpin.'

'Jessie's quite capable of doing it herself. She's nothing else to do all afternoon,' said one of the girls obviously annoyed and so they trooped out again.

'She can come and watch the tennis,' chorused the boys as they reluctantly left the clubhouse.

They hadn't been gone five minutes when there was a crackle in the heavens and a zig-zag of lightning flashed through the clubhouse window. Immediately afterwards there was an enormous clap of thunder and the heavens opened. The players all fled inside. No more tennis today.

'Now quines,' said one of the young men, 'since Jessie has so very kindly made aa the tea for us all, I really do think the rest of you should dae the washing up and let Jessie chat to us.'

Jessie knew this was her moment of triumph. Her moment of realisation that she was attractive to the opposite sex. She had the wind in her hands.

CHAPTER FIFTEEN

First to Leave the Nest

THE INJECTION of money into the farm and years of hard work and mean living with all of the family pulling together had made a difference. By 1912, even although farming in general was in a poor way, things were definitely looking up at Dartfield.

By then the oldest son William was getting restless. He was in his early twenties and wanting to see the world. He was tired of the daily slog. Tired above all of days and days spent behind the plough in all kinds of weather. Even when it was raining the plough had to be kept going unless the ground got too wet. Worst of all, was working in the biting winds so prevalent in this part of the North East. No number of old coats piled, one on top of another, would keep out the knife-edge cold. Even worse to young William than the cold was the boredom of it all. Was this all that life was about?

Since the railways had come more than half a century before and nowadays that motorised vehicles were seen more and more on the roads, it wasn't so difficult to get out of Aberdeenshire. He read in the *Aberdeen Journal* of sunnier, warmer places where there were exciting things happening. He heard of fortunes being made abroad in other countries, of land being almost given away in distant places. So much was happening outside Buchan. Here, in farming, it was difficult to make enough to live on, let alone a fortune no matter how hard you worked. Like many young people through the ages with adventurous inclinations, young Willie did dream of making a fortune and seeing the world. Buchan was boring. He had no wish to go into a bank like John had done. That didn't appeal to him at all. Nor did he wish to try and find some sort of office or shop job in Aberdeen. He had no notion to live in a town – he did want to be associated with the land but he did want to get away.

One of his friends, a young man called Alec had gone to Africa several years before. He had had one or two short letters and had heard from Alec's mother, a little of what life was like in British East Africa. A sunny pleasant climate up in what was called the White Highlands where wild animals roamed, herds and herds of them, elephants, zebras, wildebeest, lions. It must be fantastic to see these animals in the wild. Willie could hardly imagine it.

One day the opportunity came along quite by chance and suddenly. One of the neighbouring farmer's sons, Dod by name, had been all set to go to Africa under the auspices of the son of a local Peer. This particular Peer's son had been in the land that was to become Kenya for a few years and had acquired several farms. He was in need of one or two strong young farmer's sons as overseers for his various projects of putting virgin land under cultivation and implementing other schemes to do with livestock. He was desperately in need of one man immediately. Dod was that man. At the last moment Dod had broken his leg. His father paid a visit to Dartfield.

'What aboot young William?' he enquired of father Jaffray. 'Has he ony notion o gaun tae Africa?' He told him of his son's misfortune. 'He canna gyang wi a broken leg and he was tae sail from Southampton in a couple o week. A grand opportunity missed. What aboot young Willie? I've heard that he's restive like. Would he like tae gyang? These young loons can end up wi decent sized places o their own, mak fortunes.'

Father Jaffray was reluctant at first to let Willie, his oldest son, go but he knew there was not a living for all his sons at

Dartfield and that William was wanting to get away. He had been dour and unhappy at home lately.

When father Jaffray told Willie of the proposal that evening, after the latter had had a long exhausting day thinning turnips, there was no hesitation at all. This was his moment.

'Aye, I'd like fine tae gyang,' he said.

'But hoo will you manage, faither?'

'I'm no wanting to see you gyang, loon. You've been a fine son tae me and a hard worker but I've sae little tae offer you here and this does seem to be an opportunity tae get a fairm o your ain, maybe at a later date. If you dinna like it you can aye come hame. Dinna worry aboot us. We'll manage. Things are looking up a bit. I'll manage to get some ootside help wi the hairst even if it's only the tinks and I think we can afford to hire anither loon come Michaelmas.'

For the rest of the Jaffray family, feelings were mixed and all were stunned at the suddenness of it. Mother Jaffray's eyes filled with tears whenever she thought about it – so soon – this was the breaking up of the family – her chickens were beginning to spread their wings. John in the bank and beginning to live his own life, not always with mother Jaffray's approval. He was, she felt, a little too fond of the good life, drinking a bit too much, getting into debt. It would be Jessie next. She would be off come October to the university if she had passed all her exams. It would never be quite the same again. Jessie and Fanny, however, were excited about the project.

'If you go you'll write to us often.' Jessie said, 'Tell us aa about it – aa these wild animals and birds and braw weather, how exciting. One day you'll hae a fairm of your own and we'll aa come ower and see you.'

John, to tell the truth, felt a pang of jealousy when he heard of the proposal.

'You lucky old sod getting oot o Aberdeenshire jist like that and me aye in this boring ald bank.'

Warning signs flickered momentarily in mother Jaffray's eyes. So her beloved John of whom she had such high hopes was getting tired of the bank – he was getting restive too, wanting away. Her dearest hope had been that he should, in time, become a respectable bank manager but she wasn't so sure now.

The younger children weren't wanting their big brother to go or at least not unless he came back soon and brought them exciting presents.

The very next day Willie went over to see Dod and his father. He found Dod sitting in the kitchen in front of the peat fire resting his broken leg up on a chair.

'I'm sorry it's at sic short notice but as you see I just canna gyang richt noo. I'm foonered, and Carmichael is desperate in need of help as soon as possible. I'll gie you the ticket. It's aa paid for and some o the kit I've got for going abroad if you like. It's no aa that expensive and it'll save you howking around at the last minute for gear. Fortunately we're both of much the same heicht and build. I'll show you the letter I got from Carmichael explaining things.'

With that Dod stretched over to a small table beside the peat fire and handed Willie several sheets of cream foolscap paper. The address at the top of the first page was embossed in deep blue and read, Government House, British East Africa. The writing of the correspondent was big and bold and Willie read it with interest. Much of the contents of the letter was about the sort of land Carmichael had acquired and all that he was hoping to do with it. He had had trouble with cattle lately.

> . . . some gastro thing. I think I'll get out of cattle. Sheep are the brutes I am going to concentrate on. What I would want you to do to begin with is take over my original plot, do a little dairying and superintend the ploughing, crops etc, and pigs – just ordinary farming while I go to my newly acquired bigger place which I

hope to get into order soon. I am also hoping to get an even bigger 20,000 acre plot in the future under the slopes of the Aberdares and in full view of Mount Kenya, with its peak and glaciers, when the land office in Nairobi makes up its mind what it is doing and gets on with it. They're so slow. If I do get it and if you are satisfactory and wish to stay on you could come and help me up there. You would have your own house and control of the boys. I never interfere in a man's work.

Now to more detail – I have got little money to spend but I offer all I can afford. The following is my offer:

1. I offer rs (rands)150 (which equals 10 pounds) per month as salary, as the outside to which I can go at present.

2. A weatherproof house, rough but sufficiently comfortable, to yourself.

3. The salary could be paid monthly or quarterly as you prefer.

4. I will pay your passage (3rd class) free, with no deduction from salary. In fact pay your passage to Mombasa (Kilindini) and second class railway fare to Nairobi.

5. Whatever farm you are on you will get milk, butter, vegetables free if they are available.

6. As to the length of the engagement. It would hardly pay me if you signed on for less than a year. Of course if things work out and we get on well together I would hope it would be for more like ten years. On the other hand it is possible that you might not suit or might dislike the work or the country or both. How would a year's engagement from the time you land in Mombasa suit? At the end of the year we will know if it's working or not and if it is I will offer, in the normal course of events, that is, if you suit in every way, another engagement of four years. You would of course be

at liberty to go at the end of the first year. I mean the first
year to be a trial period for both parties. If things are
looking up at the end of the first year I might be in a
position to raise your salary or offer you a part of profits. . .

Now, how to get here. You'll will get a B.I. boat from
Southampton that will take you to Mombasa. When you
arrive you can go to my agents Boustead and Clarke
and I will leave instructions with them what to do next.
It will probably be to take the train to Nairobi where I
will meet you.

As to clothes. You ought to have a suit of good strong
khaki, and a sun helmet (khaki), good thick flannel
shirts and shooting boots. Bedford cord breeches and
puttees would be useful. It is sometimes quite cold so
don't make the mistake of bringing out only tropical kit
although, some thin things for the Red Sea would be
rather necessary – but really, for here, your ordinary
Aberdeenshire kit is good enough. I would advise tin
trunks of smallish size to carry your clothes in, no
leather or wood containers.

You will get this letter about the middle of July and
perhaps you could sail in the first half of August to
reach here by September.

Things are looking up here and I really believe the
country is going to do. Had a topping 'Safari' in
Laikipia and around, hunted lions with the Masai who
speared two. Self, shot a fine rhino.

At the moment I am staying with the Gov. for a few
days. This house is most palatial for this country – two
stories, electric light, hot and cold baths, and every sort
of luxury. I hope you will be able to come very soon.

Yours,   Bob Carmichael

Willie was determined to go. Here was an opportunity not to be missed. There was no time to waste. Willie accepted and paid for the kit that Dod was offering but mother Jaffray was determined to get him more clothes. No son of hers would go from home without being well and truly clad so they had a shopping spree together in Aberdeen.

Mother Jaffray was the only one who had raised any ethical doubts about Scots procuring farms in a black man's country. To allay her fears the family read all they could about Africa from material gleaned from Peterhead library. She had no time to read the books herself but they assured her it was all right. Even more than all right. The British were helping the black people to have a better life. Missionaries were out there persuading the natives to change some of their evil practices! The railway line that had been built reached right through to Uganda and was helping to eradicate the slave trade outlawed in Britain since the days of Willberforce. When Willie was born at the beginning of the eighteen nineties Africa was known as the dark continent, that the German's were in danger of claiming for their own. It was the unconsidered wilderness that stood between the Queen's peace and Uganda, the country to which they carried the Christian Faith and the Flag. At that time, before the days of the railway line, Nairobi was unnamed, a piece of swamp at the edge of the Kikuyu uplands, the last camp before the tiny outpost known as Fort Smith in Kikuyu which offered the first civilised comfort after weeks of safari. It was a wild swampy plain inhabited by herds of game and myriad birds into which the Nairobi river dispersed itself.

What they did not tell mother Jaffray was, that beyond Nairobi, now attempting to be a prosperous town, the forest concealed the less than hospitable Kikuyu. Nor did they tell her about the ever prevalent outbreaks of plague.

Apart from the Kikuyu there were no other inhabitants around except the nomadic Masai who, from time to time, built their manyattas on the higher ground. Long before the eighteen nineties, however, slave traders and explorers had brought back to the Sultan of Zanzibar tales of what this no-man's-land was like. A man called Holmwood wrote in 1885 of the wild and beautiful uplands, 'A more charming region is probably not to be found in all Africa not even in Abyssinia' – undulating uplands at a general elevation of 6,000 ft, with varied and lovely scenery, forest-crowned mountains, a land in fact where there is little to suggest the popular idea of 'tropics'.

In 1897 an explorer called Lord Delemere came by the northern route from Somaliland. He stopped at a place called Baringo to prospect the Highlands which he fell in love with and where he eventually began farming, always encouraging others to join him. He saw great opportunity for fellow countrymen. In spite of being close to the equator here was a climate the British could live with.

Somewhat mollified by this extra knowledge, mother Jaffray was more content. If missionaries approved of what was being done it must be all right.

In two weeks time Willie, his tin kists packed, was ready to go. On a day of intermittent rain and sun the whole family went to see him off at the station. The undemonstrative people of Buchan hated to show emotion especially in public. The Jaffray family were no exception. The hope was they would all be able to keep back their tears at Willie's departure for the unknown. They had had a small farewell party for him the night before when the thought of his going suddenly filled his mother with such grief that she found it impossible to hold back the tears. In order to hide them she had rushed through to the kitchen and started to stir furiously at the big black pot of soup hanging from the sway and simmering away for tomorrow's dinner. Willie had seen her hasty departure and followed her into the kitchen. Gently he put his arm round her.

'Dinna worry Mither,' he said. 'I'll be aricht.'

'Fit if you dinna like it,' she said speaking through her tears.

'Och, I'll jist come hame again but I'm sure I'll like it and in time I'll mak siller, even get myself a fairm, and I'll come hame tae see you aa. Maybe you'll be able to come and see me. It micht tak a few years but I'll keep in touch.'

No one in the family really wanted to see Willie go. The first to leave the nest, there was a certain fear in the hearts of his parents, a fear of the unknown. Apart from father Jaffray and his trips to the west coast, none of the rest of them had been further than Aberdeen. Having been brought up in a happy home and a relatively safe environment, the fear in the children was less pronounced. They looked on Willie's departure rather as a great adventure from which their brother would return triumphant. Jessie was the most enthusiastic

'Fit a gran opportunity,' she said to Willie and then, always the romantic, went on to quote a passage from Julius Ceasar that she had been studying for her school leaving certificate.

There is a tide in the affairs of men that taken at the flood leads on to fortune. . . On such a full sea are we now afloat, and we must take the current when it serves or lose our ventures.

'You'll mak a fortune Willie and be able to come hame and see us all.' Jessie reckoned Willie's tide had come but just the same she cried herself to sleep that night silently so that no one would hear.

Mother Jaffray had insisted that every one dress in their Sunday best to see Willie off at the station. There was a great bustle that morning in the Jaffray household. They arrived at the station with not much time to spare. Soon the train came along drowning out the sound of the curlew, lapwing and lark that had been the music of young William's youth The voices of the birds were muted now that summer was well underway and their busy springtime work of bringing up chicks almost over. Their young were also preparing to leave the nest.

In no time at all Willie's tin trunks were stowed in the guard's van and he shut into a carriage. He levered the window down by its stout leather strap to wave goodbye. As the train began to move they all took out their clean white handkerchiefs that mother Jaffray had made sure that everyone had. They waved until Willie was out of sight and then rather to the children's astonishment their father put his handkerchief to his eyes to try to stem the tears that were running down his cheeks. They had never seen their father cry before.

None of the family were ever to see Willie again apart from Charlie, the youngest, who followed his brother out to Africa twelve years later.

Chapter Sixteen

Aberdeen University

THE JAFFRAY parents didn't have much time to brood on their eldest son's departure. With Willie gone they had more work to do than ever. And it wasn't long until the next excitement when the important news came through that Jessie had passed all her exams. She could hardly believe it. She was delirious with joy. The rest of the family were impressed, happy for her and proud of their sister.

Mother Jaffray, at the few afternoon teas she either held or attended, could now hold her head up high with her neighbours. Not many of the farmers around had daughters going to university and she began to think that perhaps it wasn't such a bad idea after all. Things were going better than she had dared to hope, what with Willie as overseer on a farm in Kenya, John working in a bank, albeit in a lowly position at the moment, and now Jessie accepted by Aberdeen University – and a quine at that. She found that this impressed her neighbours most of all.

For Jessie it was life with a capital L beginning. Nineteen twelve and she had just turned nineteen. The thought of attending university filled her with awe. She would be based mostly at King's College, the ancient and awesome building in Old Aberdeen. Jessie thought it beautiful with its huge quadrangle, its arches, its towers built by master craftsmen of yesteryear to withstand all weathers. She considered it the very seat of learning itself and the professors in their flowing robes, strolling the hallowed corridors, were the font of all wisdom. She was going to be a part of all this. This was what she had dreamed of, ever since she could remember. This was what she wanted. This was life itself.

Her worries were fewer now. The farm was beginning to pay and her father and mother were able to get in hired labour again and there was still enough left in the kitty for the university fees. She must find herself a place to stay in Aberdeen. A landlady with a flat in Union Street was advertising for a student and the terms seemed reasonable. After living all her life in the country, how wonderful to wake in the morning to a bustling street to be able to look out of the window and see so much activity and so many people.

'I'll gyang to Aberdeen wi you to see the landlady,' said her mother. She was determined to watch over this wayward daughter of hers whom she knew was still ignorant of the world and who had a great trusting innocence about her.

The landlady in Union Street turned out to be satisfactory. 'A widow woman, a decent sort of body,' her mother told her husband that night.

Jessie would have a room to herself, very plain and simple but all she needed. For the price also she would get breakfast and an evening meal. A tram would take her to the university in the mornings on bad days although Jessie was determined to cycle in the good weather and save the fare.

To begin with, the university wasn't all plain sailing for Jessie. For the past few years, having been accustomed to studying on her own for much of the time with the help of books, she found it difficult to listen to the various lecturers and concentrate on what they were saying. She learned, after a while, to take copious notes and find books from the library from which she could learn more easily. Also she wasn't sure if the lecturers approved of girl students which left her thinking that girls would have to work twice as hard as boys to impress them and pass the exams. Jessie felt their attitude was that learning was for males and what did females need with education? They should be in the home where they belonged and that lecturers were wasting their time teaching girls who, at the end of the day, probably wouldn't be able to pass the more difficult exams anyway, being too scatterbrained. If they did finish the course, which was unlikely, they would meet up with some young man, get married and that would be the end of that. All that wasted education.

In her first year Jessie studied English Literature and the Humanities. English Literature, of all subjects, was her favourite and she hoped she would excel in it. She found the going tougher than she had expected. She admired one of the lecturers above all others, Professor Grierson, even although he didn't take much time to explain things to his students, taking for granted they would know more than they actually did. But she loved his lectures just the same and hung on his every word, never doubting that his opinion was the right one when he told them that the English writers were the ones to be revered above all others. The Scots came rather a poor second although he did concede that he thought Burns the greatest lyricist of love poems of all time. She was rather sorry he didn't have such a high opinion of Byron as he was the poet Jessie loved above all others. She was pleased, however, that he did spend a lot of time on poetry, her favourite subject.

Jessie found that in order to keep up she had to spend a great deal of time studying in her small room. To begin with she wasn't always feeling well enough to do so. Most of her life she had had problems with a rather delicate stomach and was given to bouts of bad indigestion. With eating the landlady's food these bouts became worse than ever. It wasn't that the food was bad or the amount meagre, rather the reverse, but that it was badly cooked and stodgy. The landlady was definitely no cook. Jessie hated to disappoint her by leaving any on the plate and she knew she would have to do something about the situation.

One day, after a particularly painful bout of indigestion, she got the opportunity to explain to her landlady about the problem.

'I wonder if it would be aaricht' she said, 'to bring my ain food frae hame. I could have a sma paraffin stove in my room and cook and eat when I feel like it.'

The landlady hummed and hawed a bit but she could see for herself that Jessie wasn't well and she was a kindly soul.

'Ach weel, I can see you're nae richt, quine. If you think it would help, but I wouldna be able to tak doon your rent aa that muckle. Jist what it costs to feed you.'

'That wouldna maitter,' said Jessie glad to get a reprieve. 'I wouldna expect it.'

She went home that weekend and told her parents what she had done and why.

'Do you think I could tak some food frae hame, mither?' Now that Jessie was at university she spoke mostly in English when the need arose but reverted to the Doric when she was home on the farm. Jessie's suggestion was not unusual. Many of the poorer country students survived by getting food from home, cooking it themselves on stoves supplied by landladies, thus saving money on keep.

'Fegs aye, if you think it would help,' her mother said and so Jessie went back to Aberdeen laden with packages of food – oatmeal and oatcakes from the girnal, eggs, butter and cheese from the dairy, hard fish and salt herring from the barrel, potatoes and turnips from the pits. She could buy milk in Aberdeen and anything else she should need and could afford.

A new two-burner stove was installed in her room. The landlady had taken it upon herself to do this while Jessie was away, being careful to get one that she considered safe. She also provided for Jessie a couple of pots, a kettle and a frying pan. When she thought about it she was pleased with Jessie's proposal.

She didn't really like cooking and now she would have more time to herself and be less tied to the house. She knew she could trust Jessie. She was proving to be a hardworking girl and wasn't in danger of bringing a lot of wild students to the house when she wasn't about like some of her young men students had done in the past.

Things were better for Jessie health wise after this. Now she could eat what and when she wanted and was able to put more effort into her studies.

Although, in that first year the glamour and wonder of being one of the students in those ancient and impressive halls of learning was substantial, there were some disappointments. Before she went to university she had not been able to think what it would be like to be one of a bunch of students, only that it would be exciting. It was in a way, but it did seem to her that women were treated as inferior beings by many. Male students had their Union where they could congregate, have fun, sing their student songs, have amazing discussions and be loud and boisterous if they wanted to. The girls had a separate Union which was quite small. Jessie seldom went there. She got on less well with women. She herself had a straightforward personality lacking guile. She had no aptitude at all for the clever catty remarks in which some of her fellow women students indulged. In a way she had a great innocence about her with enthusiasm for everything and everyone. Perhaps this coupled with her obvious happiness was what annoyed some women and occasionally there would be a nasty remark that came as a great surprise to her and hurt. Some let it be known that she was just a farmer's daughter.

It was perhaps as well, she realised, that the social life was less than she expected as she knew she would have to study hard if she wanted to get through the first year's exams. She did, however, manage to meet up with the opposite sex after lectures, from time to time, and enter into what she considered to be fascinating conversations. The boys were drawn to this bright attractive girl, brimming over with life and obviously interested in what they had to say.

One or two of them appeared to think that because Jessie had a friendly open way with her and emancipated about learning that she might be emancipated in other ways also. Jessie soon put them straight about that. It wasn't so much that she had been strictly brought up. Perhaps if she had, she might have thrown over the traces and defied her parents' teachings. It was more the culture she was brought up in that influenced her. There were certain things you did not do on any account and allowing young men to have their way with you was one of them. Jessie never questioned it. The consequences could be too serious. How often had she heard it whispered that some young girl had got into trouble.

'Aye, Mary had an unwanted bairn and she was jist seventeen – life ruined and the peer wee, illegitimate cratur – a bastard all its life and nae its fault – the jade, no better than she ought to be.'

The 'cutty stool' was seldom in use these days. In the past some ministers in the Church of Scotland had the errant girls sitting on stools confessing their sins and repenting of them in front of the whole congregation but everyone knew of a girl whose life had been 'ruined'.

'Fit decent man would hae her and her faitherless bairn aifter that?'

A young man's stature was not exactly enhanced by getting a girl into trouble either. If at all possible he would be encouraged or forced into marrying her 'for the bairns sake at least' if it had not been his intention to do so in the first place. But he was not condemned to the same degree. Men were different. It was to be expected. The girl had to be the strict one. It was her unquestionable duty. If she was dutiful, she and her unwanted child would be the ones to suffer most. There was no use thinking that she might get away with giving in to the passions just one time. How often had it been the one and only time a girl had given in to her lover that had ended in an unwanted birth. Hadn't mother Jaffray, in the old days, always given a dose of salts to the servant quines after a night out? Not that there was any guarantee that would solve the problem. Nor was abortion a way out. Abortion was illegal and dangerous and there were more doctors in prison over giving some girl an abortion, because they were sorry for her desperate plight, than for any other reason. Besides, it was a disgrace to the whole family and they had a position to keep up in their society no matter how lowly.

'Dinna listen tae a young man who says he'll mairry you and gie you aa thing he has in order to mak love to you. Aifterwards he may forget aa aboot sic promises.'

Mother Jaffray talked very little about sex to her girls. She expected them to learn from the day-to-day living with the breeding animals around her but, from time to time, when the opportunity arose, she would give words of advice.

'Dinna let your passions get ower you. Dinna excite a man ower muckle. Men are different frae us, canna control themsels the same. Aye remember that the greatest gift you can gie a husband is your virginity.'

On such occasions, as on others, Jessie loved to argue with her mother.

'But fit if you just looed someone mair than your hale life and for some reason he couldna mairry, maybe aff tae war or something?'

'But me, nae buts. There's nae circumstance. . .' Mother Jaffray was quite adamant.

'Och mam, are you no a wheen ald-fashioned? Things are changin.'

'They're nae changin that muckle. I'm nae ald-fashioned, just practical and sensible.'

Outwardly Jessie may have argued black was white with her mother but inwardly she had learned her lesson well. She had no intention of giving into any young man no matter how much she loved him. She would wait. She wanted to finish her course and then see what kind of a job she would get. Marriage would have to wait. She found, however, that most young men treated her with the respect they had been taught to give to 'good' girls. There were, just the same, one or two young men who seemed to think otherwise. Jessie kept them at arm's length. She had to be careful after the lesson of the tennis match. She now knew she was attractive to men.

There were times, of course, with her romantic nature, when she would have loved some young Lochinvar to come along, sweep her off her feet and take her flying off on one of these exiting new motorbikes and make passionate love to her, but she would keep these sort of thoughts as dreams for the future.

That first year at university was the most difficult one for Jessie. She worked hard but because everything was new to her, she found she often got distracted. She felt her essays were not as good as she would have liked them to be. She knew she was often writing what she thought would impress her lecturers rather than to please herself and succeeding in neither. She didn't quite manage, either, to establish a rapport with Professor Grierson whom she admired so much. He tended to ignore her. For some reason her brightness and charm didn't work with him. Perhaps he thought, being a woman, she was not serious enough about the importance of literature. Perhaps he mistook her cheerful optimism for an over- confidence which she didn't actually possess when it came to writing or scholastic abilities.

Whatever it was, Jessie felt a sense of disappointment. She had enjoyed Professor Grierson's lectures very much and was vastly impressed by his knowledge and for all the rest of her life never forgot his teaching. He had, however, given her little or no encouragement to write, something she had always wanted to do. She felt he had not appreciated the style of writing that had got such praise from her masters at school both for its skill and its fresh outlook. Perhaps this lack of interest, on the part of this professor, was what made her lose confidence, to a certain extent, in her ability with the result that, in later years, she confined her love of writing to penning copious letters to her two sisters.

She went home in the summer to the farm to help out as best she could. She was not at all sure if she had passed all her exams so was happy when the results came through and she found she had, although with no great distinction.

Several years later when she was collecting references from her professors, she was a bit disappointed with the bare-bones write-ups that some of them gave her.

UNIVERSITY OF ABERDEEN
I hereby certify that Miss Jessie I. Jaffray attended the
Ordinary Graduation Class in English Literature
during the session 1912/13 with sufficient regularity,
and her essays and class exercises were satisfactory, and
that she passed the prescribed examinations.
(Signed) H. J.C. GRIERSON,
Professor of English Literature.

and from her Humanities lecturer:

UNIVERSITY OF ABERDEEN
Miss Jessie I Jaffray attended the Graduation Class of
Humanity during a complete course Session 1912/13
with due regularity and performed the work of the class
satisfactorily.
(Signed) A SOUTER
Professor of Humanity

CHAPTER SEVENTEEN

Letters from Abroad

IT WAS during one of her weekends home in that first autumn term at the university that the anxiously awaited letter came from Willie. The address at the top of the page was 'The Norfolk Hotel, Nairobi'.

Dear Everyone,

It has been a long journey but not altogether a tedious one. The ship I sailed on transported more cargo than passengers. The cabin I was allocated was in the bowels of the ship, tiny but not uncomfortable. We had no great storm at sea and I wasn't seasick for which I was grateful. We called at various ports – Lisbon, Marseilles, Port Naples, Port Said, Aden and then Mombasa. Later on in the voyage I was glad of my tropical gear. I've never felt so hot in my life.

Mombasa is also hot, very hot, hot and humid which makes for lethargy. It is a port bustling with humanity of all races, Europeans, Africans, in varying shades of blackness, and Asians.

I found 'Bousesteads and Clarke' without too much bother and there a letter awaited me with a train ticket to Nairobi. Bob Carmichael had got the message that I was replacing poor Dod with his broken leg. The journey to Nairobi was interesting. I could never have imagined so much uninhabited country and all these herds of wild animals we glimpsed through the carriage windows. Unbelievable!

How can I describe Nairobi? I got off at the station, a long low building constructed only a few years ago. Nairobi is very young. It only really began at the beginning of the century, not long after the railway line from Mombasa reached this place where they had decided to make a base and construct workshops and stores. All sorts of other people moved in also – traders, explorers, adventures, Asians, Africans, and Europeans and set up camp. Already it has become a town but a very strange town to my eyes.

When I arrived I got a sort of rickshaw thing to take me to the Norfolk Hotel, a rather grand sort of building surrounded by trees. A white picket fence runs the full length of the hotel which is long and low, like the station. The Hotel has a wide cool veranda stretching its whole length. It is full of people at the moment – white people, mostly men down here from the farms for 'The Races' which seemingly last ten days or so. My boss Bob Carmichael is here for the occasion like the others and when the races are over, which will be tomorrow, I go with him up to a place called Nakuru which is not far from the farm I am to be looking after.

The rest of the town is a mixture of houses and stores with wide streets in between. One or two of the houses are rather attractive in an English kind of a way. The busiest part of the town is the Bazaar where much of the trading goes on. It is mostly inhabited by Africans and Asians and on the wide road between stalls one finds carts and carriages, bicycles and the odd cow or buffalo wandering around. It could do with some work from your barn brush, father, and your scrubbing brush, mother, and the latrines are awful.

I've been taken to The Races which engender a lot of excitement and afterwards, at night, this town resembles some Western American frontier town that one reads about that, for some reason, I didn't expect to find here in Africa. There is a lot of drinking goes on and even from this hotel, pot shots are aimed at targets like the street lamps. Even Lord Delemere, I have been told, the explorer who first saw the potential of the land beyond here for farming, has been known to indulge in this sport. Last night it got wilder than ever with men setting up bottles in the bar to shoot at. Everyone owns a gun here. Seemingly its not at all uncommon to come face to face with both lion and tiger on the outskirts of the town. Bob Carmichael says he will give me a gun when we get to Nakuru. I'll need it, he tells me, to protect myself against the marauding leopard, lion or charging rhino and perhaps even the odd Kikuyu. The Kikuyu tribe are more friendly than they used to be, I've been told, but you can come up against a dangerous one now and again. I don't like the idea of all this killing but it could be a case of me or them and I am glad, just the same, that I learned to shoot at home.

There are a lot of men here with very 'Coonty' voices and I am surprised to see how badly dressed many of them are in well-worn and sometimes none-to-clean breeches, puttees or leather leggings and wide-brimmed hats or pith helmets. On the whole it's a rough place which in many areas doesn't exude wealth. It is also a strange place absolutely alien to anything I have ever known.

Yesterday I saw a Camel Caravan laden with ivory and driven by Somalis going down tree-lined Station

Road. A company called the Boma Company (strange
name) have opened up the Northern Frontier and trade
as far as Addis Ababa (Arabian night country) for ivory
and precious metals. It is all very new to me and exciting.

Not far from here the Ali Khan has an attractive
bungalow. He came here seemingly in 1904 with a mob
of horses picked up somewhere along the Benadir coast.
He is a true explorer respected by all. His rickshaws, gigs
and landaus are all part of the picturesque scene. Is this
romantic enough for you, Jessie?

Another name you hear mentioned with awe is
that of John Boyes, a trader and adventurer who, some
time ago, began trading with the Kikuyus. He gained
their respect when, during a smallpox epidemic which
swept through the country, he vaccinated many of the
tribesmen against the dreaded disease. He is now self-
styled King of the Wa Kikuyus and it has made them
less dangerous and more favourably disposed towards
the whites.

The weather here has been hot but comparatively
dry. I have been told that in wet weather, in the rainy
season, the roads in the town are a muddy mass of pot
holes, a nightmare

I must stop now. The noise of merriment from
the bar gets louder and louder. It's the last night of The
Races and if yesterday is anything to go by, fights could
break out any minute. I am keeping out of the road and
hope to get to bed reasonably early to be fresh for my
journey to Nakuru tomorrow. I'll send an address to
write to as soon as I know it myself. Hope everything
goes well back home and that Jessie got off to the
University.

Yours Aye,
Willie.

On Jessie's next weekend home another surprise awaited her, something completely unexpected. Her second brother John was getting ready to go to Malaya. Like Willie's departure before him, this situation had arisen very quickly.

One day in the bank in Peterhead, a stranger came in to withdraw money. He was a well-dressed man around thirty five years of age of military bearing with a neat handle bar moustache and an English accent. His name was Edward Hisart. He struck up a conversation with John telling him that he ran a rubber plantation in Malaya and was home on furlough. His wife was the daughter of one of the bigger farmers near Peterhead whom John knew of and he was here staying with his in-laws for six weeks or so. John took to this friendly man and the next time he came into the bank to withdraw money, a short conversation ensued. This time Edward Hisart quizzed John about himself and a rapport grew between them. But what he was asked on his next visit to the bank took John completely by surprise. That particular day there happened to be no one else at the till when Edward came in. Edward seized the opportunity to put his proposal. He wasted no time, the other teller might be back at any moment.

'How would you feel about coming back to Malaya with me? I am sore in need of a young fellow like you to help me with the accounts. Things are getting out of hand now that the rubber is running. I can offer you a reasonably good salary which will increase as more trees come into production and you will get leave to come home every so many years. But you will have to let me know quickly. There will be much to arrange for your journey and it would be easiest for you to come back with my wife and me in a few weeks' time. I think I could swing things if you could tell me soon – tomorrow perhaps. Go home and think about it.'

With these words the other teller, who had been out on an errand, returned and Edward Hisart took his cash and departed.

For the rest of the day John had a problem concentrating

on his job. That night he had little or no sleep. He hadn't told his family anything about the proposal thinking that to do so might cloud the issue. Almost certainly he would have opposition from his mother. By morning he had made up his mind. He would take up the offer. Didn't Jessie always quote that 'things taken at the tide lead on to fortune'?

When Edward Hisart came into the bank the next morning John was ready for him.

'The answer is yes,' he said.

That day he gave a month's notice to the bank. That evening he went home and told his family what he had done. As he had feared, his mother was the most difficult to reason with or console. Although not given to weeping, tears were running down her cheeks.

'Dinna gyang, son,' she said. 'You'll dae weel eneuch here. It's an afa lang way and its very hot, I heard, and you'll maybe nae like it.'

'I'll like it fine, mither. Don't you see its a grand opportunity. It's nae easy to get to these jobs and you allowed Willie tae gyang awa. Why nae me? Besides, he's promised me a good salary and holiday's hame, so I won't be awa forever.' John loved his mother and hated to grieve her but he knew he must go.

Ever since the letter had come from Willie he had wanted to go to somewhere more exciting with greater opportunities. He wanted to see other parts of the world and it would be a long long time, if ever, that he would have the chance to do so again.

'But hoo div you ken that this man's honest and is wha he says he is?' Mother Jaffray wasn't going to give up easily.

'I have made some enquiries and you'll ken o his wife's people.' He mentioned their name and mother Jaffray had to confess she had heard no ill of them. She knew she was defeated.

Next morning there were no more tears from mother Jaffray, just a steely determination to take some of her butter money to help outfit John to the best of her ability in the tropical clothes he would need.

Jessie's reaction to the news was one of excitement. She forgot for a moment all her disagreements with her brother

'Hoo wonderfae for you, John. Of course, you maun gyang, tak the opportunity while it's there. Fit an adventure. Maybe you'll become the richest o us aa. I've read about these new rubber plantations starting up in Malaya.'

Before Jessie came home for the Christmas break, John was away. The farm seemed a quieter place. Mother Jaffray threw herself into her daily work harder than ever. She had become rather withdrawn, Jessie thought, but she'll get over it. She has to let us go.

Before Jessie returned to Aberdeen after the Christmas break another letter came from Willie giving a box number address for the family to write back. This time the information was mostly about the farm he was now on.

> . . . As I was promised I have a small house of my own, if you could call it a house. It is a roughly put together shack, fashioned out of logs and divided by a flimsy partition into two rooms. It is adequate and no more sparse than the chaumer in the loft back home.
>
> At one end there is a bed of sorts and a mosquito curtain and in the other a table and a couple of chairs plus a few shelves and that's about it. Cooking is done on a stove outside. I will however be able to make more furniture for it when time will allow.
>
> I am kept pretty busy. We have cattle, sheep and pigs. We grow sisal, coffee, potatoes and general crops for feed. Farming is very different here. I am not supposed to do much of the physical work myself as there is an abundance of natives to do it for me. But I always do lend a hand although I sometimes get into trouble with the boss if he finds me at it. My main job is to try and keep the natives working and make sure they

do things properly. This is not so easy as you think. They want the jobs. They want the little money that they get but they are not so keen on physical work and on the slightest excuse will down tools. They do require to work quite hard but no harder than we do at home.

This is a rather wonderful wilderness. I am living so close to the equator yet here in the highlands, 6000ft above sea level, the climate is temperate and I wake up to clear light and sunshine. Later in the day the weather may break down a bit and we can get rain but who could feel downhearted for long in a climate like this?

There are many wild animals around. True to his word, Bob Carmichael gave me a gun not long after we came here. I haven't had to use it yet but it is needed. I am finding it a bit difficult to come to terms with living in daily danger but I expect one gets used to it. I have to admit also to feeling homesick. Sometimes, how I wish I was back in Buchan where one feels comparatively safe. Also I miss you all: our rumbustious happy home that was, and sometimes I think if only I could get home, how I would plough. But all in all this is a wonderful place to be for anyone seeking adventure and hoping to get on in the world.

I'll end on a cheerful note and try to describe to you some of the many wonderful sights I have seen. How I wish, Jessie, I had your powers of description.

Nakuru, our nearest small town, if you could call it that, is built on the shores of a soda water lake where often thousands of birds called flamingos feed. They are truly both strange and magnificent birds with large oddly shaped bills, wonderful pink bodies toppling on high stilt legs. At certain times they all fly away together. How can I best describe how this exodus looks? Its like one of these brilliant Buchan sunsets that is left after the sun has gone over the horizon. Instead of fading and changing colour, however, this one flies away spread out against the sky leaving the white sands at the edge of the lake and moving towards the blue green hills in the distance.

I have already seen great herds of wildebeest, zebra, rhino and different types of deer, marvellous! and I saw something yesterday, much smaller but that absolutely fascinated me – a lizard-like creature with a long tail and protruding eyes called a chameleon. I hardly noticed it at first, it blended in so well with the green leaves it was amongst. I had been told about its amazing powers and that it was harmless so I caught hold of it, took it inside and placed it on my yellow bedspread. It immediately turned the same colour. How can this happen? You have always said it was an amazing world, Jessie and much bigger than Buchan but how I wish I was there with you all right now just the same. . .

It was well into Jessie's second term at university before they heard from John. His letter was shorter than Willie's letter and didn't go into such detail.

. . . The journey has been long and boring. Nothing to see but waves, day after day. However I have made some good friends aboard ship. After a while at sea, however, you do begin to wonder if you will ever get to your destination. The ship was full of both people and cargo and quarters were rather cramped but bearable. At last we sailed into the South China Sea and made for Port Sweetinham where most of the trading ships dock. Afterwards I went with the Hisarts up to Taiping where I am told most of the rubber plantations are. The first

147

rubber trees, which came from South America, were
only planted at the beginning of the century and didn't
come into maturity for ten years but it seems to be a
successful venture and rubber is running well.

The Hisarts live in quite some style although in
rather a roughly put together house. It has two storeys
with a veranda that has a thatched roof. They have
already got a garden in place and spend quite a bit of
time sitting out in the evenings when it is cooler. It's very
hot and humid here, that's the worst bit, that and the
ever-present dangers of which I have been warned. I
hear about them but have not come into contact with
them yet. It certainly adds an excitement to life. It almost
seems as if we are living in a clearing in the jungle which
I suppose we are. It's not all that picturesque. Perhaps it's
too new. There are fallen trees everywhere with a lot of
brush still not cleared away which gives the land an
untidy appearance. This house looks out on to acres of
very young trees. Everywhere else is forest – a bit
claustrophobic. I live with the Hisarts at the moment but
am shortly to have my own bungalow down by the
factory which will also serve as the office for the estate.

The forest holds a wonderful array of creatures, I am
told, from long-armed gibbons to ant eaters and a most
wonderful assortment of colourful exotic birds. There are
also, within its frightening depth, snakes of all sorts, some
extremely dangerous. They are all over the place, actually,
and one has always to be on the outlook for them.

There is human danger also in the form of native
head-hunters who infiltrate these forests coming from
Sarawak intent on stealing rubber. However, don't
worry mother, I live in comparative safety. I enclose a
couple of photographs which were taken not long ago
after my arrival here. . .

The family poured over the photos taking in every detail. One was of the barn-shaped factory with rows and rows of young rubber trees in front. In the background stretched unremitting jungle against a long low horizon. There was a tangled mess of torn-down trees and through the bare acres of young rubber trees a couple of pale tracks criss-crossed to the far left of the picture.

The other photo was of more interest. In the background was a portion of the veranda of the Hisart's house with its thatched roof held down by inconsequential thin branches of trees. In the foreground Mr and Mrs Hisart were sitting on cane chairs that boasted impressive intricately woven oval backs. Mr Hisart's chair had an extension which let him have his feet up and that gave him, in his light cool tropical suit and white open-neck shirt, a relaxed air without taking away his look of distinction and authority. Mrs Hisart was dressed in a white Edwardian gown with a lace collar. On her feet were white boot type shoes. Her hair was up in a bouffant style. She would have been pretty had it not been for a rather grim expression about her eyes and mouth. Behind them stood John, a hand on each of their high-backed chairs, a handsome dark-eyed, dark-haired callow youth in a long dark somewhat rumpled jacket with an uncertain smile flickering around his mouth. Their John – out to find adventure and make his fortune.

CHAPTER EIGHTEEN

Flights of Fancy

IT WAS in Jessie's second year at university that she met Rory. He was one of the older students and in his final year. A clever fellow and a hard worker, he intended to stay on and take honours. He was taller than she was with a strong handsome face that, at the same time, had an air of sensitivity about it. His hair was as fair as Jessie's was dark, as curly as her's was straight.

She had noticed him first in the midst of a crowded meeting held for students of both sexes. It had been a good night ending in a rumbustious rendering of student songs which Jessie loved and many of which she already knew off by heart. As the evening was ending the singing grew louder – *Oh my darling, Clementine, Riding down from Bangor*, finishing with *Gaudeamus Igitur* (Let us Rejoice).

The next time they met was in the middle of one of the university's long corridors. They were going in opposite directions to separate lectures. She caught his eye and her heart missed a beat. The next chance meeting was out in the huge quadrangle on a bright sunny day. Their eyes met and she knew there was more there than just mere interest.

Eventually a mutual acquaintance introduced them and left them to converse. Jessie was fascinated by his conversation – there seemed to be nothing that he didn't know. She hung on his every word. He asked her out to a concert. Jessie didn't particularly like classical music but because he did and he had asked her, she enjoyed it better than she thought she would. She wished it would last forever and then realised it was not so much the music that had her feeling this way but rather the fact that he had slipped his arm round her waist and she never wanted him to take it away.

That night, when he escorted her back to her room in Union Street, before they had quite reached it, he guided her gently into a cold, dark close nearby, kissed her gently on the lips and said, 'I love you, Jessie.'

Nothing more was said but walking up the cold winding stairway to her lodgings seemed like walking downstairs into an enchanted land. She lay on her bed that night but did not sleep, reliving the kiss and his words over and over again. So this was what love was like!

Once, sometime after their night at the concert, he took her to see his parents. They were well-to-do shopkeepers in Aberdeen and lived in a grand house in an affluent part of the city suburbs. It wasn't an altogether happy meeting. Jessie was apprehensive, feeling she was not altogether welcome especially by his mother. The air was at times tense. Afterwards Rory attempted to explain.

'You see,' he said. 'My folks have great ambitions for me. They want me to take Honours and hope I will become a lecturer at some university or other. They don't really want me to get mixed up with a girlfriend until I'm finished studying and have got well into a career. But they'll come round. I know they will.'

Jessie wasn't so sure. She felt they saw her as a country girl, not polished enough for their son, but she said nothing. The kissing grew more passionate that night but Jessie knew she must not let things go too far, however much she might want to.

Each of the arranged meetings with Rory after that evening was like an oasis in a desert of hard slog. Times to be savoured and dreamed about over and over again. Jessie made the rules of how much kissing was allowed and Rory obeyed.

Jessie was more determined than ever to do well in her exams. She read history and found it a vast and interesting subject but once again didn't do as well as she would have liked. She also took French and, much to her pleasure, found she did well in this subject. The hark-back theory to ancient ancestors floated to the surface again.

Nearing the end of the last term of her second year, something happened that Jessie never forgot. With the exams mostly over the students were feeling more relaxed. A fair came to the university and one of the attractions, perhaps the biggest one for the male students, was that a biplane was to land and give one or two of them a short flight. Aeroplanes, of any sort, hadn't been long in existence and this was a wonderful opportunity and a great thrill.

It was mostly male students that surrounded the flimsy biplane. It had landed on a long stretch of grass not far from the fairground. There were, however, a smattering of girls among them of the more adventurous type. Jessie was there with Rory.

'It's truly wonderful what can happen nooadays,' she said to Rory. 'Not long ago I read in the *Aberdeen Journal* of a Miss Trehawkie Davis. I mind her name because I thoucht it rather strange. She was taken up in one of these planes at the London aerodrome where, for the first time with a passenger aboard, the pilot looped the loop. Two perfect loops the article stated and afterwards a fine landing. When she landed she said it was the most thrilling experience she had ever had in her hale life. So you see,' she said turning to Rory with a teasing smile, 'women are jist as capable of takin risks in adventurous enterprises as men.'

Just at that moment the pilot of the plane was asking for volunteers to go up with him.

'Jessie will,' Rory shouted, with a twinkle in his eye. 'Jessie's fearless.'

'Yes, let Jessie, let Jessie go first,' the other male students shouted in unison. 'She's fearless.'

Jessie was a great favourite with these young men for her fun, her dauntless nature and her adventurous spirit. Before she knew it she was rigged out in a long leather coat, with a leather helmet strapped beneath her chin, wearing goggles and sitting beside the pilot in his open-to-the-elements tiny cockpit. To begin with it was thrilling to speed along the grass and then take off into the air and climb up, up, up to a blue sky with scudding white clouds. Jessie dared to look down. How unbelievable it was to have Aberdeen spread out beneath her and to be able to pick out well-known landmarks. At its curving edge was the blue sea with waves coming in like long wrinkles. Exhilarating to feel the air rushing past. She would have liked to speak to the pilot, ask questions, but the noise of the wind and engine combined was deafening. And then, suddenly, without any warning, she was looking at Aberdeen from upside down. It all happened so quickly that the plane righted itself before she let out a scream which blew away in the wind. Before she had time to say anything he had looped the loop again.

'No!' she shouted above the wind. 'No, no more!' She saw, to her consternation that the pilot had a broad grin on his handsome face and again they turned over. Six times they looped the loop in all. Six times she screamed to no avail. Only the wind heard her. Jessie's delicate stomach was by this time playing up badly. Was she going to be sick? Soon after the sixth loop the pilot came down out of the skies and made for green grass and the edge of the fairground. The figures beneath her were getting larger. Every one was standing, necks bent backward, watching the plane. It was, for many people, the first time they had ever seen one. As the plane came to a halt and Jessie stepped out, a great cheer arose. Jessie's face was ashen. She could barely stand. Her legs had gone to jelly.

Rory seeing her pale face rushed over.

'Darling, are you all right?' He put his arm solicitously around her, and said, excitedly, 'It was fantastic, you know.'

'Rory how could you?' She was almost in tears but, beginning to recover, she gave a wan smile.

'But think of it,' he smiled that bewitching smile that she had grown to love, 'you are probably the first woman to have ever looped the loop six times.'

'Six times,' she said. 'It seemed like a hundred and six. I was terrified.'

To Jessie, towards the end of that second year, apart from the occasional blip, the world was looking rosy. But something was to happen to change all that. For a while, among the student community, and elsewhere, there had been rumours of war. Jessie with her usual optimistic nature thought it would all blow over and never come to anything. But she was wrong. What was to become the Great World War was declared and nothing was to be quite the same ever again. Although there was despondency among the students at this event there was also an excitement especially among the young men. They were enlisting all over the country. The troops were gathering. There was something glorious about fighting for your country and having a chance to become a hero and, at the same time, see the world at your country's expense. Many young women were not altogether averse to the idea either. So many daughters were kept strictly at home until they got married. Now was an opportunity to get out in the world. Like the young men they were needed. Many signed up for the Red Cross.

It wasn't too long after war had been declared in 1914 that a personal bombshell was dropped for Jessie. Rory asked her out to a meal. They went to a more expensive restaurant than they usually did. Jessie wondered why but said nothing. There was a table ready for them in a quiet candle-lit corner. They had ordered before Rory spoke.

'I've something important to tell you,' he said. 'I don't know quite how to say this.' His voice was low and gentle. 'I know it will upset you. It's upsetting for me to have to tell you but yesterday I went to the recruiting office of the Gordon Highlanders and enlisted.

'Enlisted?' Jessie's voice was shocked and scared.

'Yes, enlisted. Jessie, try to understand. I just had to do it. I've been wanting to ever since war was declared but put it off because I knew you and my parents would be upset. I haven't told them yet. I wanted to tell you first, but I will do. I have to go. Please see it Jessie. The country needs all the young fit men it can get otherwise we will be overrun by the Germans. I really do feel compelled to do my bit, no matter what the consequences are. I can't let all these other young men, some of them my friends, die for me and not do anything about it. I would never forgive myself. Never. I've got to go now.'

It was a while before Jessie could speak. Her eyes filled with tears that ran down her cheeks. When she could speak she said, 'Yes I div understand Rory. Oh hoo I wish the war could be over afore you get to the front.'

'Perhaps it will be. Who knows?' Rory gave a wan smile. 'Don't cry, Jessie. I can't bear to see you cry. I'll come back all right. I've always been lucky. I'm one of the lucky ones, you'll see.'

Jessie tried to smile through her tears.

'I've got something for you,' he said, taking a small parcel out of his pocket and gave it to her to unwrap.

Jessie eased off the wrapping paper to reveal a black velvet box. She opened it gingerly and there within was a ring – a beautiful ring: a moonstone set in gleaming gold. It gave off thin flashing strands of blue, gold and green light in the dimly lit restaurant.

'Do you remember how you admired it once in that jeweller's window and told me it was a moonstone. I would give you the moon but perhaps this will do till I come back. And then if I'm lucky, you'll say that you'll marry me.'

'I will Rory, I will,' said Jessie through her tears. 'Please, please come back and never leave me again.'

For a while the letters came frequently. Always hopeful letters, letters of love saying how he couldn't wait to see her again and how he hoped the awful war would soon be over.

Once he was posted abroad she heard less often and the letters sometimes came heavily censored. So much so she found it difficult to work out where he was or what dreadful things were happening. And then the letters ceased. One day she plucked up courage and went to see his parents. She could feel she wasn't overly welcome. She could see they were worried and unhappy.

'He's missing,' they told her. 'We got a telegram. . . we can only hope he's still alive. We'll let you know if we hear anything further.'

They didn't ask her to stay.

For a time she buried herself in her studies and didn't socialise much. It was dreadful this not knowing, this daily waiting for a letter that never came. It was awful this not being sure if he was alive or dead but gradually, always optimistic, and remembering what he had said about being one of the lucky ones, she convinced herself he was a prisoner of war somewhere without the opportunity to write. She would wait till this terrible war was over that was taking the lives of so many young men. Surely we would win and then, perhaps, when all the prisoners were released, there he would be on a troop ship, thin and tired. But she would nurse him back to health and they would get married and live happily ever after.

Chapter Nineteen

The Sacking of Bancar

THE GREAT WAR affected everyone and everything in one way or another. Jessie felt it fortunate that her beloved father was past the age for being called up and her brother Andrew was too young.

In one of Willie's letters home, early in the war, he had told his family that he, along with other white settlers from the Highlands, had ridden down to Nairobi soon after war was declared and there organised themselves into fighting units, Bowkers Horse, Ross's Coles and Wessell's Scouts. Rather rough and untutored units they were to begin with without a uniform, their only equipment being their horses, water bottles, shooting rifles and knifes.

At the beginning of the war there was only one official army battalion in British East Africa and that was the King's African Rifles. There was concern because, shortly after the onset of war, a British cruiser had opened fire on Dar es Salam the capital of German East Africa and the precious railway line ran near to the border with German Tanganyika. It was thought that the Germans would be sure to retaliate and try to overrun the British colony. Soon several units of settler volunteers joined together to become the East African Mounted Rifles, a protective force that proved itself very useful before more regular troops arrived. Their first official weapons were bamboo lances made in the Nairobi railway workshops now turned over to war production.

In September, in that first year of hostilites, they took off for the frontier with Tanganyika but no great battle ensued. There was a skirmish at Lake Victoria but Kenya's main concern was to protect itself. When the East African Mounted Rifles returned to Nairobi they found fresh troops had arrived. The volunteers proved very useful in introducing these troops to strange ways and a foreign land but after a while many of the volunteers drifted back to their neglected farms.

Willie didn't tell them all this at the time not wishing to cause undue alarm and thinking that letters might now be censored anyway. It wasn't until the war was over that they heard the full story.

A letter from John in Malaya said less about the war directly but mentioned how busy they were because of it. He, by this time, knew a fair bit about the rubber trade. It all began with the need for rubber because of John Dunlop's invention of pneumatic tyres for bicycles. The natural habitat of the wild rubber tree was the rain forests of the Amazon Basin and in the beginning the main supplier of rubber to the world was Brazil. With the upsurge of motorised vehicles of all sorts, the need for rubber grew and by the time Henry Ford went into mass production with his 'Tin Lizzie' America was importing 40% of the annual world total of rubber. Demand just kept growing and growing. The price of rubber went through the roof.

In 1878 a naturalist explorer called Sir Henry Wickham collected many seeds from the wild rubber tree and brought them back to London's Kew Gardens. A small percentage of them germinated but Kew scientists quickly realised that these trees would not do well in a cold climate such as Britain's and speculated that, outside their natural habitat, the equatorial belt of South-east Asia might be the place where they were likely to do best. Twenty two precious seeds were sent to Henry Ridley, director of the Singapore Botanic Gardens, who treated them with great care and with persistence they flourished. By 1904 the first rubber plantations were being laid out. and now with the vast new war machine calling out for rubber the demand was endless. More and more jungle was being slashed down in Malaya and other places in South East Asia. More and more rubber trees were being planted. Rubber planters were making fortunes. John had been promoted from accountant to under-manager with two young accountants underneath him and had a good salary. He had met a girl called Molly to whom he had become engaged. She was Australian by birth although her parents had lived in Malaya for several years. They worked on the neighbouring estate He meant to get married next year, he wrote, and hoped the war would be over by then as he planned to come home with Molly on a visit. Perhaps some of the family might manage over to the wedding although he warned them it was a long long voyage.

In 1915 Fanny too had been accepted by the university. Her parents would be hard pressed to afford two girls at the university and although Jessie would be finished by the time Fanny began, she still had a year to do at Teachers Training College. Finding it difficult to get any kind of job with an MA degree, Jessie had enrolled for the college.

Fanny, knowing that it would not be easy to get the coveted bursary, had bicycled the many miles to Fraserburgh and back most days for a year or more to attend a course that would help her pass the bursary exams. She spent maximum time swotting and all her efforts brought success when she won the bursary. This turn of events pleased Jessie greatly as she knew that this was what her sister wanted so badly.

As with all wars there are always advantages for some people. The Great War was no exception. Farmers in Britain at last felt they were needed and they were now better paid for the food they produced. Courted by government and populace alike they were encouraged to grow as much as they could. Farmers in fact became important to everyone for the duration of the war. Father Jaffray was keeping reasonably fit these days with the worrying pressure of lack of money eased and was able to afford a loon or two, not yet of calling-up age, to help on the farm. He also had young Andrew who was working full time and enjoying it. All he ever wanted to do was farm. He was a big strong fellow, almost six feet tall already, and as he had been working for his father off and on for quite some time, he knew the ropes. There was a new enthusiasm about the farms, and great camaraderie among the farmers. They were doing something of importance for the good of the nation while making money for themselves at the same time. They would show what they could do.

Peggy also did what she could to help, working in the house or with the animals, making cheese and butter for her mother, feeding the hens and pigs, helping with the milking. She also had left school and had no wish to go to university like her sisters. She did enjoy reading, however, and in the short time off that she had, could be found curled up with a book.

The day of Jessie's graduation was a magical, unbelievable day. Aberdeen put on her best dress for it. The whole of the Granite City sparkled with light. It seemed as if both sea and city were studded with diamonds. Mother Jaffray had made herself a new outfit and Jessie, who had learned how to make hats, made her a fabulous one for the occasion. Father Jaffray bought himself a new suit. He hadn't bought himself one for years. In spite of making more money since the beginning of the war the Jaffrays were still parsimonious in their spending, knowing that the good times in farming wouldn't last for ever. But with Jessie's graduation, caution was thrown to the wind. They were proud of their daughter and they wanted their daughter to be proud of them. Mother Jaffray had changed her opinions somewhat on the matter of education for girls. The war had changed thinking to a degree. Girls were doing all sorts of things these days and were much needed too.

Jessie looked well in her graduation gown and cap. This was her moment of triumph and there it was in a photograph to put on the parlour dresser for her folks to show off whenever they had visitors.

In June 1916, Uncle John died. Even although they had never been very close, William was unhappy to have lost his only living brother. The bulk of John's estate went to his wife. Neighbours had been surprised at John Jaffray's sudden death of a heart attack. He had always appeared much healthier than his wife Fanny, who had suffered from heart trouble for years and was very much overweight. When John died she gave up the hotel side of their enterprise. With the advent of war the hotel business had been somewhat in decline in any case but, against everyone's advice, she kept on her wee shop. But things went into decline. The shop got dirtier and dirtier and Aunt Fanny herself wasn't overly keen on washing. The shop was pronounced 'foul' by the neighbours and less people went to it but Aunt Fanny, being a hoarder, still bought all she could lay her hands on for stock. By the end of the year Aunt Fanny was dead too. She had left no will. She had no near relations on her side and it fell to the lot of William Jaffray to make all the arrangements for the funeral. The wake was held at Dartfield several days after Christmas.

Neighbours and Jaffray relations came from miles around to attend. Jessie and Fanny were at home on holiday. There was a full house at Dartfield that night. Once all the neighbours had departed they were left with relations, mostly William's sisters and their spouses, who lived at some distance. It was a dark and bitterly cold December night and they were persuaded to stay till morning. They didn't often all get together these days and the lure of the big peat fire burning in the great stone hearth in contrast to the cold outside was the deciding factor. The whisky bottle did its rounds for the menfolk and there were constant cups of tea for the women made from the water steaming away in the big black kettle hanging from the sway. They all sat up most of the night in the kitchen as it was the warmest place and, by the light of the pale lamp glow supplemented by the leaping peat flames, they talked of family matters. They hadn't had such a good yarn in years. The main topic under discussion, however, was the distressing news that they had learned from the lawyer earlier that day. Aunt Fanny had left no will and as the couple had no children, no direct heirs, the fear was that everything would go to the crown.

'Uncle John wouldna have liked that ava,' Jessie said at one point in the discussion. 'Fitever else he was, he was a faimily man.'

'You're richt aboot that,' said her father, 'but there's naithin we can dae aboot it.'

'Och I dinna ken,' said Jessie jokingly. 'You could arrange the sacking o Bancar.'

Jessie's head, after all the history and literature that she had assimilated, was full of sackings and pillagings and because of her lack of worldly experience they were rather romantic ideas.

'Fegs aye, we could jist that,' said Margaret Sutherland, always the most practical one of William's sisters. 'Fit's tae stop us? The croon will get quite plenty wi that grand hoose but fit's tae stop us takin some o the stuff that's richtly oors. The hoose and shop must be fair stappit fu.'

And so the seed was sown and the rest of the night taken up with hatching the plot amidst numerous swigs from the whisky bottle and cups of tea. The dark deed was eventually arranged for the following weekend, New Year's Nicht.

'Ilka ane will be soond asleep that nicht aifter Hogmanay,' William Jaffray agreed.

'Fit aboot the bobby at Lonmay ?' asked Margaret Sutherland.

'Ach he's aricht,' said her brother.

'He likes a fell dram at New Year himsel and onyway he's a bra chap. He doesna bother you muckle and likes tae be neebourly. Even if he was aboot, which is unlikely, he'd like as naw turn a blind e'e an keep oot o the way.'

And so it was arranged. Mother Jaffray carried the lamp through to the parlour and by its dim light peered at the grandfather clock that had on its brass face the phases of the moon.

'No muckle moon that nicht,' she came back and told the conspirators. 'But if you aa come ower here early and bring your cairts and gigs and things, we'll easily mak oor way doon tae Bancar. It's nae far and the hoose is at the roadside. I could gyang there blindfold. It'll be aa the better for being dark in case there are ony Nosey Parkers aboot.'

They all agreed. Any sense of illegality of the plan didn't bother them. The way they saw it was that this was their legal property to be shared out between them and would have been but for the omission of the making and signing of a will. It was illegal that it should belong to the Crown.

New Year's Day dawned clear and very cold. Nine am and there was a wonderful sunrise, all rose and gold with just the hint of that mysterious greeness one sometimes gets in a northern sky. The ground was rock solid hard with frost and a glimmer of white rime clung to every bare branch and twig. Relations from surrounding farms and villages began arriving in the afternoon with gigs and with farm carts – the Ironsides, the Morrisons, the Sutherlands, the Piries. Mother Jaffray had made a big pot of barley broth and an equally large pot of stovies for the occasion.

They planned to set off about ten in the evening. By that time on New Year's night, most people would be in bed. Hopefully there wouldn't be anyone travelling on the road and there were no houses to pass between Dartfield and Bancar.

Their one fear was that it would snow. Even if there was just a small scattering of snow the wheels of gigs and carts and the feet of people would show up and there might be speculation about all the unexplained activity around a dark and desolate house. There was much tapping of the old barometer to see if the weather was going to change. As darkness fell, after a glorious sunset when a fireball sun had slipped into the sea, it was still too cold to snow and relief was felt all round. At ten the horses were all bridled and ready to go with everyone clad in their warmest coats, hand-knitted gloves and scarves. The air had softened a little and the crescent moon, like a slice of melon, came and went under cloud. When the moon was completely hidden, it was pitch dark and all one could make out were the bobbing storm lanterns in this strange cavalcade of vehicles.

William Jaffray led the way down the winding Dartfield track onto the narrow road that led from Peterhead. It didn't take them long to arrive at their destination and to disappear round the back of the hotel and prise open one of the downstairs windows. The back door opened easily from the inside and as there was a door from the hotel directly into the shop there was no problem getting in there either. Most of the rooms had their thick wooden shutters closed so the light of the hurricane lamps would not be noticed from the outside. And in that dim light what a treasure store they found.

Uncle John had been a *bon vivant*. He had treated his paying guests well. In a cool roomy larder he had his wine cellar with a few good wines stashed away for special guests. He also had barrels of rum, brandy and whisky which, because guests had been in short supply lately, were almost full. There were lots of books in the house and some attractive pictures and trinkets. Each one took what small thing he or she fancied, also some furniture – not much, just the odd rocking chair, desk or bookcase and by the time they had finished it would not be apparent to a stranger that anything had been removed. After the Jaffray tribe had gone through the house systematically removing the barrels of spirits and wine, they repaired to the shop.

Here they found a kind of chaos. The shop hadn't been cleaned since Uncle John died more than six months before. What's more, mice had got in. They had nibbled their way through cheeses, butter, stale bread and left their trademark amongst barley, rice and flour. There was much that was unusable but because the shop was so full of goods of every variety from wool and thread to shovels and pots and pans there was much that was of use to those thrifty Jaffrays. Besides, a lot of foodstuff was in jars including a variety of sweets from humbugs to striped balls.

It took till about three in the morning until carts and gigs were loaded up. They took time to leave the house and shop in good order with an untouched look. The horses champed impatiently outside until at last the blankets, brought to put over their backs to keep them warm, were removed. By the time they were ready to go, however, huge flakes of snow were falling softly on the hard ground. They trundled their way back up the winding dark road to Dartfield, weary but triumphant.

There wasn't much sleep for anyone that night and the visitors all left at staggered intervals next day. There was nothing unusual in this. It was quite customary to have many family visitors staying over the New Year, weather permitting.

Their dark deed was not discovered, or if it was, not mentioned. There were rumours going around that on New Year's night there was some strange happenings at Bancar. Perhaps it was haunted. Someone had seen pale lights bobbing in a strange fashion – ghosts perhaps or German spies. But other events happened and speculation soon died down

Amongst the Jaffrays, however the 'Sacking of Bancar' became a legend, talked about, from time to time, whenever a few of them got together, a happening that any Jaffray alive at the time never forgot. One of the little Pirie girls, barely five years old at the time, remembered, seventy five years later, her delight at the beautiful satin rose-coloured ribbon given to her by her mother after a visit to Dartfield all these years ago.

CHAPTER TWENTY

Jessie Jaffray MA

JESSIE had liked the idea of becoming a teacher when she was younger. When she thought it through, however, to be cooped up in a small school in Aberdeenshire with a class full of children, was not her idea of bliss or progress. In her last year at university she had looked into all the jobs open to her that would require a degree. For women there were very few, even with so many young men killed or away at the front.

'Weel, fit dae you want tae dae?' her mother said to her one day annoyed with her dissatisfaction at the thought of going to the Teachers Training College.

'Och I dinna richtly ken but somethin exciting or somethin that would gee me eneuch siller to traivel to France, at least, aifter this war is ower.'

'Women dinna traivel on their own,' said her mother.

'Why not? Isabella Bird did and her faither was a meenister.' Jessie had just been reading about her. 'She was an ailin, shelpit wee body when at hame but totally different when aff on her traivels. It's truly amazing where she got to – Asia, Japan, the Gobi Desert, America – climbed ane of the highest peaks in the Rockies, aince, in just ordinary shoes and clothes. She wrote books aboot some of her journeys, good books.'

'Weel you're nae Isabella Bird nor the Queen of Sheba either,' retorted her mother but this didn't stop Jessie dreaming.

The training college it had to be. She must start earning money soon. She didn't want to be a burden to her parents any longer. She enrolled for the obligatory year. At the college she was much fêted by the young male students most of whom had failed to get into the army because of flat feet or some other defect. There were a few girls on the course, girls like herself with a degree but no clear idea what to do with it other than teach.

One day after what seemed like an age of uncertainty and not long after she had started her college course, Jessie received a letter addressed to her lodgings. It was the half-expected and long-dreaded letter from Rory's parents. It was brief and to the point. They told her that they had just received information that their son Rory had been killed in action. She would naturally be aware of their great grief and they would be grateful if she had no communication with them at this time of coming to terms with their loss. The letter didn't mention Jessie's loss. She felt desolate.

That night she cried herself to sleep caressing the moonstone on her finger. The next morning she decided to tell no one of her grief. She wouldn't be able to prevent herself from bursting into tears if she did. She wouldn't remove the moonstone from her finger either. She wanted to feel him still there in some way however small. Hard work she found to be the best antidote to grief and she stuck into her teacher training with renewed energy drowning out other thoughts as much as she could.

As time passed and the grip of grief lessened she began to realise that in some ways she was mentally better off. Not knowing whether he was alive or dead had been a great strain. Now she must get on with her life without him and she repeated to herself from time to time, a maxim often quoted by her mother. 'It's better to have loved and lost than never to have loved at all.' Not that she intended not to love again if the right man came along. She was twenty three now and crafty nature saw to it, as she does with so many women of that age, that to have a child of one's own seems to be one of the most desirable things on earth. How she was going to fit everything in she wasn't quite sure.

One thing that did help Jessie that year was having Fanny in Aberdeen. She had separate digs but sometimes, of an evening, the girls would meet up. Eventually Jessie told Fanny about Rory and found a most sympathetic shoulder to lean on. Although there was a certain rivalry between the two sisters, which gave impetus to each one to reach greater heights, there was also a great friendship and understanding. Fanny was determined to be upside down her sister for whom she had a great admiration, if not to beat her. She wanted to be as like her as possible which annoyed Jessie at times. Why couldn't she do something different?

'Imitation is the sincerest form of flattery,' her mother used to tell her when Jessie complained about this trait in her sister.

Fanny had a different personality from Jessie's and the older the sisters grew the less alike they became in both appearance and character. Fanny had not grown as tall, had mouse brown hair, and a rather long Scottish face. She was however, a pretty girl with a pleasant disposition but without that sparkle that gave that unaccountable charm to everything Jessie did. This was not something strived for, but as natural as her dark and shining hair.

One evening shortly after the Christmas break, Fanny confided in her sister.

'I've met this absolutely winnerfu fellow called Raymond. He's in his second year at 'varsity and seems to have taken a fancy to me. He's a communist through and through and has some truly winnerfu ideas. He thinks a lot aboot the disadvantaged fowk in life. The only thing is he is aye needin money for his cause and I dinna really have muckle tae gie him. I wish I did. It's a winnerfu cause and I'm really interested.

'Well for guid sakes dinna join the Communists,' Jessie warned. 'These activities really div tak up ower muckle o your valuable time. I was pressurised occasionally to join the Suffragettes. I'm glad I didna. Not that I dinna agree with fit they are daein in attempting to get the vote for women and other lang owerdue richts but it's the time factor if you get involved. Besides I like to be my ain woman. Do things my way.'

'You're ower self-centred,' berated her sister.

'Weel maybe I am. At the moment onyway, till I've feenished my training.'

Jessie met Raymond once and didn't like him. He had lank hair, a swarthy complexion, hollow cheeks, shifty eyes and a permanently tired look. Words from Shakespeare came into her head – 'I like men who sleep o nights'. For the life of her she could not see what Fanny saw in him but said nothing. One way in which the sisters were very different was that Fanny could be persuaded to take up a cause which she would stick to vehemently considering that everyone should espouse the same one as herself. Jessie was not so gullible.

During that first year in Aberdeen Fanny made several journeys back to Dartfield to beg for money for this marvellous man. To begin with she managed to wheedle some out of her parents much to the annoyance of the rest of the family. One day she took Raymond out to meet them. They didn't take to him any more than Jessie had.

Towards the end of Fanny's first year she went to see Jessie in her digs with a shock announcement.

'Raymond and I are going to get married. It's going to be a quiet affair, a secret wedding. Raymond wants it that way – the registry office, two witnesses and a meal afterwards. Will you help? Will you be my bridesmaid and one of the witnesses? I'm not telling mother or father or the rest of the family and swear to me you won't tell them either. I know they don't like Raymond and won't approve of what I am doing, but I don't care. I'm going to marry him anyway. Please, please say yes. You always have been the one to help me out.'

Jessie was not at all happy about the situation. There was something about Raymond that she didn't trust. She tried to talk her sister out of doing so foolish a thing when she knew so little about his past life.

'Find out a bit more about him first,' she advised her sister but Fanny was adamant.

'Fit mair div I need to ken? I love him and trust him. He is a winnerfu man trying to dae sae muckle for the poor.'

Jessie promised to support her sister but privately decided to do a little sleuth work before it was too late. The wedding was due to take place three weeks hence and she hadn't much to go on. Jessie confided in James, one of the students at college whom she knew was a communist sympathiser and would know Raymond. She asked him if he could possibly find out something about him before the wedding came up. As luck would have it, James and Raymond had a mutual acquaintance in London. James wrote to him and what he came up with the day before the wedding was that Raymond already had a wife in London.

'Hooever am I gaun to tell her?' said Jessie to her student friend.

'Leave it to me. Afore you say onything, I'll tackle Raymond.'

On the eve of her wedding Fanny was handed a letter. She opened the sealed envelope and immediately recognised the handwriting.

Dear Fanny,
Circumstances have transpired that make it impossible
for me to marry you. By the time you read this I will be
on a train to London. Please don't try to contact me.
It has been fun knowing you.

Love
Raymond

Jessie arrived at Fanny's digs shortly after she had received the note and found her sister in tears. It was one of the hardest things Jessie ever had to do in her life to explain to her sister why Raymond had sent the note and her hand in the affair. For quite some time afterwards Fanny blamed Jessie for interfering and ruining her life but eventually she realised what a lucky escape she had had and Jessie was thought more of than ever. Raymond was never heard of again.

The summer of 1916 saw Jessie looking for a job and helping out at home. Jobs for women were few and far between. She gathered together all the recommendations she could from her ex-professors and from the headmasters of the two schools she attended. But in spite of being armed with these and some other glowing credentials, all she could come up with were one or two jobs in small schools in outlying parts of Scotland and a position as matron of a girls' school down south which she didn't fancy. The nearest of the small schools with offer of employment was at Crudie, a village not too far distant from her home although she would have to catch two trains to get there. She chose Crudie School as it would be cheaper to live at home and she might also be able to be of use to the family in this time of war.

Although Jessie liked teaching and was good at it, this was not at all what she had envisioned after leaving the university. As far as Jessie was concerned this was back to square one. This was disillusionment. It felt like being trapped in the Buchan she loved but at the same time wanted to break out of. Life must hold more than this. University had in many ways been wonderful. Being a student in these great and beautiful buildings was a pleasure. She enjoyed the lectures and loved being in a world of books where anything could be discussed. Life must be more than the prospect of home in Buchan. It wasn't fair. If she could travel, see more of the world, that would be something but how could she get money enough? And anyway there was a war on. Perhaps she should have gone into the Red Cross but she had never felt cut out for nursing and it was too late now.

The dominie that Jessie found herself teaching under had a different personality to that of her own. He was strict and stuck in his ways and treated Jessie almost like one of the children. She had to do exactly what she was told. Teach the children the way he told her to. Jessie would have liked to be a little inventive in how she taught. Get the children interested, excited about learning the way she had been. She had been fortunate with her headmasters in the small schools she had attended. They had been stern but men of wide vision who had seen the varying potentials in their country children and done their best to bring them out. They had an amazing amount of success. But this man, Jessie felt, was narrow-minded and would never be anything else. Stoically she taught the three Rs but she wasn't happy. This wasn't life.

Unlike her usual optimistic self, Jessie began to see a bleak future. She was twenty four. By twenty five, it was said, a girl was 'on the shelf' with little chance of getting married. Above all she wanted children of her own but what chance had she here, shut up in a small school, of meeting any suitable suitor? Besides most of the eligible men that weren't away to war were married by this time and there was still terrible carnage going on. Would any of the others come back? Hadn't her own dear love been killed in the war. There was nothing for it but to slog on and hope the war would soon be over.

She spent the following summer helping on the farm as labour was getting hard to find these days. Jessie loved working outside and her summer was a happy one. She loved to feel the wind about her skirts, the sun on her face. She went back to school with a golden glow about her but once there her depression returned.

Although the distance from home wasn't far, Jessie had a long day. Two trains to get her to her destination meant delays especially in the afternoon when she had a couple of hours to put in at Strichen Station before the train to Lonmay was due.

Fortunately she had an aunt in Strichen whom she quite often went to visit. It wasn't a big village and her aunt, Mrs Pirie, lived fairly close to the station. Jessie would discuss her problems with her. What could she do? Her aunt couldn't come up with much in the way of suggestions herself but one day she said to Jessie, 'Why do ye no gyang and ask some o your former professors or some one you ken in authority? Maybe they would be able to come up with some ideas.'

On the way home in the train that afternoon Jessie pondered over the question of who she could ask. It was a bleak and miserable afternoon in late November. As a rule Jessie spent the train journey looking out at the familiar landscape – rather beautiful, she thought, in its stark way at any time of the year. On the way home she passed the bare but gentle slopes of Mormond Braes, Buchan's one claim to a hill of any consequence. Once, before her time, her father told her, it had been covered in small crofts, a hundred or more, but the landlord had evicted the crofters and used the land instead for rearing cattle. Today the hill was dull and dreich, barely discernible in the grey air. She became influenced by the thought on that train journey home that nothing stays still. Things were constantly moving on and that is what she needed to do too, move on in some way or another. Who could she go to for advice?

The Christmas break was not far off. She would have time then. She could make a journey into Aberdeen and go and see some of her old professors. All of a sudden someone else flashed into her mind, Captain Chaplin. Why not go and see him at the estate office? He might be able to come up with something. She hadn't seen him for ages and he had always taken a fatherly interest in her problems.

Before she went to the university he had said to her, 'You will find it a very different world than the one you have been accustomed to. If you have any difficulties with your studies or anything, come and discuss them with me in the office. I'll always be pleased to see you and I might be able to help.'

Quite a few times she had taken up his offer when home for a weekend and paid him a visit on Saturday afternoons when the clerkesses had knocked off duty but he was still working. He had been helpful. He had so much knowledge that she felt if he did not know the answer to her problems he would at least point her in the right direction.

She had even gone to him once or twice after Rory had gone missing. He had told her not to give up hope. He might be in some prison camp. War was like that. He had made her feel better. Once, some time after that terrible letter had come from Rory's parents telling her their son had been killed in action she had gone to him. He had been kind and sympathetic and had said, 'But Jessie life must go on. A vibrant person like yourself mustn't waste her life by being forever in mourning. Life is for living. You are young and you have so much to give.'

Captain Chaplin had always given her confidence in herself. He was always positive when it seemed to Jessie that her parents were sometimes negative. On that last visit however, a constraint had grown up between them that Jessie couldn't quite explain and she hadn't been back since. Just the same she had felt better after it. Still she wondered why she had kept away so long. She had long ago lost any dislike she had for him in the past and always enjoyed his company. It was time to go back.

The very next Saturday she got on her bike. The wind in her face coming in from the sea was brisk and cold and kept her from bicycling fast. Straight from the Arctic she liked to tell herself. Why she should think the Arctic romantic she couldn't quite explain. Overhead she heard the familiar gaggling cry of geese. She took her eyes off the road for a moment to look up and saw a thin straggle of them moving across the sky like writing on an enormous empty grey slate. They were fighting against the wind as she was. How she loved their music. Every winter it had been with her for as long as she could remember,. Just now they would be making for the Loch of Strathbeg, that flat stretch of water near to the sea. Soon they would land on its grey waters or its flat shore, a comparatively safe resting place. The afternoons were short at this time of year. Darkness would soon be upon them but she loved this wild land with its summers of long light, its winters of long night. What did she really want to move away for? Where else would she see these wonderful skyscapes, crimson sunsets, streaked with Arctic green, and be aware of these huge silences? Her spirits began to rise. She hoped Captain Chaplin would be in.

CHAPTER TWENTY ONE

Secret Wedding

WHEN JESSIE arrived at the estate office she rang the front door bell, entered the hall, knocked at the office door and, without waiting for an answer, walked in as she was accustomed to doing. Captain Chaplin was sitting at his desk writing. He was all alone as she had hoped he would be. His eyes brightened when he saw her.

'Good afternoon, stranger,' he said, 'and how can I help you today?'

'Problems,' said Jessie, 'aye problems.'

Jessie waited silently while he addressed and sealed an envelope.

'That is that done,' said Captain Chaplin with a sigh of relief. 'I've been down here most of the afternoon trying to compose this damn thing. The fire upstairs in the sitting room will be nearly out by this time. Come up with me, Miss Jaffray, while I put on more peat. It's more comfortable up there.'

Jessie had never been in his living quarters before. She followed him obediently upstairs. She was curious to know how he lived. He took her into the sitting room, a spacious brown parlour with rich red curtains draped at either side of the window and held back by gold-tasselled cords. The fire in the hearth was almost out but the room still retained a certain warmth. It was a dark afternoon and Captain Chaplin pulled the two seater brown leather couch closer to the hearth and motioned Jessie to sit down. Then he stoked up the fire from a huge basket of peat. Then, remarking on how dark it was, he went over to the Aladdin lamp that stood on the sturdy round table placed in the middle of the room. Carefully he removed its long graceful glass funnel and held a match close to the fragile white-net mantle while, with the other hand, he twisted the knob that gave it the paraffin it needed. A blue flame began in the mantle turning to soft yellow as it grew. He replaced the glass and the room was diffused in a soft silent light. The newly stoked fire showed little signs of life so he returned to it and took up the embossed brass bellows lying on the hearth. After squeezing a few times and, blowing wind into the fire, flames gradually began to curl and dance round the black peat.

While he was thus engaged Jessie had time to look round the room. The wallpaper had a deep beige background with a brown regency stripe through it. The room was simply furnished. Against one wall stood a long mahogany bookcase filled with books. Against the narrower wall, facing the window, a rolltop desk also had a mahogany sheen to it. Opposite the couch on which she was sitting, sat a matching easy chair. It had a low small table close at hand on which sat an ashtray, a pipe and a leather pouch of tobacco. Beside this chair were piled two neat stacks of newspapers – the *Aberdeen Journal* and the local farming paper.

She liked what she saw. There was a richness about the room. Everything was quality but there was also a bareness. It was a batchelor's room – it lacked a woman's touch. There were no cushions on the couch or the armchairs to bring extra comfort and relieve the brownness. There were no ornaments about, no knick-knacks, no flowers. The high carrara marble mantelpiece was bare except for the green onyx clock in the middle with two matching ormolu at either side. As she waited the clock rang out four golden notes.

When Captain Chaplin had finished plying the bellows Jessie

had expected him to occupy the armchair opposite but rather to her surprise he sat down on the couch beside her.

'Well, young lady,' he said, 'now to the problems. Fire away.'

'I'm stuck,' confided Jessie, 'well and truly stuck.'

'Stuck in what way?'

'The only job I could get on leaving university was assistant teacher at Crudie. It's nae the sort of thing I want ava.'

'Why not? It's a start. It's a worthwhile job having all these young children to influence, educate, point in the right direction.'

'I'm nae allowed to point them in ony direction. I must do strictly what I am told and by the time I get hame at nicht I am too exhausted to help on the farm let alone do onything else and there's nowhere to go in the evenings even if I was able. After university I must say it's a huge let-down.'

'Oh come now, living in Aberdeenshire is not that bad.'

Jessie looked round at him. He was looking at her and smiling in a kindly way. And then, for some reason, all her misery tumbled out.

'But don't you see,' she said, 'I'm stuck. I've nae future. I'm almost twenty five. The man I loved is dead. There are nae eligible bachelors aroon. There have been so many young men killed in this dreadful war that there is a real scarcity of men and it's not ower yet. Women are on the shelf at twenty five. I'll be an ald maid, worse than that – an ill-natured teachery ald maid.'

'Well, marry me then.'

Jessie could not believe what she was hearing. Was he teasing her again? Startled she looked round at him and then she knew he was in deadly earnest. His eyes looked directly into hers. Not even Rory had looked at her like that. His eyes had become liquid pools of love touching her very soul. There was no mistaking that look.

'But, but I couldna possibly.'

'Because I'm too old? As old as your father perhaps. Well I have to admit I am sixty on my next birthday and yes there is a huge age gap, but I don't feel old and with luck I've lots of life in me yet.' He was almost pleading with her now.

'But, but my parents would never let me,' Jessie heard herself saying.

'Your parents don't own you, Jessie.' She noticed he had dropped the Miss Jaffray and she rather liked it. 'You have your own life to live. Sometimes I think they don't understand you too well. I know that in your eyes. I'm old. I only wish I could put the clock back. Had I met someone like you when I was young my life might have been very different. I might not have got into the scrapes that I did. I've never loved any one as much as I've loved you. I think I've loved you from the very first day that I saw you standing holding on to your bicycle. I've watched you grow into a beautiful young woman from that gawky girl you were then. How often I wanted to tell you that I loved you but promised myself that I would not say a word until you had finished at the university. When you came and told me about Rory I thought I had lost you and then when you told me he had been killed I knew I must say nothing in the midst of your grief. There hasn't been the opportunity to say anything to you until now. Love is not the prerogative of the young, Jessie. I love you more than I can say. Could you find it in your heart to love me just a little?'

Jessie didn't know what to say. For once she felt completely without an adequate response

'I dinna ken. I just dinna ken. It's such a new thoucht. I do like you, like you a lot. An I aye feel safe with you and sort of kind of at hame. But love. . . I'm nae sure what love is ony mair. I thoucht I could love no one else but Rory at one time.'

'There is something very special about first love and it will never come again but it does not mean you cannot love again. You are a beautiful woman. I have had the great privilege of watching a fantastic butterfly emerge from its chrysalis and how I wish that butterfly could be mine. Will you at least give it some consideration. I don't expect an immediate answer. I could give you so much. As my wife you would enter my world. I know you think it's a wonderful world. You have told me so often. Perhaps it's not quite so wonderful as you think and I can't offer you riches. I made a mess of my early life recklessly throwing everything away. I was sent down from Cambridge and then went into the army, the Scottish division of the Royal Artillery. That sorted me out a bit and I eventually became a Captain. I was stationed in South Africa for quite some time but eventually fell ill with black water fever from which I was very lucky to recover. That was the end of my army career. I was invalided out, tried out a few jobs here and there, and then my dear friend, the Earl, give me this job which I have been in ever since. I don't want to tell you any lies. My only failing, since coming here, is the occasional bout of hard drinking. The last time I indulged I was told by the doctor I must not be tempted again as, besides being a nuisance to every one around, it had damaged my heart slightly but otherwise I'm perfectly fit and could live a long time.'

'But children,' said Jessie. 'More than anything I would like children of my own.'

'So would I,' said Captain Chaplin. 'I love children and have always regretted I had none. I would love to have a son especially. About the time you went to university I inherited a couple of small estates from a distant relative. These estates are entailed and I was the closest male heir. When I was very young my parents had my name changed from Robertson to Robertson Chaplin so that I would inherit them. However by the time they came my way they were in hock to an insurance company and I had no money to get them out of hock and run them. I can't see that I ever will be able to but a son would inherit. There is no saying what he might do.'

Jessie didn't know what to say. Her heart went out to him but this was such a new thought and she knew how very much her parents would be against it. 'Throwing herself away on someone old enough to be her father and with the reputation he's got.' She would not be able to talk herself round that one.

'I'll need time, Captain Chaplin,' she said.

'George, please at least call me George,' he said. 'Of course you'll need time and I can wait. I've waited a long time already. It's difficult to see you or get in touch with you without arousing suspicion of being up to no good. I've so much to tell you. So much to explain. I can't offer you a fortune. They don't pay me that much but I can offer you a different life. One that I know you will enjoy. Would it be possible for you to come again next Saturday and tell me a little of how you feel about it?'

'Yes,' said Jessie simply.

It was then that he very gently put his arm round her waist and kissed her lightly on the cheek.

Jessie had almost forgotten what it felt like to be kissed by a suitor and a thrill went through her.

She left shortly afterwards. Her mother would be wondering where she had got to. She mounted her bike and, switching on the dim light, flew home as if on air. It was dark and it was cold but she didn't notice. Could this really be happening to her? Just when it seemed to her that life was over, the exciting wonderful part of it anyway, this most unexpected thing had happened. She consulted her parents and family on most things but this she knew would have to be kept secret. This time she had to make a decision all on her own.

When she got back to Dartfield her mother was waiting.

'You've taen your time,' she said

'Mither, I'm no a bairn onymair,' Jessie remonstrated.

'Weel, fit did he say then? Did he gee you ony ideas?'

'He has ane or twa. He wants me to come back next week and he'll look out some addresses for me.'

With that her mother had to be satisfied. She didn't want to tell lies but what else could she say?

Jessie ate her supper, helped with the dishes and then escaped as soon as she could to the bedroom she shared with

Peggy. Peggy was still downstairs. Jessie's mind was in a turmoil.

She tried to analyse her feelings for him. She had never before remotely thought of him as a lover or husband. He was too old and too out of reach. Could she love him in that way . Did she love him in that way? The words ceased to make any sense. This feeling of compassion and pleasure in his company, was that how love began? It had been different with Rory. Then she had had no doubt she was in love but Rory was gone. And there were other considerations. Captain Chaplin, George, (would she ever get used to calling him by his first name?) wanted children and soon and so did she. He was right, too, when he said he could give her many of the things she wanted from life. That handsome big house to live in. She loved big houses. She always had done. And to be in among the nobility. Well, it had always been one of her dreams ever since she watched them all coming and going at the station. What a wonderful life they seemed to lead and in what splendour. Not that she would ever have considered going as a maidservant. She was far too proud for that but her gift to the farm had sorted that one out – none of the family were obliged to go into service for the County. She heard from time to time what servants had to do. A lady's maid, for instance, her friend Annie had told her, 'had to hold out the towel when her Ladyship steps out of the bath.'

'Can they dae nothing for themselves?' she had said to Annie. But this hadn't put her off wanting to enter their society. Like the university had been, it was a dream to which she sought entry. Up till now she could see no way.

Then there was his age. That must be taken into consideration. He didn't seem so old to her now as he did when she was younger. Fifty nine, sixty. It was old but he was still a handsome man. She relived the way he had put his arm about her waist and kissed her tenderly, taking no liberties. Yes, perhaps it was the first stirrings of love on her part. She would go and see him next Saturday and tell him that she would need to make sure what her feelings really were. He would understand. Perhaps he would kiss her again if no one was about. Yes she would like that. The thought of it filled her with pleasure and the beautiful things he had said to her – a butterfly emerging from a chrysalis. How romantic it all was. She wished she could share it with someone, tell her parents but she knew this would be impossible.

It was also impossible to see him much alone. A buzz of ugly gossip would soon get up. He wouldn't dare take her out anywhere or even go a walk with her. What a scandal that would be. This was the worst thing about living in a small community where everyone knew everyone else for generations back. There was nowhere to hide. How she would love to go out walking with him along the leafy Crimonmogate tracks or down to the shore of Strathbeg. But it would be impossible. Someone would be sure to see them.

The following week was one of the longest in Jessie's life. She thought it would never end. The children were badly behaved and the dominie was cross with her. How wonderful when the end of the day came and she could get on the train and dream about Captain Chaplin. George.

The next Saturday was a grey and miserable day when Jessie set off on her bike for North Lodge. It was early afternoon. She hoped no one else would be there. To her surprise a clerkess appeared at the office door as soon as she entered.

'Miss Jaffray, Captain Chaplin had to go to Forfar on some urgent business. He gave me this letter to give to you when you came.'

Jessie, somewhat stunned, recovered enough to thank the clerkess. She put the letter in her pocket and turning her bike round went back in the direction she had come.

On the way home it started to rain more heavily. Her long nap coat, the one that she thought suited her best, was not waterproof. She hoped the letter would not get wet. Once home she waited for the opportunity to go off and read it on her own.

When it came, she opened the letter with trembling fingers. It had got wet and the ink had run a bit but not to the point where it was impossible to read.

> Dear Jessie,
> Because of an unforeseen emergency I have to go to
> Forfar this weekend. I cannot say how disappointed I
> am. I do hope you will be able to come to North Lodge
> next Saturday and above all I hope that your reactions
> to my proposal will be positive. I truly love you.
>
> George

He wasn't off the idea then. Her heart leapt with joy. She must really be in love with him. She had been so disappointed when he had not been there and wondered if perhaps the contents of the letter was to tell her that he had thought better of the proposal and that the age difference, on thinking it over, was too much to cope with. To her relief this was not so. Impulsively she made up her mind. She would say yes.

It would have to be a secret wedding of course. She didn't like to deceive her parents but she knew there was no other way. They will accept it, she thought, when it is a *fait accompli* and they are powerless to do anything about it. After all, she would become somebody in the district. She would be the factor's wife, a woman of substance. A great happiness came over her. Who would ever have foreseen something like this?

The following Saturday Captain Chaplin was at North Lodge alone. Their meeting was that of true lovers planning a life together. George agreed it would have to be a secret wedding and it would be better to be soon. No point in putting off any more time.

'I don't think the Southesks will go for it either. They will tell me that I am a foolish old man and that these things never work.'

'Of course it will work,' said Jessie optimistically, 'because we love each other and you're still as young at heart as I am.'

Captain Chaplin lost no time in arranging the wedding. They would be married by registrar in Aberdeen early in February. They would need two witnesses. He chose one of the clerkesses he knew was absolutely trustworthy and would tell no one. Jessie, with much heart-searching, decided she would tell Fanny and ask her to be the second witness. Fanny was in Aberdeen anyway so it would cause no suspicion. She went to see Fanny one Saturday in some trepidation. How would she accept it? After all, had she not been the one to bring Fanny's wedding crashing down? Would Fanny try to do the same with her? She didn't think so but she couldn't be sure. Fanny and Jessie had mostly told each other everything and they had always kept each other's secrets.

'You're a fine one,' said Fanny when she heard the proposal, 'trying to stop my mairriage when you thoucht it unsuitable and noo you come tae me with your mairriage plans. Captain Chaplin is totally unsuitable for you, Jessie. For a start, he's far too old. He's had his life. Yours is just beginning. And what about children? I thought you wanted children.'

'So I do and so does Captain Chaplin.' Jessie still hadn't got into the way of calling him George, 'and there is no earthly reason why we couldn't.'

Plead with her sister as she might, Jessie was adamant.

'Well if you won't help me, I'll just have to find someone who will.'

'Och, I'll help you aa richt. I just dinna think you should do it and I winna tell a soul, I promise.'

'Thanks Twi,' said Jessie. 'I kent I could coont on you and it winna be such a bad thing, you'll see. I'll be in amongst the County, meet aa sorts of interesting people and George told me he has actually got twa entailed estates. They're in hock because of lack of money. If we could just make some money somehow and get them out of hock, wouldna that be grand?'

Fanny pricked up her ears at what her sister was telling her. She, like Jessie, had a romantic notion about the County. She would love to get into their company. And two possible estates? Well, that would be something. Slowly she became keener on the idea. She would have to make the best of it anyway, for Jessie's sake.

'We've got three weeks afore the wedding. I'll mak you a dress, Fanny, and one for myself. Yours will be blue because you look richt bonny in blue. Mine will be white. I'll get the material the day and get started. They will both be quite simple. I'm back at school teaching so I'll have to sew at night. Mother is accustomed to me running up dresses and to my nocturnal habits. She knows that working all hours of the night is how I got through my exams.'

These three weeks when Jessie had to keep this huge secret to herself were perhaps some of the most difficult of her life.

On February the 7th 1918, a bitterly cold day in the granite city in war-torn Scotland, Jessie Isobelle Jaffray married George Robertson-Chaplin before a registrar. Jessie was aged twenty five and George Robertson-Chaplin was sixty.

CHAPTER TWENTY TWO

Nineteen Eighteen

JESSIE AND GEORGE had a one-day honeymoon in an expensive Aberdeen hotel. Next day, Monday saw them both back at work. To keep their secret safe Jessie had not asked for time off school.

When the news broke, to say that her family, friends and neighbours were surprised would be to understate. They were stunned into disbelief. It was the 'claik' of everyone around. It had come as a complete surprise. No one had the slightest inkling that there had ever been anything between them.

'A young attractive quine mairrying an ald man. Fit a feel thing tae dae. How did her folks ever lat her?' was heard wherever a wee group, a clamjamfrae of Buchan folk, got together.

Her family's reaction to this latest act of impetuousness was much as she had expected. 'Jessie, Jessie fit hae you daen?' her father said, 'Mark my words, you'll rue the day!'

'Weel you hae made your bed and you'll jist hae to lie on it' was her mother's angry reaction to begin with. But, as time went on, she became secretly pleased, in one way, when she found her status had gone up in the outside world. Her daughter married to Captain Chaplin, the factor for Crimonmogate estate, a friend of the Earl and someone who had once been engaged to the Earl's sister.

The reaction from the Southesks was on the whole more

favourable. They had a fond regard for George and were happy that he had found, at last, someone he could love and who would hopefully look after him. Their only fear was that because of the age difference, things might not work out and he would end up with a broken heart. She was not the person they would have chosen for George had they had any say in the matter. She was not of his class, only a farmer's daughter from one of their farms, but at least she was educated, which was certainly something for a girl in these days. They did know also that she had saved her parents from going bankrupt and having to give up farming some years back. No ordinary young woman.

Not long after their marriage the Countess arranged a party for them, a small reception in the great hall with Jessie's nearest relations, Captain Chaplin's very few relatives and with the guests staying at Crimonmogate at the time. Jessie was rather overcome by it all. Crimonmogate House itself, was awe-inspiring and it did, at times, give Jessie a feeling of smallness although, as a rule, this feeling was alien to her nature. Jessie didn't altogether like the look of the great house from the outside. Because the building material used was granite it had a rather angular and severe appearance and on days of overcast skies, the stone took on a dull grey colour resembling the cloud overhead. There was nothing angular however about the huge neo-gothic pillars that ornamented the high porch. They were smooth granite, unfluted. Such honing had been put into their making that when Jessie ran her hand down the surface of any of the pillars they felt as smooth as silk.

If Jessie didn't exactly love the outside of the mansion she certainly fell in love with the interior and its sixty five rooms. Never had she seen anywhere like it. On the main floor the ceilings were high and hung with chandeliers. The windows were also high, stretching from near floor level. There were plenty of them letting in a lot of light, unusual for these days. Each window had sturdy wooden shutters and curtains of velvet in a variety of rich hues. On the polished floors lay Persian carpets and rugs. Rich wallpapers decorated the walls.

The outside porch, almost as high as the house with its many pillars, led directly into the great hall which also boasted tall columns. These were different, however, being fluted. They rose from a marble floor and led up to a cornice and a coffered ceiling with a glazed dome at the centre. Doors, exactly designed to be seen between the columns, lead out of the great hall on either side. To the left ran the main wing of the house. Here, surprising for the times, was a semi open-plan layout with one huge room leading off into another with enormously wide doors, partitions really, that could be opened or closed as required. Here first of all was the elegant drawing room where guests were entertained and then the family sitting room with its huge marble fireplace that Jessie, when she first saw it, was sure could take half a small tree. The room was well furnished and bookshelves lined the walls. But for all its size it had a cosy air. On the other side of the great hall was the library, billiard room, and dining room with its many portraits hanging on the walls, its huge sideboard gleaming with silver and its long dark mahogany table with matching chairs that boasted embroidered seats.

Upstairs the many bedrooms were all of different shapes and sizes, many furnished with four poster beds, mahogany chests of drawers and wardrobes. Each also was furnished with a marble-topped washstand holding colourful china ewers and basins. The larger bedrooms had dressing rooms off the main room and one or two had strange looking kists which, on lifting the wooden lid and looking inside, revealed full length baths. The bedrooms, to the front of the house, had an impressive view over the well-kept lawn replete with its eighteenth century sundial decorated with Prince of Wales feathers. Beyond, just a vastness of trees in the two hundred acre policies stretching right to the horizon to merge with the rim of the great bowl of sky. There was no other habitation in sight which gave the view a wonderful feel of uninhabited wilderness which was actually false. Beyond lay the many farms the estate called its own.

Downstairs there was another world entirely. Darker with smaller windows lay the basement headquarters for the use of the staff of which there was a considerable number. For the housekeeper there was a suite of rooms almost like a house within a house. There was a spacious octagonal dairy, a big kitchen for the preparation of food for the family and their guests, and another long kitchen for the use of the maids etc. Also sleeping quarters for the rest of the staff. It was hard for Jessie to reconcile the two worlds. The world of harsh reality for all those that worked for them (which included the small tenant farmers and their families on the estate which Jessie had been a part of as a girl growing up) and the life of comparative splendour of the so-called upper crust. For Jessie, their life had an air of unreality but it didn't stop Jessie loving being part of it. She didn't question too much the rights and wrongs of things, just accepted that this was a way of life that she most certainly was enjoying.

She was also very happy indeed with George. She hadn't realised just how lonely she had been, how very much in need of a husband she was. He was a good lover and filled all Jessie's romantic needs as well as her more earthly ones. They had never been able to have a courtship but made up for it now and were often to be seen in the lengthening Spring evenings wandering in the woods of Crimonmogate or down by the shores of Strathbeg watching the geese fly in to their resting grounds.

That year the Great War was drawing to a close. Britain was tired and grieving – so many young men had been lost. At the end of the previous year, Andrew had been called up, even although he was in a reserved occupation. They were desperate for manpower. He joined the Gordon Highlanders and went down to England to train. He hated to leave. Unlike his brothers, he didn't seek to depart his home land and was happy working on the farm helping his father. That left young Charles, the only other male in the household at home to help. All the farms were now short of manpower.

Gentle, slim Peggy could now be seen out in the fields ploughing, a job for which she had no relish. Jessie, taken up with her new life, was not able to be of much assistance. Now that she saw an end to teaching, she began to enjoy it a bit more and was gaining confidence. She no longer worried about the dominie's bad temper and dared to put some of her own thoughts and ideas into teaching. She got on well with the children. Weekends were a busy time sorting up North Lodge to her liking. They had received quite a few wedding presents, a mahogany table for the dining room from the Southesks, silver cutlery and ornaments from some of their friends, delicate fish forks and knives with white bone handles, silver salvers and servers in plush velvet lined boxes, delicate teaspoons and, Jessie's favourite, a pair of fruit spoons with silver backs and grapes embossed in their gilt hollows. There were ornate vases, a silver tea set and one or two heavy crystal bowls. More mundane but useful things came from neighbouring farmers and relations – linen, towels, pots and pans. George and Jessie were popular with the farming community round about and because of this people gave them presents. Jessie brought over her silver chest from Dartfield which had sat in her bedroom unopened since Dr Blackhall had died and laid her silver out on the long sideboard. The house began to take shape, showing a woman's touch.

Sometimes she would sit up for a good part of the night and sew. She needed dresses to dine with the Southesks, as they did quite often, especially when they had small house parties. The Southesks were rather intrigued with this new person in their midst. She was somewhat different, entertaining to have at a dinner party, not shy. It was good to sit her beside some retiring guest to draw him out. Jessie relished the meals. She also loved meeting all these different and exciting people, so many of whom were noblemen and their wives, and feeling almost one of them.

But they were different, They had manners and an etiquette that Jessie must learn and did, amazingly quickly with George's help. They all spoke in what sounded to Jessie a beautiful English, the Scots among them having been educated at English schools. Jessie did her best to emulate them and used fewer Scottish words but failed to lose the Aberdeenshire lilt. Her new-found acquaintances found this rather charming and would tell Jessie so.

Not long after their marriage, the Southesks gave them the use of a pony and gig. Captain Chaplin still had his horse but they thought he might want to drive Jessie around. To begin with, while she was still teaching, he drove her to the train in the morning and fetched her home at night.

At Easter they went on a delayed honeymoon for an out-of-time week. They spent it at a small hotel on the shores of Loch Sunart in the west of Scotland. Jessie couldn't get over how very different a world it was from the one she had come from. Quite a number of the people spoke Gaelic although many could speak good English as well and did so with a softer lilt. Everything seemed softer, the gentle rain that stubbornly showered upon them on some days, the contours of the mountains, the women's faces. There wasn't however the lushness of grass for the grazing of animals, nor many cultivated fields. Instead there was the constant feel of wetness. Lichens hung like long grey beards from the indigenous trees or in contrast patterned the many rocks in soft shades of yellow, red or white, like maps of some unknown country. Mosses replaced the greeness of grass.

Even at Easter there was a warmth in the filtered sun. Sun diamonds sparked off Loch Sunart and there was a wealth of wild-life about that Jessie hadn't seen before – red deer running on the hill, dainty yellow siskins hiding in the trees and one day, to her delight, she glimpsed a pine martin on the red brown branch of a Scots pine.

It was a wonderful week for Jessie but when it ended she was happy to get back to the new life that had miraculously taken off for her, on the same estate where her ancestors had lived for hundreds and hundreds of years.

Each Sunday she accompanied her husband to church. This was the Scottish Episcopal, which was in close proximity to the Church of Scotland, the one she had attended as a child. She was captivated with this faith that was new to her. So associated with the Jacobites had it become in the eighteenth century that it had been more or less outlawed. No more than five members were allowed to gather together in church so they took to gathering for worship and intrigue in kitchens and attics. It was all kept very quiet and it enabled these zealots to keep their church alive albeit in a very modest way. In the nineteenth century, with the danger of the Jacobites gone, and with the new Christian movement at Oxford helping to give it impetus, the Scottish Episcopal Church began to recover with the new-found zeal of the Bishops. Jessie loved the services. More high church than she was accustomed to, she revelled in the pageantry of it. The Canon in his long robes, the kneeling on the long padded stools and the responses taken by the whole congregation. It all seemed to her to have a more beautiful, spiritual and airy quality about it, different from the mundane, down-to-earth Presbyterian kirk with its delight in making you feel guilty for your sins.

One day she said to George, 'I would like to join your church.'

George was pleased and soon Jessie took part in a confirmation class and in due course was confirmed into the Scottish Episcopal church by the Bishop of Aberdeen.

Fanny finished university that Spring. Having learned, from the experience of Jessie, how difficult it was to get any kind of job with an MA degree,she made a special effort to find something different. She heard of a secretarial college in London that gave courses of a year's duration. The only snag was they were expensive. She had no money. She would have to ask her folks. She did not have the same hesitation about asking for money as Jessie had had. She felt it was her right. After all, had she not had a bursary and been of very little expense to them over these last three years.

'Please, faither, please. It'll mak all the difference to my life. After I'm feenished I'll get a guid job doon in London. I just know I will.'

'We're no made o siller, quine. We've done better on the fairm lately but ilka penny needs tae be a prisoner. You just dinna ken fits gaun tae happen the morn.'

'Please, please, faither. Life will just be hopeless for me if I dinna get. Aifter I'm feenished I'll most likely get a guid job and be able to pay you back.'

Mother was brought in for consultation. She too was reluctant to give Fanny all she would need but Fanny remained adamant. She would just die if she didn't get it. So it was agreed but for one year only.

That year, nineteen eighteen the Great War came to end. What troops that were left made their weary way back to their homes. There was great rejoicing. People started to rebuild their lives as best they could. Andrew was demobbed without having to go to the front. He was glad to be home.

Chapter Twenty Three

Interlude

IN THE SPRING of 1921 William Jaffray died. His death was sudden and unexpected. Although he had suffered for a considerable time with stomach ulcers and had become thinner, he had seemed reasonably fit for his sixty one years. But things weren't improving and the doctor had recommended an operation. It was decided to dip into savings for William to go into a nursing home. He died on the operating table.

His funeral was held on a balmy Spring day when the earth was buoyant with renewed growing. The rowan and lilac trees in the garden had unfolded their very different leaves but as yet had not burst into blossom. Fields of grass were a vivid emerald and the grazing cattle were already becoming fat after their winter spent indoors in the reeds. Lambs were growing almost as you watched and in the evenings would gather together in bunches to teeter and dance on any handy hummock. Strong shoots of oats and barley, that William himself had sown not so long ago, were pushing through the ground with amazing speed turning bare earth green. Swallows had returned from Africa to their familiar nesting barns and the curlews keened overhead while peeweets tumbled about the sky like so many acrobats. Gorse brightened Dartfield's farm road so that even on a dull day it seemed as if the sun was shining.

The brightness, on the day of the funeral, was in sharp contrast to the dark and solemn horse-drawn cortege that wound its way to Lonmay Kirkyard. No expense was spared for William's 'waygo' and there was a great gathering of farmers and relations from all around. He had been well liked. Several weeks later, a tall grey stone was erected in the high-walled graveyard beyond which lay an inland sea of barley. At this time of year, on days of fresh wind, it moved with the motion of land-locked waves. The gravestone was almost as tall as some of those of the fisher folk from St Combs. Below William Jaffray's name was engraved the name of Robert William, Andrew's twin, the son they had lost in infancy.

William's death was a deep blow to his wife. She had always loved and relied on him and to be without him seemed like half of her very self had gone. Jessie was also devastated. This was the first close bereavement in the family. She had never really contemplated her father not being there. It was unthinkable. How she wished she had talked to him more and told him of her high regard and love for him. For a while, after her marriage to George Chaplin, relations had been a bit strained but lately they had been getting on much better together. For that, at least, she was grateful.

The farm was left to William's widow and to Andrew. They continued to farm as before. Jessie spent what time she could with them to help out.

John in Malaya, on hearing of his father's death, wrote that he was coming home on leave and bringing his wife Molly and his little boy Peter, barely one year old. He had been meaning to come for a long time. How he wished he had come before his father had died. The visit had a good effect on mother Jaffray. Her favourite son with his wife and her first grandchild. It was a time of happiness which helped to lift the gloom. Jessie didn't take too well to John's wife thinking she was an awful boast, always ranting on about her Australian forebears and how well John had got on and in what luxury they now lived. Jessie did have a rather possessive attitude towards members of her family and it would have been difficult for any wife to have been just right for any of her brothers had they not been chosen by Jessie herself.

Her father's death had been a great shock to Jessie. Life with Captain Chaplin had been happy and carefree up till then. When George wasn't away working at the estate in Forfar she was his constant companion. On his visits to various farms he would take her with him in the pony and gig provided by the Southesks. She took great interest in his work and helped him in that she could discuss with him what real poverty was like from experience and the real difficulties many of these farmers had. The only cloud on the couple's horizon had been that there were no children forthcoming. To begin with, after Jessie had left her teaching job, she had been quite happy that she had not become pregnant too soon but as time went on her optimism began to wear thin. After her father's death and realisation that the unthinkable was possible, a serious doubt grew in her mind. Would she and Captain Chaplin ever have children? More than anything else on earth she wanted to have his child. Jessie became despondent. The sparkle in her dimmed.

George Chaplin knew he must do something. It was difficult for him to get time off to go on holiday. This didn't bother him personally. He was happy where he was. He had seen quite a bit of the world in his youth and was content to be in Scotland. He had promised his wife that he would save whatever he could and when he semi-retired at sixty five, which he intended to do, they would go off on the grand tour as the nobility did and see much of Europe at least. But now he knew he must do something sooner than that. The opportunity came quite unexpectedly.

One morning, on opening his mail, he asked Jessie, 'How would you like to go to France?'

'Go tae France? But I thoucht it would be impossible for you to get away.'

'Well it is at the moment,' he said. 'But here's a letter from Belinda and Bertha. They are going to Paris in two weeks' time and they have asked if you would like to go with them. They know how much you have always wanted to visit France and they say that they would insist on paying for the holiday as your company would give them pleasure. You are so young and bright and interested in everything you see.'

Bertha and Belinda were George's two spinster sisters and lived together in a flat in a respectable district of London. They had come north once or twice to meet their new sister-in-law and to have a holiday. Jessie had got on well with them.

'I would just love to gyang but how aboot you? How would you manage?'

George laughed, put his arm round her slim waist and gave her a kiss.' I managed for a long time without you. I can manage again, but don't stay away too long. I need you and I'll miss you very much.'

And so it was arranged for Jessie to travel down to London. It would also be an opportunity to visit Fanny who had finished her secretarial course at St James and, as she had predicted, had landed a good job. She was now secretary to the Socety for the Prevention of Cruelty to Animals under the immediate direction of the Duchess of Hamilton. The Duchess had rung up the college one day, near to the end of Fanny's course, looking for a secretary for her work Had they anyone they could recommend. Fanny was the one chosen. She loved her new job. She had, in fact, become a little fanatical about it and was a strict vegetarian. Also, like Jessie, she loved being amongst the nobility.

Jessie did not have time to see Fanny before the visit to France. Never had she been so excited in her life. To achieve what had in her youth sometimes seemed the impossible, to visit France, the place of ancient ancestors she insisted on feeling kin to, was the stuff of dreams. She was not disappointed.

They spent two weeks in Paris and surrounding area and

then back to London. There was so very much to see here also but first she must go and visit Fanny.

She found Fanny highly delighted with life although still pleading poverty. She was pleased to see Jessie and relapsed somewhat into the Doric in her company although English was the only thing she normally spoke nowadays.

'It's sae expensive living in London you jist wouldna believe it and the nice freens I've made recently. I have to keep my end up. I'm afraid I've been telling some white lees. Letting folk believe that my people hae a sma estate in Aberdeenshire, not just a sma fairm. So when you meet some of my freens, dinna let ony cats oot o the bag.'

'You shouldna deny your parents. These people should accept you for who you are,' said Jessie.

'Oh but you dinna understan.'

'I do understan perfectly weel. The Southesks know who my parents are and accept me for who I am. Oh what a tangled web we weave, when first we practise to deceive.'

Fanny had always found it irritating to have her sister bring out appropriate quotes from the vast repertoire of poems and pieces from literature she had packed into her head. Jessie wasn't finished yet.

'Remember one of the pieces of advice Kipling gives to his son in his poem 'If'. 'To walk with Kings nor lose the common touch. You are in real danger of losing the common touch.'

Fanny hotly denied this observation and Jessie said no more other than promising to be discreet when asked questions. Despite all this, Fanny was pleased to see her sister. It made her feel less homesick.

On the way home on the ferry, with the Channel like a mill pond, Jessie had written a letter to George telling him what a wonderful time she had had in France and that she intended staying a few days longer in London.

George's sisters were eager to show her some of the sights

of London, the home that they loved. Jessie was much impressed by all she saw. Secretly, and not even wanting to admit it to herself, she found London more impressive and awesome than Paris. They took her also to one or two parties and introduced her to some of their friends.

One evening they attended a concert in the Albert Hall. Music was not a particular love of Jessie's but she was impressed at the size and grandeur of the hall and its huge audience out for the evening, a glittering array of people dressed up for the occasion. They also took her to a play or two. She was particularly thrilled to see 'The Merchant of Venice' her favourite Shakespeare play. How often had she imagined herself as Portia?

Before anyone realised it, time had slipped past in an alarming way until one day, a letter came. The postmark was from home. The address was typewritten. Who could it be from? George never used the typewriter when writing personal letters.

Jessie tore open the envelope. Inside was a letter in George's handwriting. It was short and to the point. What was keeping her? She had said three days. When was she coming back? It was signed with a scrawl that Jessie hardly recognised. Inside the envelope there was another short note, this time typewritten and signed by Jane the clerkess who had been the witness at their wedding. What business had she handling a letter to her from her husband was Jessie's first reaction, until she read the note. Jessie read.

> Dear Mrs Chaplin,
> Your husband asked me to send on this letter hence the typed envelope. I also feel it is my duty to tell you that your husband is not at all well although he told me not to mention this because you would be home soon. I do feel you should know this however. Please forgive the liberty.
>
> > Yours Sincerely,
> > Jane.

A mixture of panic and remorse flooded through Jessie. She had neglected George. Every day there had been so much to do that there seemed to have been no time for letter writing and true, she had said she would be back in a few days. Wherever had time gone to? What was the matter with him? He had been perfectly alright when she left. She must get back as quickly as possible.

CHAPTER TWENTY FOUR

Back to Reality

IT WAS a long anxious journey back by train to Aberdeenshire. How glad she would be to get home. She was going to surprise George. Just arrive without letting him know she was coming. She would leave her luggage at the station and walk. It wasn't all that far.

It was dark by the time the train drew into Lonmay station. She had almost forgotten how dark it could be in this far north land away from the influence of city lights casting a blush on the night sky. It was well into October now and the nights drawing in. Fortunately it wasn't raining. Instead there was a touch of frost in the east wind.

Out on the empty road all was silent apart from the rustle her feet made on crisp leaves. It was pitch dark: there was no moon. After walking for a while, however, her eyes grew accustomed to the dark and it didn't seem quite so inky black. She tried to keep her mind off what she would find at home and took to thinking about all these people in Paris and London and other big cities, many of whom would seldom see a really black night. She began to feel a kind of pity for them living in the city. How much they missed of the natural wonders. She herself was totally unafraid of the dark. If there were bogies she did not see them, nor had she ever met any.

Eventually, there at last was a welcome ray of light from North Lodge. Soon she would be in the arms of George and all would be forgiven. Perhaps he would be better now from whatever was ailing him but if not she would soon nurse him back to health. She wouldn't leave his side until he was well again. With this resolve she confidently turned the brass handle on the outside door at North Lodge. This door was never locked. The door of the estate office was locked every night but not this one. Jessie turned the handle, pushed the door and nothing happened. It was locked.

What had happened? Fear rose to the surface. Perhaps there was no one in. Perhaps George had been taken to a nursing home. The bell hadn't worked for some time so Jessie knocked loudly. Soon she heard someone running downstairs. It didn't sound like George. Who could it be? She was sure it was a man's footsteps.

The man who opened the door was a complete stranger. This couldn't be. Something strange was happening. Something out of time. Neither spoke for a moment and then the stranger tumbling to who this unfamliar lady at the door might be said,

'Mrs Chaplin?'

'Yes,' she said, 'and wha are you? Far's my husband? Fit's happening?' As she was talking Jessie stepped inside the house and pushed the door shut.

'I'm John Kerr,' said the stranger. 'The Countess hired me to look aifter your husband. I ken this maun be a great shock to you,' he hurried on before Jessie could get a word in edgeways, 'and I am sorry it's me that has to tell you the bad news. We thoucht we would get warning o your arrival and the Coontess wanted to see you immediately. She meant to tell you hersel but noo it has fallen tae me. I think you micht ken that your husband used to occasionally gyang on binges when, for days on end, he would tak far tae muckle tae drink. For days and days he would hae naethin tae eat, only drink until he became a danger tae himsel. Eventually he would decide to come aff it or would allow someone to help him tae. The trouble was at thon stage he would invariably gyang intae the DTs. I'm nae sure if you ken fit that is, Mrs Chaplin, the delirium tremens.'

'Yes, yes of course I ken,' said Jessie impatiently.

'Weel I've nursed him through this afore. It hasn't happened for quite a number o years noo. His marriage tae you has helped him a lot but seemingly a day or two aifter you left to gyang tae France he decided to hae a drink. Just one, but these kind o folk just canna dae that. One leads on till another and another. He was trying to get aff it afore you came back and it resulted in this.'

'I must gyang tae him at once,' said Jessie.

John Kerr barred her way to the stairs.

'No, I'm afraid you canna do that,' he said. 'You wouldna want to see him the way he is jist noo. He michtna even ken you or he micht hairm you in some way. He's locked in his room.'

'I dinna care. I maun see him. Please let me past.'

'I'm afraid I canna do that.' John Kerr was adamant. 'My instructions were to phone the Coontess as soon as I heard frae you. I'll phone her richt noo and she'll send someone for you.'

Jessie hardly heard him finish the sentence. She had pulled open the door and was out into the dark and running for the big house. If she had thought it dark before it was doubly dark now as she stumbled her way up the soft pathway through the trees. She was glad when she saw a glimmer of light coming toward her. It was the Earl himself carrying a lantern. He took her arm and led her the rest of the way without saying anything at all. When they got inside he led her through the great hall and into the sitting room and sat her down beside the Countess who put an arm round her shoulder and said,

'What a dreadful homecoming for you, my dear.'

'Before any more is said,' spoke up the Earl, 'a glass of brandy is called for,' and he rang for the butler.

Jessie sipped the burning liquid as the Earl insisted she should. She felt it warming up her whole body, relieving the awful numbness that had set in.

'Now, my dear,' said the Countess, 'this has happened to George before. He has always recovered. Don't despair. You have made all the difference to his life. I have sent for his doctor to come here to explain things to you himself. Fortunately I got him in. He will be here shortly and will be able to explain why it is imperative that you don't see him just yet.'

Soon the sound of a motor was heard outside and the doctor was shown into the drawing room so that he could speak to Jessie in private. A small fire, hastily lit, sputtered in the hearth. It was cold. In days before central heating these big houses were cold but the people inhabiting them dressed accordingly. Thick tweeds and woollen jerseys were the garb of winter and sometimes summer too. Jessie shivered in her London clothes and yet barely noticed.

The doctor was a kindly man

'I know how you must be feeling, Mrs Chaplin. It maun be a great shock to you returning home to be confronted by this situation. It would be unwise for you to see your husband just yet. It is likely to upset him more than he is already and we have his heart to consider. As he will probably have told you he does have a slight heart problem and we don't want to risk any more damage. Besides it would be really upsetting for you. At this stage he may not even know you. But he will recover and be back to his normal self in a day or two, rest assured of that. I ask you to please be patient.'

Jessie didn't argue. Instead, huge hot tears welled up in her eyes and began to run down her cheeks.

'I know what a shock it must be,' the doctor reiterated. 'Are you alright? Can I give you something that will give you a good night's sleep?'

Jessie didn't reply immediately. She was too absorbed trying to keep herself from crying, breaking down altogether, but eventually she was able to say, 'No thank you.' She didn't have much faith in drugs and didn't like to be under their influence.

'Well then, let's go and find the Countess. She'll look after you.'

Back in the sittingroom a huge fire burned and drinks were handed round. Once again Jessie was handed a goblet of brandy. Jessie didn't drink as a rule and asked if she could have something else to dilute it.

'Oh, but my dear, that would completely spoil it,' said the Earl.

The Countess came up with the solution. 'I'll tell you what. I've just ordered coffee. Wait till the coffee pot comes and we'll pour the brandy into a cup of coffee . Nothing better, Cognac and coffee, most relaxing. The Countess knowing of Jessie's antipathy to strong drink, went on, 'Just for once it will not harm you. It'll do you good, in fact.'

Jessie did as she was told and sipped slowly at this strange delicious coffee. Slowly her body warmed and she began to relax. There was a hazy buzz of conversation around her that she barely noticed and then she heard the Countess say , 'I think it would be best if you stayed here for the night. I've got a bedroom prepared for you.'

Jessie didn't argue. She didn't feel she could take much more. Shortly after the doctor left she was shown up to her room. There was a bright fire burning in the hearth and a winceyette nightdress was laid out for her on the bed. She wasn't expecting to sleep but sleep she did, lulled by the hiss and sputter from the burning logs and the brandy seeping through her veins. She awoke to find bright sunlight flooding a strange bedroom.

The next few days seemed some of the longest of Jessie's life. The Countess had managed to persuade her to stay with them until it was advisable to see her husband again. Jessie had reluctantly agreed. Perhaps it would be best. If she was in North Lodge she didn't know how she would stop herself going to see him. She didn't make any attempt to go to Dartfield either. They wouldn't know she was back from London and if she did go home and tell them, all she was likely to get would be 'I told you so'.

It was several days before she was allowed to see George. When she did he was the same calm, kind George she had grown to love so much although he looked somewhat shaken and hollow-cheeked. They held each other close, saying nothing at all.

Eventually George whispered, 'I'm sorry.'

'You're sorry,' responded Jessie. 'It is I wha should be sorry. I should never have left you and stayed awa sae lang.

Both of them were overcome by feelings of guilt but it hadn't destroyed their love for one another. Jessie vowed never to leave home again without him.

In the days ahead she noticed, that although he was the same old George, he tired more easily. The doctor told her that his heart was not too good and that he would always have to be careful not to overtax himself. Jessie helped him all she could and did all he would allow her to do on the estate. The Southesks also, were most helpful. They were fond of their friend and factor George, and Jessie had seeped into their affections too. They recognised how much she tried to help and what an asset she was to him. In spite of everything, however, as the year went on George became less and less able. The Southesks decided to get someone else to look over after their estate near Forfar.

The Chaplins had to take a drop in salary. Jessie had been brought up thrifty and knew how to cope and it made life easier for George. As time went on however, he gradually lost the power of his legs and eventually took to bed, a much dispirited man.

The Southesks wanted to get a resident nurse for him at their expense but Jessie would have none of it. She would look after him herself. Sometimes she was up day and night with him. Sometimes she would ask her sister, Peggy to look after him at night while she snatched some sleep or went to look into something important that had happened on the estate. One day she brought him his breakfast as usual. He seemed a little brighter, kissed her and said how much he loved her and how sorry he was to be such a burden. Jessie assured him he was no such thing. Five minutes later he gave a great cry of pain and fell back on his pillows. He was dead.

CHAPTER TWENTY FIVE

The Woman Factor

IT WAS 1925. A motorbike sped along the narrow winding roads that looked as if they had been gouged out, on this fine October day, from golden fields some of which were still embroidered with standing stooks of grain. In others, farmers were pitching sheaves from the stooks into farm carts and leading them to the stackyards to wait for the threshing mill. Many fields were completely shorn and empty of crops. Only the bristle of golden stubble was left marking the end of another growing year.

It was hard to tell who was on the motorbike, as the rider was dressed in a long brown leather coat, a matching helmet and goggles. Had the locals not known, in that day and age, none would have expected it to be a young woman. It had been the 'claik' of every farmyard and village around when Jessie had first got the motorbike. What would this rebellious young woman do next, this small farmer's daughter who defied convention?

On reaching North Lodge Jessie dismounted and propped her bike up close to the narrow front garden and removed her goggles, coat and helmet. She shook out her shining black hair before deftly twisting it into a bun at the nape of her neck. Under her coat Jessie wore a deep pink blouse, frilled and feminine and a navy divided skirt that she had made herself for riding on her bike. She was as attractive as ever with her healthy outdoor complexion, her bright grey-green copper-flecked eyes with the sparkle quite returned after several years of widowhood. There was a general air of happiness, hope and confidence about her. It was a surprisingly hot day for late October. In fact the whole past week had been an Indian summer much appreciated after a poor wet year.

Her mind was full of the farm she had just been to visit. The farmer's wife had taken her up to the attic in her old farmhouse to show her the devastation caused by a wet year. Rain had been coming in all over the place. The house needed re-slating; there was no other solution. She would have to approach the Earl and get his sanction for the job. Jessie had become good at this lately but she knew there must be compromise. The estate would provide the slates, the farmer would do the work.

Jessie got on well with the Earl. She found him to be a considerate man, even if out of touch somewhat with the ordinary world. It took quite a bit of explaining to let him see things from a tenant's point of view the way that Jessie did. She wondered if he sometimes regretted having employed her. She had got the surprise of her life when shortly after Captain Chaplin's funeral, that dreadful day, he had suggested to her that she should stay on in North Lodge and become the new factor for Crimonmogate Estate.

'Me?' Jessie exclaimed in astonishment, 'but I couldna possibly. I'm a woman.' Inwardly, Jessie didn't believe this at all but she had been so conditioned all her life that this was her first reaction.

The Earl was smiling. 'But I thought you always maintained that women can do anything.'

'So they can,' said Jessie, 'but I just wasna expecting this.'

'I've put quite a bit of thought into it. Everything is all right in Forfar, I've got a good chap there. He's fitting in very nicely. But I don't think he would take kindly to coming here as well. You mention about being a woman but since the war women are entering all sorts of professions that were once men's territory. You are well-educated and well-respected in the district and you know the job. You helped George so much with it latterly that I can't think of anyone better. I can't afford to pay you a huge salary, I'm afraid, but if you would consider managing on what George was paid in the past year. . .'

'The pay would be fine,' said Jessie whose main concern for work done was not money, 'but would the tenants accept me, a woman, being factor for your Lordship?'

'They would just have to, wouldn't they?' said the Earl. 'I think there might be a bit of difficulty with one or two of the older tenant farmers but we'll be able to sort that out. Of course you'll still have a clerkess to do the donkey work who will be completely under your control.'

Jessie, always impetuous, decided quickly.

'Yes I'll do it,' she said. 'Thank you for your confidence in me. I shall do the very best for the estate. I need something to do to keep me from dwelling on my loss.'

'Well that's settled then.' The Earl seemed pleased. He was smiling, 'Perhaps you are the first lady factor in Scotland. In Britain for that matter. I shall boast about it at the Club. It will make me feel quite modern, moving with the times and all that. Besides, why shouldn't you do this job? You are just as capable . You have proved that already. By the way I don't know if you are aware that my small grandson, David, because he can not pronounce your name properly as yet, calls you Chappie and I'm afraid it's become a habit of the household to call you that now. Do you object? Just in the family, of course. To everyone else on the estate it must be strictly Mrs Chaplin.

'Not at all,' said Jessie, 'I should like that. It would make me feel as if I belonged in some way.'

'We're all fond of you, Chappie,' said the Earl. 'You brighten up our lives considerably. We would be pleased if you would still join us for meals when the occasion arises and hope that things won't be much different from when George was alive.'

In the weeks that followed Jessie did not regret her decision. She was glad she didn't have to move away. She did not want to leave the house where George and she had been so happy together. She wanted to be able to talk of George to people who knew him as a way of keeping his memory alive for as long as possible.

Because she had helped George with his job before he died, she was not afraid of tackling it now. There was one thing she wanted to change, however, and that was the mode of transport. A horse and gig was old-fashioned nowadays. She had never really liked working with horses anyway and ever since she had been at university she had dreamed of having a motorbike, a fast and exciting mode of travel. Captain Chaplin hadn't left much in the way of worldly goods but there was enough money to buy a new Enfield. She told no one of her intentions, but just went to Aberdeen one day to choose one. Every day, after it had been delivered at North Lodge, Jessie could be seen whizzing along the tracks on Crimonmogate estate breaking the silence of the woods. At least everyone knew when she was around and could keep well out of her way. She found it a most exhilarating experience, especially after she graduated to the narrow network of public roads.

She always had to be careful, however. Nowadays as well as the few Rolls Royces, Rileys, Bentleys and various other big and beautiful cars owned by the County, there were more and more small Fords, 'Tin Lizzies' they were fondly called, on the roads. More and more farmers were buying them. Sometimes their owners were not the best of drivers, considering the road their own and dawdling along examining their fields and those of their neighbours from the driving seat and paying little attention to any other traffic. Also, some had the bad habit of rounding bends on the wrong side. Jessie began to think that farmers must have a code of practice different from others because this became generally recognised and others took evasive action.

Jessie loved to feel the rush of wind and rain on her face and despite many people's predictions that it would not be long before she had a bad accident on that dangerous machine, it had not happened. One day, however, having got off her motorbike at a farm she was visiting, she hadn't propped it up well enough and it fell on her ankle. She had had to lie up with a broken ankle for a month or two. While she was laid up, the Southesks insisted on supplying a nurse to look after her. They were patient with her difficulties.

Jessie loved her job. She had been very grateful also that she had not had to move away from North Lodge, a house she had grown fond of. And it was good to be kept busy. True, there were some problems particularly from older farmers. Some, point blank, refused to deal with a woman, refused to take any of their problems to her or to pay her the rent. The Earl himself dealt with these awkward few which somewhat mollified them. Jessie found it an interesting and challenging job with many facets to it. She knew the farmers' very real problems from experience and was totally aware of both the workers' problems also and those of her boss. In the end it all came down to money or lack of it and how it was to be divided out.

Depression was setting in again, as it so often did in the countryside after a war. Jessie could never quite understand the town people's attitude to those living in the country. It seemed to Jessie that they looked on food at a low price, sometimes even below the cost of production, as a right they were entitled to. Of course, politicians encouraging cheap imports from the Empire had a lot to answer for. Farmers were constantly fighting that battle. She was most impressed by the young dynamic Robert Bothby MP for East Aberdeenshire, affectionately known as Bob, whom she had met several times at some of the Southesks' dinner parties. They had many a rousing discussion. She admired the way he had gone round and learned about the various very real problems people had. He was the champion of the fisher folk and those that worked on the land and the people loved him for it.

In a smaller way she tried to play the same role for the people who earned their livelihood, in one way or another, on the estate. The farms were in need of cottar houses to house the workers with families rather than the bothies that housed only single men. Improvements were always needed in farm steadings and to drain and cultivate the land. There was so much always to be done but money was limited. The County also needed to keep up the style they were accustomed to. It would be unthinkable not to send their children to the best of schools, to have the latest in modern transport, holidays abroad for those who wanted them, servants to do all the menial jobs and sometimes a flat in London where they could spend the winter. All that plus keeping up and trying to improve the infrastructure of their estate. With hard times this was apt to deteriorate and it happened also in Crimonmogate House itself which was not redecorated and kept up as often as it needed to be.

Jessie's job was a varied one and she found she did have some influence in making things better. That awful cottage that had been used, when she was young, as a poor's house where single old or disabled people ended up if they were without relatives to look after them, was no longer there. It had been quite close to Dartfield and she remembered once being taken there, along with her younger sister Peggy, by their mother who was delivering scones. She had been horrified at the miserable conditions of the inmates. The stench of urine was all-pervasive. Nothing was clean and they were looked after by a man even although most of the patients were female. Afterwards Jessie had asked her mother what they were given to eat.

'Mostly porridge and chappit neeps and onything fairmers roond aboot can afford tae gie them. Some o them have nae teeth so their diet is limited.'

Peggy in particular was never to forget that visit. She never did marry and fearing sometimes that she might be left without any close relative explained, to a certain extent, why thriftiness degenerated into an unreasonable meanness with herself and everyone else. She never quite lost her fear that she would be left destitute. In actual fact she ended up a rich lady and lived until she was ninety five.

Occasionally, in the course of her job, Jessie had to attend the law courts in Aberdeen about some petty wrangle between estate and tenant. Sometimes some neighbour would ask if she would speak up for them as she was good with words and they were not. Jessie liked these opportunities of being able to help people in this way. She took delight in doing a good job.

What she had not succeeded in doing was finding a new husband. At first, after George Chaplin's death, she couldn't consider this, but as time went on and the memory of her loss became less painful, she knew she wanted to marry again and above all have children. How she yearned for children.

The Southesks had family, some of whom were around Jessie's age. There were two daughters amongst them, Catherine the eldest and Mary. They came home to Crimonmogate quite often. There were grandchildren – a boy David and a little girl called Marriotta. Jessie got to know the children well. She played with them and read them stories and sometimes, when nanny was needing a break, took them off her hands.

She also spent some time with Lady Mary when she came to visit. They had a hobby in common, making hats. Lady Mary would bring ostrich feathers, artificial flowers and rich satin ribbon from London and share them with Jessie to add style to those hats they made.

The Southesks had also several sons, Charles being the oldest and Duthac the youngest in the family. At one time Jessie thought she might herself win over one of the nobility, perhaps some of the young friends of the Southesks when they came to visit but no such luck. They all had their own agendas, all became engaged and married to people of note and influence. With one or two of the men she met it would have been easy to have an illicit affair or have become some Lord's mistress but in this area Jessie was adamant. She didn't compromise. It was marriage or nothing and they accepted and admired her for it.

Occasionally Jessie was sent down to London to the Corn Exchange on business. She loved these excursions and would stay with George's two sisters who were always glad to see her. It was also a wonderful chance to visit Fanny. Jessie found little time to write letters these days and Fanny loved to get news from home. Things had changed at Dartfield since their father died.

CHAPTER TWENTY SIX

A Visit to London

JESSIE was glad that she lived near to Dartfield, her childhood home. Things hadn't been easy for the family since William Jaffray died. By 1923 there were only three of them left at home – Andrew, Peggy and their mother. The farm had been left jointly between Andrew and his mother. Charles, the youngest member of the family and everyone's favourite, had worked at home for a while. He was a cheerful and helpful young man who had always got on well with the rest of them in an undemanding sort of way. He had been glad to leave school and work on the land but realised that there would not be enough room for two brothers to make a living on Dartfield and the chance of being able to afford starting up in a farm of his own was slim. It would take a lifetime. Besides he sought adventure and wanted to get away. He wanted to be like some of the older members of the family who seemed to lead much more exciting lives than he did.

In William's letters home, which were now less frequent, he would mention, from time to time, how he kept hoping some other member of the family would come out to Kenya.

'If you want to farm there are certainly opportunities here,' he wrote in a specific letter to Charlie one day, 'and to eventually get a farm of your own wouldn't be too difficult. The powers that be in the Land Office in Nairobi have a new policy whereby they want to sell land to the smaller farmers rather than those hoping to become huge landowners and they are making it easier for this to happen. Why not come out? Give it a try. There's a chap here, Willie Dawson. He is a relation of the Dawson's of Phingask who farm near Fraserburgh. Mother will know of them. He is a decent fellow and is looking for someone from home to help him with a farm he has recently acquired. I mentioned you. He jumped at the idea. You may have had a letter from him by this time.'

The letter duly arrived and Charlie was off. He worked for Willie Dawson for a couple of years until the lure of gold got to him. There was gold being mined up north in the Kakamega goldfields. Charlie's last letter had come from that area.

'So far I am not having much luck but I could strike gold any day and could make enough money to buy a farm outright and come home for a holiday. This place has its own sort of beauty, hard to describe. I am living kind of rough at the moment and it is hot, hot and dry. How I wish I was there with you all and could feel the fresh cold winds of Buchan coming in from the sea and the rain.'

John had never been a very good correspondent but now that he was married his wife Molly took on the role and wrote fairly regularly. She informed the family that John was doing well and that she had given birth to another boy. It would probably be a year or two before they could manage home again. How mother Jaffray longed to see John and her grandchildren and wished they didn't live so far away.

Jessie still had half of her money in the farm, the other half having gone to pay for her university education. She took no loan interest on her money. She never had and nowadays took nothing at all from the farm in the material sense. She did like having a say in the running of it, however. The farm interested her greatly. She now no longer had the desire to escape from Aberdeenshire, the land of her ancestors for hundreds of years back. She felt the strong pull of the land and knew that, had she been a boy, she might have been a farmer. It was in her blood. That couldn't be denied. Her mother thought it was only right that she should have some say in the running of the place because of the money she had invested in it and because she had once saved them from disaster. There was many a late night discussion round the fire. Farming was in recession again but they were managing. Jessie was always optimistic that the recession would be over soon and that times would be better again. Her attitude was a boost to morale.

Jessie noticed a change in her mother lately. She did not seem as able as she once was, always complaining of feeling tired and making excuses frequently to stop and have another cup of tea because she was so thirsty. Jessie persuaded her mother to go and see the doctor but he came up with nothing specifically wrong.

'You are in your fifties now. You've had a hard life. You can't expect to be as able as you once were. You've got a daughter at home. Try to take things a bit easier,' was the advice the doctor gave.

Peggy worked harder than ever to make up for what her mother could not do, although they were still able to afford a 'kitchie deem' who took a lot of the rough work off their hands.

It was in the autumn of 1926 that Jessie once more had to pay a visit to the Corn Exchange in London. By this time Fanny, living in London, was able to afford a bigger flat so their was plenty room for Jessie to live there for the duration of her stay. Now they would be able to sit up half the night discussing their childhood, the farm, the people of Aberdeenshire and Fanny's affairs in London. Like Jessie she was well pleased with the job she had acquired and found it absorbing. Like Jessie she had got in with the nobility and could now feel upsides her sister.

On this particular visit a surprise was waiting for Jessie. She hadn't long arrived when Fanny held out her left hand for Jessie to see the glittering hoop of diamonds on her third finger. Jessie let out a yell of pleasure

'Fanny you're engaged. How winnerfae. Why didn't you tell us. Wha's the lucky fellow. I hope it is somebody suitable.' A slight note of apprehension had crept into Jessie's voice as she remembered her sister's disastrous affair with the communist.

Fanny had noted the change in tone.

'Dinna worry,' she said. He's nae a communist, the very opposite in fact. I ken you'll like him and approve. He's richt up your street. And oddly he's a Captain as weel. Captain St John Eyre-Smith – afa weel come.' Fanny reverted to her Aberdeenshire tongue which she didn't often use nowadays. 'You'll get to meet him as lang as you promise you'll be discreet. Like everyone else of my acquaintance here, he thinks my parentage hicher up the ladder than it really is. His faither was somethin quite hich up in the navy I think.'

It was many years before Jessie found out that when St John was born his father was plain Harry Smith, 21 Railway Street, Chatham and that his mother was Annie Smith née Eyre, and realised that both Fanny and St John were, in a way, both romantic pretenders.

Fanny had been correct in her assumption that Jessie would approve and like her fiance. She did. He had a pleasant disposition, good features, was of slim build and very dapper. His dark hair, receding somewhat at the temples, was short and brushed well back from his high forehead. His ears, Jessie noticed, stuck out a bit but this didn't detract from his overall appearance. He had a neat dark moustache. All in all he was a handsome man with a countenance that exuded a cheerful confidence. He was six years older than Fanny. In those days five years older was considered to be the perfect age for a husband. Jessie was charmed by his good manners and upper class accent and his easy way of talking to her. Their first, and as it turned out, their only meeting, was when he turned up one evening to take Fanny and her out to dine in an expensive London restaurant.

The whole evening seemed like a dream to Jessie. The

bustling streets of London were busier than ever and rather strange in the foggy lamp-lit glow of evening. Every time she came down to the capital there seemed to be more cars and fewer horses and cabs in evidence. The restaurant, where St John had booked a table, Jessie thought very grand indeed with its plush red carpet on which you couldn't hear a spoon drop, marble pillars and sumptuous velvet curtains. In an alcove, almost hidden in greenery and imitation palm trees, a small orchestra played unobtrusively. Scattered among the marble pillars of this vast Victorian building were dazzling white-clothed tables, set out with a glittering array of silver cutlery and shining crystal. Some tables boasted an ice bucket with tinkling bottles of champagne. Busy waiters were in evidence everywhere in formal black evening suits but what interested Jessie most of all were the other diners, an impressive display of grandeur in keeping with the age of British Empire. The men all wore smart evening suits complete with cummerbund and bow tie and the women in the fashion of the day, daringly short skirts, some up to the knee, indeed. On their feet they wore a variety of high heeled shoes with pointed toes and straps across the instep. The material of their dresses was often filmy but there was every sort and Jessie didn't feel out of place in a dress she had fortunately brought with her. The dress had been given to her by Lady Mary who had worn it several times and was tired of it. The colour of the dress was of a deep green which suited Jessie and brought out the green in her eyes. It was waistless and covered in sparkling sequins. Fanny was dressed very differently in a short, beige filmy dress falling softly to her knees. Her hair was short and teased out at the sides just enough to take away from the length of her face. Her soft blue-grey eyes glowed with happiness and Jessie thought she had never seen her sister looking more beautiful and told her so, which got the evening off to a good start.

Once they had settled down and ordered the first course and the wine St John turned to Jessie and said,

'I've heard so much about you that it's fabulous to meet you in the flesh.'

'What you have heard has been good I hope,' responded Jessie.

'Oh certainly good. Fanny tells me about the inspiration you have always been to her and all your family. She calls you Twi because you think of yourselves as twins but now, having met you, I can't say you look alike. I've heard all about your remarkable university career and how you have become, your sister tells me, the first woman factor in Britain. Quite an achievement for a woman in this day and age, what!'

Jessie noted to herself that Fanny must have been exaggerating again but thought it prudent to say nothing.

Over the leisurely meal the conversation was kept fairly general. Fanny knew quite a few of their fellow diners and kept pointing them out to her sister. One or two came over to speak to them and be introduced. Jessie drank a little more wine than she usually indulged in and felt a warmth glowing inside her.

It was over the coffee and cognac that the real conversation began. Jessie had become really interested in St John and was keen to know more of this man who was about to marry her sister. She could see that they were very much in love. Jessie found him easy to talk to and he didn't seem to mind being plied with questions. He was an outgoing sort of fellow.

Because of her genuine interest, St John didn't object at all to being quizzed by this attractive woman. Jessie spoke in her best English as she had been warned to do by her sister.

'When you first left school what did you do?' Jessie asked.

'Well I was always of an adventurous nature and always wanted to know what went on in other countries, other civilisations, how different people lived. At school I learned several languages as I thought they might be useful on the travels I was determined to make. As luck would have it my father, who was in the navy, knew someone with a ranch in Brazil. He wrote to him and asked if there was any chance of a job for his young son on his ranch. The upshot of it was I travelled to Brazil and for three years, worked on the ranch there learning about tropical agriculture, cattle ranching, horse breeding what have you.

'And afterwards?' said Jessie taking another sip of the cooling coffee.

'Afterwards, well the war came along, didn't it, and like most other young chaps I felt the call and was determined to go and fight for King and Country. Besides it was a way of seeing more of the world that would have been difficult to achieve otherwise. And true enough I did see a goodly chunk serving as I did in France, Belgium, Germany and Turkey but, if you don't mind, I'd like to get off the subject of war. I don't speak about it if I can help it. It's over and done with. We had some dreadful experiences that are best forgotten. There is nothing glamorous about war. You'll find most other chaps who have been in action feel as I do.'

'He won't tell you either,' said Fanny, 'that he was mentioned in dispatches for bravery in the field and that he won the Military Cross. He didn't tell me. One of his friends did.'

'All in the line of duty,' said St John. 'You just did what had to be done. We were all in the same boat. But let's get off the subject. There are much more pleasant things to talk about than that.'

'So what next?' Jessie continued with her questioning. 'After the war?

'Well I wasn't quite sure what I wanted to do but I did know I wanted to work in some developing country and be of some use to people. I rather fancied Africa. With that aim in mind I spent a year on a Colonial Administrative course at the Imperial Institute learning civil and criminal law, Mohammedan law, tropical agriculture, tropical hygiene, African languages and anthropology. I got a smattering of each and after the course was appointed to the Colonial Administrative Service in the Gold Coast. It was a place I knew very little about other than it was often referred to as 'the white man's grave'. It got this reputation because in the past so many white people had died there from malaria, yellow fever and other tropical diseases. But things are better now. I have been there for four years and I'm still around.'

'And are *you* going out there?' Jessie turned her attention to Fanny.

'I most certainly am,' said Fanny. 'In a couple of months in fact. St John has to sail next week as his leave is up but I want to work out my notice with the Duchess. We're getting married not long after I get there.'

'Getting married in the Gold Coast?' There was a note of both surprise and shock in Jessie's voice. Fanny had omitted to tell her sister any of these plans up till now.

'Yes, why not?' said Fanny. 'Why so shocked? I always thought you were supposed to be the romantic one in the family and what is more romantic than getting married in a place with a name like the Gold Coast where beaches are long and white and studded with palm trees, or so St John tells me,' she said smiling over at him lovingly.

Jessie omitted to say what she was really thinking which was that's a clever way to get out of anyone you don't want coming to your wedding. Fanny would ask all the family, of course, but could be pretty sure they wouldn't attend. She could understand her fears. Andrew, for instance, going down to a London wedding, would not even attempt to alter his broad Doric speech. St John might find out that Fanny had been telling lies about her lineage.

'Yes, but it is so very far away,' was all Jessie could come up with.

'The beaches are beautiful,' St John continued.

'The Portuguese came to this part of the west African coast in the fifteenth century and exploring inland found so much gold between the rivers Ankobra and Volta that they called the place Mina, meaning mine. When the English colonisers came along they changed the name to Gold Coast knowing of its history and finding many of the coastal women wearing gold bangles and other jewellery.

'But where will you both live? In a mud hut perhaps? I've heard it's still pretty primitive out there and isn't it all a bit dangerous?'

'Well, where I'm stationed in the Northern Territories I have to admit it's primitive,' St John said. 'But not long before I left, Princess Marie Louise came to visit us. She takes a great interest in the Gold Coast and I was rather ashamed of where she had to be housed. We had so little to offer her. However she didn't seem to mind at all. I had the great honour of getting a very kind letter from her after she returned home. It took a bit of deciphering, I have to admit, because of her almost illegible handwriting. She seems to have been most satisfied with the treatment she got from the chiefs and myself. She sent one of the chiefs, Bassana by name, a medal ribbon with which he was delighted. In her letter she also asked me to look her up whenever I come to London. Actually, I have made arrangements to see her tomorrow. I wrote back telling her what a very great honour it was to have her with us and that at a meeting of chiefs, they had said what a thrill it was that the granddaughter of the 'Great White Queen' had come to visit them and for one of their chiefs to be honoured in this way. That was the first time any one of royal blood had been that far north.'

'You are right, though, the house that I live in is not the lap of luxury but I'm in the process of buying a house in Accra, the capital of the Gold Coast, to take my bride to.' He took hold of Fanny's hand under the table and gave her such a loving look that Jessie could not help feeling a touch of envy.

Jessie had become really interested in the country her sister was about to disappear to. It was an adventure and Fanny was right. It was romantic getting married there.

'And what do you do? What is your job exactly?' Jessie asked St John.

'A little bit of everything but mostly, as District Commissioner, try to keep the peace. They are the nicest and most friendly people and yet the tribes quarrel amongst themselves. The most trouble comes from the Konkomba. They claim to have been there for ever but are landless and are sort of nomads. They are hard-working, however, and many have become rich growing yams. Because they are landless and because many have come across the border from Toga, territory belonging to the French, and because they have often committed some crime there, the other tribes reject them as being both landless and lawless. At the slightest hint of trouble the Konkomba have a way of rushing to each other's aid, becoming an imposing force and mini-wars ensue. Otherwise I look after the health of the people as best I can and, with my knowledge, help them to grow better crops, make better use of the land for it is wonderfully fertile soil. No one needs to go hungry on the Gold Coast.'

They spent longer than they meant to in that fashionable London restaurant and there were very few diners left by the time they went. St John escorted the two women home in a taxi and then took the taxi back to where he was staying. Fanny and Jessie talked far into the night.

'I do love him afa weel,' Fanny confided to her sister.' Sae muckle that I want to be as like him as possible. He's a Catholic, sae I've decided tae be one also if they'll hae me. I'm taking lessons richt noo.'

'A Catholic?' said Jessie 'Fitever next. Fit'll mither say?'

'That disna bother me muckle. I want tae become a Catholic. It's my life and you canna speak. You joined the Episcopal Church.'

Once more Jessie didn't say exactly what she was thinking which was 'and knowing you, you'll become more Catholic than the Catholics.'

Instead she said. 'You're richt, Fanny. You maun do fit you want tae do and I hope you and St John will hae a unca happy life thegether as I am sure you will. Hoo interesting it'll be tae hae a sister in the Gold Coast. I hope you winna gie up writing tae me. I really would love to hear aa aboot your new life. I think you're unca brave.'

'Will you dae something for me?' asked Fanny. 'Will you brak the news as gently as possible to mither. I'll write, of course, but maybe you could saften the blow and tell mither I'll be hame afore I disappear into the dark continent.'

Jessie laughed, 'You aye liked tae be dramatic but I'll most certainly dae as you ask.'

Chapter Twenty Seven

By the Loch of Strathbeg

THE VISIT to London had somewhat unsettled Jessie. She couldn't quite put her finger on what was wrong or why she felt uneasy but, for once in her life, she detected in herself the stirrings of envy. This was not for the interesting high life Fanny appeared to be living in London, nor for the impending adventure she was about to have in the Gold Coast. Neither of these. Rather it was because Fanny had found a man she could love, a husband, a lover, a companion with whom she would more than probably spend the rest of her life and with whom she could have children. Jessie did wonder how they would cope with such an eventuality living, as they intended to do, in difficult and dangerous terrain.

Jessie had to admit that, although she led a full life and had an interesting job that she liked, she was lonely without George. To begin with she told herself she would never re-marry but had modified this, as the years went on, to 'until I meet the right man.' She did meet all sorts of men. There were many visitors came to Crimonmogate House but they were mostly all of the upper crust and were either married or about to get married. As the years went by Jessie found there were fewer and fewer eligible men about. However, once she got back from London and into the swing of things again Jessie found she was too busy to brood on her dissatisfactions.

Fanny came home, as she had promised, to pay a last visit before she disappeared into the dark continent. A few months later she sent a letter from Accra telling of her wedding to Captain St John Eyre-Smith. She also sent a photograph which was much looked at and discussed at Dartfield. The photograph was posed and formal as was the custom of the day. The setting was a high white veranda bounded by tall pillars and arches. On cane seats in the front row sat the bride and groom, best man and matron of honour and at the back stood five other people that none of the family had ever met. It was the general opinion that Fanny herself looked beautiful in a filmy white gown with fluted edges and a filmy white hat that had a wide brim with downward wings framing her youthful features. She held a large bunch of almost full blown roses artistically arranged with leaves. The bridegroom looked dapper and colonial in an all-white suit with a string of medals pinned to his jacket and a white pith helmet on his knee Of the five people standing at the back, three were men, one in officer's uniform and the other two in formal dark suits. The two women were in light dresses with floppy hats similar to the bride's. No one was actually smiling but they all had pleasant expressions. Jessie had the photograph framed and placed on the sideboard in the parlour at Dartfield so that her mother could see it whenever she wanted to.

It was over a year after returning from London before Jessie did anything about her feelings of dissatisfaction. The catalyst came with an event that was to change her life again completely.

It was all because of the Honourable John who was a school friend of one of the sons of the Southesks. From an early age he had come to Crimonmogate on holiday and was almost like one of the family. Jessie knew him well and although he was the son of a Earl she just called him John like everyone else did. When they reached the age of sixteen, the boys were allowed to sit at the dinner table along with the adults.

At a dinner party one evening during the Easter holidays,

Jessie happened to be sitting next to young John. A conversation started up between them about birds. John it seemed had a great interest in birds and not just, Jessie suspected, from the shooting angle. She sensed he would have been happier just watching them or trying to photograph them although it would have appeared unmanly to admit to this. Their conversation turned to the thousands of wild geese that settled on and around the Loch of Strathbeg. Jessie was quite convinced these geese came from nesting grounds in Canada. John thought otherwise and suggested they were more likely to have come from Iceland.

'Have you ever seen them, Chappie, in the early morning rising up from Strathbeg, hundreds and hundreds of them? What a wonderful sight. I was there this morning. There's a hide not far from the shore. I've never seen anything like it.'

'No, I've seen geese on Strathbeg at sunset but never at sunrise.'

'Oh you must, you really must. I'm going down again tomorrow morning. Why not come with me?'

'Why not?' said Jessie, always one for a challenge. It would be a bit of an adventure and make her feel quite young again. It was arranged that they would meet an hour before daylight outside Crimonmogate House with their push bikes and make their way down to the hide on the shores of the Loch.

As luck would have it, it was a fine morning. There was a fresh breeze coming in from the sea which numbed their fingers and tingled their faces. The air had the scent of oceans. It was barely light by the time they reached the hide. One or two stars were still gleaming like polished silver while a full, quiet moon was paling into a disc of white tissue paper on an eggshell surface becoming imperceptibly lighter. The sky on the eastern horizon began to change colour taking over the landscape. From the direction of where they knew the sun would rise, a rose glow appeared flooding the sky. Then some unseen artist took over and added islands of pure gold, touching edges with an arctic green. No colour was still. They were always changing, getting brighter and fading, brightening and fading and becoming more beautiful every second, a moving living beauty. Cohorts of colour announcing, surely, some great coming.

From the rim of the world it came. First the curved edge of it, too bright to look at directly, the sun slowly but surely drifted onto the sky until all of its brilliant huge red-gold roundness was visible. It seemed to Jessie, at that moment, that this must have been what the first morning was like and that there was no one else in the world, only John and herself and the geese coming to life. As often happened to Jessie when she was especially moved by something, a fragment from her vast repertoire of poetry came into her head. This time the piece was from her favourite poet, Byron. She was aware, however, it was not wholly appropriate as they were not quite at the sea shore but it was near enough. Not to disturb the birds she whispered rather than spoke it out loud.

> There is a pleasure in the pathless woods
> There is a rapture on the lonely shore
> There is society, where none intrudes
> By the deep sea, and music in its roar:
> I love not man the less, but nature more,
> From these our interviews, in which I steal
> From all I may be, or have been before,
> To mingle with the universe and feel
> What I can ne'er express, yet cannot quite conceal.

With that, as if to praise the coming of the sun and honour it with a fly-past, the geese with a great clatter of wings and amazing strength lifted their heavy bodies from the pale white scarves of mist rising from the waters of the loch into the morning light.

Jessie thought she had never seen anything so touchingly beautiful. The wonder of it affected equally the young man and the older woman. What happened next however very much surprised Jessie. While the glorious dove-pink birds, with elegant necks stretched out, were settling themselves high in the sky, drifting from crazy runic writing to a variety of moving Vs, shaping and re-shaping and making for the green fields where they would feed, Jessie was aware that John, standing beside, her had put his arm round her waist. She turned round to look at him, startled.

'You don't mind do you?' he said. 'You see, I think you are the most beautiful woman I have ever seen and I want to marry you.'

To begin with Jessie was too stunned to say anything at all and then she said, 'Oh John you canna really mean it. I'm ald enough to be your mither.'

'So? Captain Chaplin was much older than you I've been told.'

'That was quite different. That's the other way roon. It happens from time to time and can work but nae a woman very much aller than a man. It would, should never be allowed. Besides you hae a certain future in front o you. It's more or less mapped oot although not in ilka detail, and it certainly doesn't involve mairrying a commoner even if she was the richt age. Besides, it would never work. When the first special love wears aff you would be sorry yoursel. The only time that your people, the gentry, mairry outside themselves and it has a chance of working, is if the woman has a lot of money, and I mean a lot, that is needed to bolster up the estate. I don't say it is necessarily a happy marriage but it can work in a way.'

'But my love will never die for you Chappie, never, never.'

'I'm afraid it micht John, if we got mairried,' she said gently knowing what he was going through. 'After a time I'm afraid it micht. I am indeed very honoured by your love. I shall nae forget this morning. It'll always remain a special day in my heart and I hope it will for you also and that on looking back you will know that I was richt. There are a lot of prettier girls in the world than me, John, and young tae. You'll fall in love again. I know you will.

Dinna let's talk aboot it any more and spoil this special morning.'

'But. . .'

Jessie didn't wait to hear any more but made quickly for her bike. They rode home in silence.

Jessie was very glad that John had to leave Crimonmogate next day and return to his last Spring term at Eton. Her conversation with him and his declaration of love had upset her more than she realised but it let her see, with a new clarity, the root cause of her own discontent and that she must now do something about it.

She did need a man, a lover, a companion, but it had to be a husband because what she wanted more than anything else on earth was a child. She thought a lot about this need. All other things now seemed to pale into insignificance.

The university, although she had loved it while she was there, it wasn't a living, flesh and blood child of her own. Crimonmogate with its fascinating people and its grandeur of house, its spacious gardens all hidden from the ordinary world by acres and acres of woods wasn't a growing living child. Now she knew, instead of all this, she would rather live in a cave and have a child of her own. No that wasn't quite correct – she would want her child to be comfortable, have enough to eat, be happy – poor in the material sense, perhaps, but happy.

The morning on the shores of Strathbeg had brought home to her also the passage of time. So busy had she been with everyday events that she had hardly noticed it. She would be thirty six on her next birthday. She remembered overheard conversations between her mother and some of her woman friends on how one got pregnant less easily as the years progressed, something most of them with big families by the age of thirty were grateful for. But then there was 'peer Mrs Scott, if she had gotten mairried just a wee bit afore she was thirty five maybe she would have had a bairn' and then there were the Bruces, 'aller parents wi a bairn that wasna quite richt'.

These conversations all came back to Jessie now and made sense. It was different for a man. A woman had only so many years. She remembered words she had read somewhere written by some Arabian mystic.She had been impressed by them at the time, the beauty of the language as much as the meaning. They came back to her vividly now.

'Behold thy daughter –
She has the wind in her hands but for a short time only.'

The full meaning of the passage took on a new and forceful reality. If she didn't hurry up, soon it would be too late. The chances of having a child would fade with every passing year. She hadn't been able to give George a child but, speaking to a doctor acquaintance, sometime after his death, he had told her that having Blackwater fever was very likely to make a man infertile. Something in her bones assured Jessie that she could still conceive but she knew that the later she left it the less likely it would become. Also, soon she might start to lose her looks. She knew she still looked young for her age with as yet not one grey hair amongst her thick black locks. Those who had just met her thought she was still in her twenties and she didn't disillusion them. She realised she must still be attractive to men for had not young John fallen in love with her. She had to admit that although she had not in any way sought his love, it had been a boost to her morale and made her feel really young again.

With the problem of her dissatisfaction properly identified, Jessie knew she must do something about it other than mourn over her fate. But what? Amongst her own folk all the eligible men, and there had been few enough of them left after the war, were married with growing families.

She saw now that she must be free of the nobility of Crimonmogate to complete her own destiny. She must have a new plan of action – change the pattern in some way or other.

But how? She must start to actively look for a suitable husband who would be a good father to her children. Aberdeen was a big town. There must be someone in the whole of Aberdeen. She would take a few weekends off. In some ways she was her own boss and could do this. She would use the little money she had saved over the years and stay in hotels on Saturday nights, good hotels so that she had a chance of meeting the right kind of man. It was a long shot but it might work. She would tell no one of her purpose.

CHAPTER TWENTY EIGHT

End of an Era

JESSIE found these first few Saturday evenings she spent in various Aberdeen hotels rather lonely affairs. Everyone seemed to be with someone else. Nowadays she knew few people in Aberdeen. All her friends had either moved away or were married and busy with their families. There wasn't much she could go to in the evenings. It just wasn't done for a respectable woman to go to the theatre or into hotel bars on her own. Had she done so she would have been seen as a loose woman and this was not the image she wanted to portray at all.

However on fine evenings she re-acquainted herself with Aberdeen. She went back to the university and wandered around its ancient precincts enjoying once more the ambience of learning, watching its current intake of students. How young they all looked. It seemed long ago now since she was one of them in another world, another time.

She also spent some time window-shopping along Union Street. She was glad in a way that they were closed and that she was not tempted to spend precious money. Sometimes she would stroll past the busy harbour with the fishing fleet coming in. What a wonderful sight that was with the raucous wheeling seagulls overhead waiting for their evening meal of unwanted small fish thrown from the boats. Further, she wandered down by the Dee.

She had forgotten what a clear and sparkling river it was, tree-lined and enhanced at times by students racing down its bouncing waters in skiffs. Once or twice, as a student, she had had the pleasure of being in one of these boats. The thrill of it came flooding back.

On cold, rainy evenings she enjoyed the warm comfort of her hotel and always took the precaution of having a good book with her. Often her eyes would stray from her reading and she would surreptitiously watch people. Making up stories about people had always been a favourite pastime of Jessie's. 'One day I will write,' she had always told herself.

Jessie persisted with these weekend visits to Aberdeen in spite of the loneliness. She tried different places. Her money was being used up. She couldn't keep this up much longer and would have to think up some other strategy to look for a husband. One more weekend she told herself and then I must think of something different. The place she chose to stay for the last weekend was a small hotel, little more than a boarding house. It was cheaper and all she could afford.

The proprietor who ran it produced a good evening meal. There were six or seven tables in the same dining room all seating four. All were full apart from the one she was sitting at and one other. At that table sat a youngish man, like herself, on his own. He was tall, slim and reasonably good-looking, clean-shaven and well-dressed in a modest sort of way. He had a rather long Scottish face with a high forehead and a somewhat larger than average nose that was ever so slightly hooked. His fair hair was closely cut, his eyes distinctly blue and his shoulders broad. At one point, after he had finished his soup, he looked in Jessie's direction. Their eyes met. How wonderfully blue they were. Afterwards, although she had been observing him earlier, she was afraid to look back again. She felt somehow he was looking at her. The meal over, Jessie went up to her room to rearrange her black hair into a softer more flowing style. She put on some fresh make-up, just enough to enhance her glowing skin, and went back downstairs with her book to the residents' sitting room. It was a gloomy wet night and most of the residents had stayed in. The sitting room wasn't big and by the time Jessie got back downstairs all the seats had been taken except one on the two seater sofa beside the young man she had seen in the dining room.

'Do you mind?' asked Jessie.

'Not at all,' said the man lifting his eyes from his newspaper. How blue they are, Jessie thought once again, as blue as the corn-flowers that appeared each year in Dartfield's crops of oats and barley. She could see he was shy by the way he looked quickly down at his paper so that he could avoid speaking to this young woman who looked much the same age as himself. But he didn't reckon with Jessie. She was quite accustomed to talking by now, to all sorts of people and was not at all shy.

'I see you've got today's *Journal*,' she said. 'Any interesting news? I haven't read the papers for a day or two.'

'Nothing special but it's always interesting to read a paper from a town other than your own. It gives you a different slant on things.'

Jessie knew by his voice that he certainly didn't come from Aberdeenshire but she couldn't quite place his whereabouts in Scotland. There was a Scottish intonation to his words and his voice was rather cultured. She decided to talk to him in her best English.

'What's your local paper?' she asked. 'Where do you come from?'

'Edinburgh,' he said. 'Can't you tell? *The Scotsman* gives the news pretty adequately.'

'Actually I've never been to Edinburgh although I've been to London quite a few times. Edinburgh's beautiful I believe.'

'It is but when you have been born and brought up there you are apt not to notice it. I've been to London too,' he volun-teered. 'I lived there for a short while.'

'You've been to London?' Jessie's interest was aroused.

'Yes when I was sixteen I went to work in the London office of Spillers grain merchants but when the war started my friend and I couldn't wait to join up. We were just old enough and no more. The day I turned seventeen we went down to the recruiting office and joined the London Scottish regiment.'

'You don't look old enough to have been in the war from the beginning,' she quizzed.

'Thank you for the compliment but I assure you that I am. I am thirty four this month.'

'It was a dreadful war,' said Jessie.

'Yes it was.' Jessie saw he wasn't going to be drawn on this topic. She had experienced this before. So many men who had been through the horror didn't want to talk about it.

'But you didn't go back to London?'

'I'm in Spillers office in Leith now, not so far from home. I'm here in Aberdeen, actually, to arrange a golf match for next weekend. Spillers is keen on the golfing reputation of its staff. It does a lot of business through golfing associations and it so happens that's the one thing that I'm really good at. I think actually that is why I got the job of manager in the Leith office.'

And so the evening progressed. All the other occupants of the sitting room faded into the distance or left to go to bed with Jessie and her companion barely noticing their disappearance, so engrossed had they become in one another. Eventually Jessie even had her new-found companion talking about his war.

'I don't usually,' he told her, 'except to some compatriot perhaps, and yes it was pretty dreadful but there could be good times too. The comradeship of my mates was wonderful. I'll never forget it. We were all in it together. In these awful trenches in France, going over the top and so many killed. I was in Africa too. I was wounded there. A bullet went right through my chest on the right side and fortunately missed anything too vital. I was carried over the desert on a camel. What an uncomfortable ride that was. But worst of all for me, I think, was the war in Salonica. We weren't even sure who we were supposed to be fighting. What a mix-up it all was and what a God-forsaken place it was then – the mud-filled trenches, the snow, the bitter cold, the snakes and the frogs. It was a great regiment to be in just the same. The Scots and the Londoners got on well together. I must say these Cockneys were cheerful no matter what. I remember one long march in particular. We were all exhausted, thirsty and hungry and knew we had only the most meagre and unappetising meal at the end of it when from the midst of the troop of soldiers the cheerful Cockney words rang out, "Anyone for a piece of cut cyke?" '

Jessie laughed.

'I'll bet you got a medal for bravery,' Jessie said at one point

'Well I did actually, bravery in the field. But any of us would have done the same as I did.'

They talked far into the night, confiding in one another as strangers often do on a long train journey. It came out eventually that both were lonely and longed for companionship but nevertheless it took Jessie by surprise when around one o' clock in the morning her new found friend took her hand and said,

'You're lonely and I'm lonely. Would you marry me by any chance?'

Jessie laughed. 'How sweet of you to ask me but we hardly know one another. I don't even know your name.'

'Henry Pollock.' He got up and gave a little bow. 'At your service. But do call me Harry. My friends do and I much prefer it.'

'And I'm Jessie Jaffray. I don't really like Jessie as a name but I seem to be stuck with it. I did try to change it to Jessica when I was at the university but it didn't stick somehow.'

'I noticed you the moment you came into the dining room. I noticed you wore no rings (Jessie had removed them before coming to Aberdeen) and I said to myself, that's the girl I'd like to marry and now that we have had this evening together I am more certain than ever.'

'But I wouldn't exactly be a young bride and as I told you I've been married before and am a widow. What would your family say to that?'

'I don't really care what they say. It's my life but I'm sure they will love you.'

Jessie had made some quick calculations and knew herself to be two years older than Harry. She had lied to him earlier in the evening, admitting to being thirty four – the same age as he. Why had she done this she wondered? She who was always on to Fanny for not telling the truth. Was it because this was the man she was looking for and she wanted to give herself every chance?

'I think we will need to get to know each other better,' she said. 'Marriage is a big step.'

'How about going for a drive tomorrow? I have my car with me. At least it is the company car. We could go down to Stonehaven or somewhere, anywhere you would like to go.'

'That would be lovely. I would enjoy that.'

That Sunday they had a happy day together and when Harry was in Aberdeen again the following weekend for his golf match they had another Sunday together and Jessie promised to marry him. Because they lived so far from one another and wanted to be together they decided to get married soon. Harry invited Jessie to Edinburgh on the following weekend to meet his people. He had told them of his intentions.

The visit was not an unqualified success. As Jessie thought, the family were not altogether keen on Harry marrying a widow whom he knew little about and certainly not in such a rush. Jessie tried to keep her end up but they thought her a bit pretentious. She was only a farmer's daughter, after all. Jessie did not find them easy company and, unusually for her, seemed to lack the language to reach them.

Harry's father had died some years before. He had been a lawyer, educated at both the University of Edinburgh and at a university in Holland. The oldest son, Walter, had carried on the tradition of the law. Jessie didn't take to him because of his aloof manner and sarcastic tongue. His two sisters also were given to sarcasm and snide remarks, something that Jessie had always found difficult to deal with. Harry's mother was an austere lady with a distinct Morningside accent. She was in a wheelchair having had an operation to remove her lower leg because of cancer. She was looked after by the daughter who lived in Edinburgh. She didn't say much and Jessie found her unbending and sensed her disapproval of this stranger, soon to be her son's wife.

Jessie felt she might never get on very well with Harry's family but she wasn't marrying the family and decided she would not have much to do with them. She formed the view that Harry was by far the best one of the lot of them and had been the least considered, perhaps even bullied to a certain extent. She knew him as gentle and kind. She had heard it said that war brutalised men but it certainly had not brutalised Harry. His failings might be that he was stubborn and, now that the war was over, unadventurous. She also felt he perhaps lacked ambition but she had plenty of that for both of them.

The wedding was arranged for the middle of July. It was to be a quiet one in front of a registrar again, but this time in Edinburgh and not in secret. Harry was anxious that his mother would be able to attend. Having had an amputation it would be difficult for her to journey to Aberdeen. Jessie wasn't all that sure how well her own mother would manage a long journey to Edinburgh. She seemed more exhausted than ever these days but she agreed and Peggy was to be bridesmaid.

Everything did not go smoothly. A month before the wedding was due to take place mother Jaffray died. Although everyone knew she was far from well and seemed to be pining away, sleeping a lot by the peat fire with less and less interest in anything, it came as a great shock to the family. Jessie was devastated. She might, in the past, have argued with her mother but she loved her just the same, and more than anything else had hoped to give her a grandchild that she would be able to see from time to time.

Mother Jaffray was in hospital for only one day. She went into a coma from which she never recovered. For the first time diabetes was diagnosed and although insulin was now known about, by the time she reached hospital it was far too late.

After the funeral Jessie made up her mind that the wedding would go ahead as planned. It was a sober affair. Her wedding photo was very different to Fanny's. Mostly everything in it was dark. The drapery against which they were photographed was dark. Jessie wore a black velvet coat with white piping round collar and cuffs over a black dress. On her head, covering every inch of her hair, was a gold cloche hat which came right over her forehead. Holding her head high Jessie looked aristocratic and serious. Peggy wore a dark suit with a wide-brimmed hat that had a high crown. They both held large bouquets of roses. The men wore tailed black jackets with grey striped trousers.

After the wedding they all went for meal at a small hotel in Morningside. On honeymoon Harry took his bride to Skye where, for a whole fortnight the mist never lifted. Not an auspicious beginning to a marriage.

Harry had rented a furnished house for them to return to in Longniddry which is some way from Edinburgh. Houses in Longniddry were somewhat cheaper and it was a fairly new bungalow. Jessie had let Harry do all the choosing as he was on the spot. What he didn't tell her was that the house was on the edge of the golf course which was, for him, part of its attraction. Jessie was happy to go along with whatever Harry chose. For her it was a new life beginning in a totally new environment and for once she didn't try to envisage what it would be like, but just accepted it.

As she had expected, the Southesks were surprised at her decision to leave them. They couldn't quite understand why she would want to. She had always seemed happy to work for them. They would miss her.

Jessie knew that in more ways than one this was the end of an era. Her mother and father were dead and all but two of the family flown from the land of their birth and unlikely to return. It didn't look as if the brother and sister, left at home on the farm, would marry. There might be no heirs. After all these hundreds of years, this could possibly be the end of Jaffrays as tenants of Crimonmogate, this dear, difficult land that they had worked so hard to improve.

Would the grey granite tombstones in the high stone-walled churchyard be all that remained to tell of their passing? Ancestors gone like the wind blowing through the rowans in her mother's garden. No one left to say who they were, these people who had helped to make this land fertile.

She knew that she would always return. In a way this land belonged to her and she to it just as it did to everyone born and raised here. She loved this land with a deep love as her father and his father had done before her. It was in her blood. How often had she heard her father say 'we farmers are the improvers and custodians of the land in our lifetime' and Jessie knew that to make barren land fertile, see green fields and fat sleek cattle where little had grown before was their greatest joy.

Little did she know it but at much the same time as she harboured these thoughts, Sir Alexander Gray was composing a poem that she, at a later date came to love.

This is my country
The land that begot me
These windy spaces
Are surely my own
And those who here toil
In the sweat of their faces
Are flesh of my flesh
Bone of my bone.

CHAPTER TWENTY NINE

New Life

ONE MORNING in December 1928 Jessie woke in the neat bungalow on the edge of Longniddry golf course and threw up. This was the third morning running she had felt unwell for no particular reason. As the day had progressed she had felt fine. Suddenly the realisation dawned. Perhaps she was pregnant. A little knot of excitement whirled round in her stomach. Perhaps, perhaps. . . Never had she welcomed sickness before, now it was positively sought after. That very day she went to see the doctor. He was a gruff but kindly man.

'Its very likely you are,' he said, confirming her suspicions.

Jessie was delirious with joy. That evening she told Harry what the doctor had said.

Harry couldn't quite believe it. He was possibly going to be a father. For some reason he had never foreseen himself in that role but he too was happy, as happy as he had ever been in his whole life. A beautiful wife and now a child.

Jessie wanted to tell everyone but there were very few people that she knew to tell in her new homeland and it wasn't something you talked about to strangers. She wrote copious letters to Peggy at Dartfield and to Fanny in Africa. Harry was worried for his wife in case her new-found joy should be short-lived but Jessie had a little knot of certainty within her that, by July, there would be a new little person in their home. Harry did everything he could think of to make life easier for her.

It wouldn't be true to say that Jessie hadn't been homesick at times in her new life. With Harry away all day at work and she left to her own devices in a strange place, she was conscious of an aloneness. Near to the sea and on Scotland's east coast, her place was much the same as back home. But there the resemblance ended. She had always been accustomed to people around to whom she could talk. Here people kept to themselves making her feel an alien in a strange land. But she had great inner resources and knew the best thing to do was to keep busy and so she tidied and cleaned her little house, made new curtains for some of the windows and new clothes for herself. She also joined the nearest library and got herself a good supply of books. For the first time in years she had time to read. Sometimes Harry would bring golfing friends home in the evenings. Jessie enjoyed these evenings. She had always got on well in the company of men. Occasionally she entertained special friends of Harry's and their wives to a meal. Now, with the advent of a baby, she began to make warm little nighties of flannelette and knit matinee jackets.

Cruel fate hadn't finished with Jessie yet, however. On the week before Christmas a wire came from Dartfield. Brother Willie has died in a shooting accident in Africa.

Harry took Jessie back to Aberdeenshire for Christmas. It was a sad homecoming – mother Jaffray gone and now their oldest brother.

It was the middle of January before a letter came to Dartfield from Charlie. Peggy sent it on to Jessie.

Dear Andrew,

I expect you received my cable telling you of William's death. It is the saddest thing I ever heard of. It happened so suddenly.

He was staying at my house at the time. I can

hardly believe it yet and need not tell you how I feel about it. I felt like clearing out when it happened but there is no good in that way of thinking as it wouldn't bring him back.

About one o'clock, mid-day, he went out to the garden with a shotgun and must have been shooting at birds or buck or something. He was passing underneath a low tree and something must have caught the hammer of the gun and knocked it off. He was found with his brains blown out and lying under the tree. He must have been killed instantaneously. I was at Nyjoro at the time and nobody saw it happen. William Morrison stays at my house and must have arrived at the scene five minutes after it happened. He saw Willie lying and ran for a fellow, Rennie, who lives about a quarter of a mile along the road. This fellow wanted to carry him into the house but saw he couldn't so went straight for the doctor and the police. They took the body to the house and had an immediate examination. They also held an inquest in Nakuru and the decision came to was that it was purely an accident so don't think there was anything wrong because the doctor said it was impossible it could have been self-inflicted because of the position they found the body in.

It's a terrible tragedy really and the saddest thing about it is that his wedding was fixed for the 20th of January. The girl, Miss Speke, is in a terrible state and it will take time for her to get over it.

I left Willie the morning it happened about six o'clock. We both had tea outside the house and he was as cheery as anything. I went to Nyjoro as I was working there that day and promised to see him that night as we had business to discuss but I never saw him again. I was determined to see the corpse as I couldn't believe it but the people just wouldn't let me see him. The funeral was held the day after as is the custom in this country. It was held from my house to Nakuru cemetery. There was a huge crowd there both men and women and ever so many natives. The people round about have all been terribly kind. They made me go away for a while so I have been staying with some friends beside Niarobi since the funeral. I just came back yesterday and feel a bit better now but I was suffering very much from shock. He and I were such good pals always. He often stayed with me and I with him and there was never a wrong word between us. All the people in the district are very cut up about this sad affair as he was so well-known and so well-liked by everyone. Even the natives felt it.

I will stop just now and write again. Please write at once and tell the others to do the same. I haven't heard a word from any of you for a long time you know.

Yours ever

Charlie

After reading the letter Jessie felt a wave of remorse go through her. She who enjoyed writing letters had woefully neglected writing to her brothers abroad in recent years. Life had been so busy for her and so interesting that her brothers had somewhat faded into the background. Fanny occasionally accused her of being self-centred. Was it true? How dreadful. Now she would never be able to write to Willie again but she could rectify matters with Charlie. How lonely he must be so far away in a strange land without Willie. She knew all about loneliness now that she was so far from home in an unfamiliar place. But she had a beloved companion who looked after her every interest and would take her home for a visit if she got too homesick.

The very day she received Charlie's letter she sat down and

wrote him back telling him of all that had happened recently and of the expected baby. She suggested to him that perhaps he could come home for a while and that might help to ease the blow of Willie's death.

It was Easter before she got a letter back from Charlie. He thanked her very much for her letter. It was wonderful to hear from her with all the news from home and of her good news about expecting a child, especially as she wanted one so much. Life goes on. There is always new life coming into the world. He had some good news also. He was now engaged to be married to a quite delightful girl. Her name was Winnie Rennie and she was a relation of the farmer he had first worked for in Kenya. A couple of years ago Winnie had come to Kenya to visit her brother Graeme who was working as a mechanic and who was a friend of Charlie's. Winnie and Charlie had been much attracted to each other and he had kept up a correspondence when she had gone back home to take up a position as a children's nurse. Last year she had come back on another visit to her brother and now she had promised to marry him. The wedding was to take place in Kenya soon. Also he was in the middle of negotiations to buy a farm of his own, something he had always wanted. Things were not so desperate as they were a few months ago.

This letter from her brother eased Jessie's sadness somewhat. Bubbles of sheer joy began floating to the surface just like those she had read of in a passage from a book set in exotic Turkey. The passage had described a river, a secret river, stretches of which, in Spring, were covered in a green skin of algae on which small turtles and terrapins rested in the sunlight. If the slightest shadow should come over them they would dive through the thin greenness and disappear swiftly and completely. Here also, now and again, blue bubbles would break on the surface coming from gases escaping from deep down beneath the river bed. Her bubbles of joy she felt came from a similar depth. She wasn't quite sure where that was, other than a deep well of which she had no knowledge. But the joy was palpable, a joy that no pain could eradicate.

Towards the end of Jessie's pregnancy problems began to develop. First it was sciatica when the baby was lying a certain way and then her blood pressure shot up. The doctors feared ecalmpsia later on and warned her that she might need to have a Caesarean section if things didn't calm down. Jessie wanted to avoid this at all costs and spent much of the day resting to give herself and the baby every chance. The baby was most obliging and decided to come a week early and although it was at times touch and go Jessie managed to deliver the baby herself. It was a girl.

Although exhausted she felt joy flooding through her. Now she understood the words her father had often read out of the bible about a cup being full and running over. They agreed to call the baby Margaret Isobel. Harry and she had decided on names before the birth. She didn't like the name Jessie or Fanny so she would call the baby Margaret after her sister Peggy and the beloved Aunt Maggie of her youth and give her her own middle name Isobel. Had the baby been a boy it was to be called William Thomas after the two grandfathers as Harry did not like his own name much either.

The fates had not finished with Jessie yet, however. Not long after the baby was born she began to feel unwell. Her condition didn't improve. Puerperal sepsis was diagnosed, the dreaded childbed fever that killed so many women. Before antibiotics came into use there was no known cure. Jessie became very ill and it was thought advisable to shift her from the nursing home to the nearest hospital. Besides, Harry would not have been able to keep up the expense of the nursing home for long. The baby Margaret was taken home to the house by the golf course where Peggy was staying. She had travelled down from Dartfield on the first hint of trouble to look after her namesake.

Harry was distraught. He spent as much time as he could at

the hospital just being near to Jessie. Much of the time she kept going in and out of cconsciousness unaware that he was there. One evening when she half woke to reality she heard the murmur of voices. She heard the voice of a nurse, one she didn't like, saying, 'I doubt if she'll live till morning', and then the anguished voice of her husband, 'She must live. She will live. She's strong.'

Inside Jessie, ill as she was, a resolve formed. Yes I will live. Harry needs me, my baby needs me and I'll prove that nurse wrong.

With that she descended into a comatose sleep once more. Her dreams were vivid. She was somewhere in a foreign land running through what looked like cleared forest. She kept stumbling over logs, breaking her way through brushwood. It was hot and breathing became difficult. There was no sign of habitation and then on the horizon she saw her brother John and he was beckoning her to climb the hill. Would she be able to? The need became imperative. She must. Eventually she reached the outstretched hand but it wasn't John standing, there it was Willie and he said, 'I knew you could do it.'

Tears poured down Jessie's cheeks. It was hot, hot, hot and humid. She felt the sweat run down her in streams and then the scene changed. The hot land dissolved into a sea of mist and she was running through the fields at Dartfield, running through the wonderfully cooling rain in Spring-time in a field full of lambs. She climbed over the fence in the horse park up through the April rain to the door of the farmhouse and ran to the kitchen. Her mother was there and she was by the peat fire feeding a lamb from a bottle as she had seen her do so often. As she stood at the kitchen door the lamb in her mother's arms became a baby. 'Who's is the baby,' she asked. 'She's yours,' her mother replied holding her out to Jessie. 'All yours.'

Jessie woke up to a morning ray of sunshine filtering its way through a long chink in the screens that surrounded her hospital bed. The fever had gone. She turned her head and there was

Harry looking down at her. He was smiling but at the same time tears were running down his cheeks like April rain. He kissed her gently on the cheek.

'I knew you would do it,' he said.

'Where's our baby ?' asked Jessie. 'Where's Margaret?'

Henry and Jessie Pollock, my father and mother, had one more child, another daughter, and after their children married and left home, lived happily together well into their eighties. My mother never got round to writing but was exceedingly pleased when, after the youngest of my seven children went to school, I started to write poetry and get it published in my mid-forties.

My uncle, John Jaffray, prospered in Malaya until it was overrun by the Japanese during World War II. In middle age he was forced to work on the 'railway of death' and his weight went from fourteen stones down to seven. He became much bothered by tropical ulcers. He died after the war was over due to the dreadful suffering he had endured. He left a wife and one son who went to live in Australia.

Uncle Charlie bought a farm in Kenya and became a successful farmer growing, among other things, geraniums for perfume. This all came to an end when the Kikuyu began their terrorist attacks and my uncle fled with his wife and two children to South Africa. They settled there where he retired and took up the driving of an ambulance on a voluntary basis.

Aunt Fanny (or Ewerdine as she liked to be called), when husband St John took early retirement after the World War II at the time when Britain was losing influnce in her Colonies and

Protectorates, went to live in Ireland. They took up residence in Lough Ine House over looking the Lough of the same name near Scibereen. She was left a widow and sometime afterwards, in her seventies, died of cancer. They had no children.

Uncle Andrew and Aunt Peggy moved into a better farm near New Deer and farmed there fairly successfully until my uncle retired due to ill health. He had suffered from angina for many years. Neither of them married and there were no heirs who wanted to take on the farm. He lived for a few years in retirement with my aunt in Stewartfield. After his death my aunt, now in her seventies, started dabbling in shares with the modest amount of money left from farming. Although for years, almost blind with cataracts, she followed the markets every day and did well. She was ninety five when she died. Out of all of this family of farmers and adventurers, she lived the longest and died the richest.

Crimonmogate estate was gradually sold off to pay death duties and other commitments until only the policies and mansion remained in the hands of the original family. Eventually they were sold to Christopher Moncton who was related through the Earl of Errol. He brought the mansion back to its former glory, raising the money to do so by manufacturing a pictureless jigsaw that he believed would take four years for anyone to solve. The prize for so doing was a million pounds. Unfortunately for him, two unemployed mathematicians, along with a computer, solved it in a year before he had sold sufficient puzzles. He was forced to sell the house to pay out the cash involved. My husband and I met him, more or less, at the time he had heard the news of the win but, nothing daunted, he showed us round the house pleased at what he had achieved in bringing it back to its former glory. This, in spite of the fact that he knew he would have to sell it. It now belongs to a Viscount from the south.

Bancar is now a thriving and popular rendezvous. The house stands much the same apart from a large function room which has been added on. It still faces a shelter belt of trees.

The farm house at Dartfield was burned down but a new one was built to replace it. The last time I was there some of the old farm buildings were still standing and the same narrow road, bright with broom, led up to it. It looked very much as it must always have looked. Still the green fields and grotesque trees influenced by cold winds coming up from the North Sea.

GLOSSARY

ae one only

ahint behind in time

ain (pronounced een) one

aricht alright

ava at all

awa away

bide wait, dwell

canna can not

dinna do not

div do

dreich dull, miserable weather

e'e eye

eneuch enough

far/whaur where

fell remarkable

feel foolish

fit what

foul (pronounced fool) very dirty

gaun going

gie give

guid (pronounced gweed) good

gyang to go

ilka every, each

loon boy

maun (pronounced man) must

peer/puir poor

quine girl

sic such

siller money

squeel school

waur worse

weet wet

For information on other books by
Margaret Gillies Brown,
or information about our complete list, write to
Argyll Publishing,
Glendaruel,
Argyll PA22 3AE
Scotland
tel 01369 820229
email argyll.publishing@virgin.net
website www.skoobe.biz